Why You Can't Catch a Rocket to Mars

Some Personal Reflections on Science and Society

by Lyndon N. Smith

To my family

The author, Lyndon N. Smith, has no problems getting transport to Bristol or London every day, but he is disappointed that currently it does not seem to be possible to get a connection on to the Red Planet or Alpha Centauri. Lyndon lives in Central Somerset with his wife, son and 2 cats.

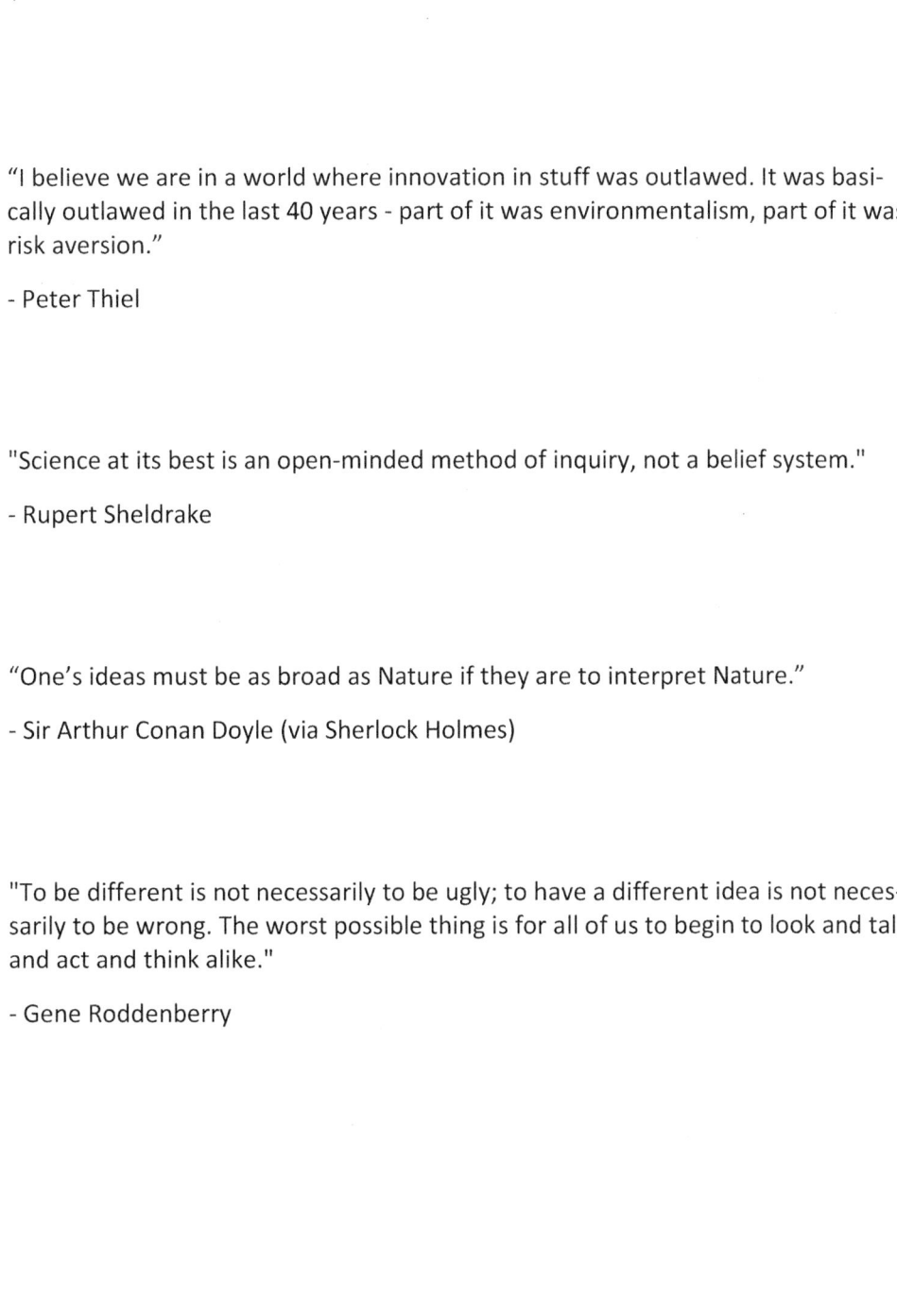

"I believe we are in a world where innovation in stuff was outlawed. It was basically outlawed in the last 40 years - part of it was environmentalism, part of it was risk aversion."

- Peter Thiel

"Science at its best is an open-minded method of inquiry, not a belief system."

- Rupert Sheldrake

"One's ideas must be as broad as Nature if they are to interpret Nature."

- Sir Arthur Conan Doyle (via Sherlock Holmes)

"To be different is not necessarily to be ugly; to have a different idea is not necessarily to be wrong. The worst possible thing is for all of us to begin to look and talk and act and think alike."

- Gene Roddenberry

Acknowledgments

Thanks to:

Les Edwards, for kindly letting me use his *I,Robot* related illustration

South West News Service, for permission to use their photograph of
The Concorde/The Clifton Suspension Bridge

Angie for the book cover concept

Dianne for manuscript proof reading

My lovely wife, Luiza, for proof reading and keeping me out of trouble (I have to say *lovely* or I *will*
get into trouble. She said that she would do it for love, then later I understood that a payment of
£100 would not go amiss!)

My son, Andy, for spiritual guidance, and for being a great kid!

Sir Arthur Ignatius Conan Doyle, for Sherlock Holmes

Eugene Wesley Roddenberry, for *Star Trek*

And, of course, Tabby; for her help in relation to Schrödinger's Cat!

Introduction

"We live in a society exquisitely dependent on science and technology and yet have cleverly arranged things so that almost no one understands science and technology."

— Carl Sagan

This book is about science and society; it addresses the potential positive effects or benefits (or lack of them) that science is having and can have for society. It is not about social science. According to Wikipedia, social science is: "the branch of science devoted to the study of human societies and the relationships among individuals within those societies". I would beg to differ with this definition, since social science does not actually comprise a scientific discipline, rather it is a systematic study of human society and social relationships. It is essentially part of the humanities and includes subjects such as economics or politics, whereas physics is an example of a scientific subject. The specific focus of the book is a cursory examination of technological progress that has been made, particularly in relation to what in the past was expected to have been achieved by now. This is followed by some speculations as to possible reasons for the identified discrepancies and potential approaches that could be pursued in order to assist with addressing our shortfalls, thereby helping to ensure that the full benefits of technological progress can be enjoyed in the future. In endeavouring to do this, it is necessary to examine several contributory factors in some detail - therefore a section is devoted to each - both to describe their nature and how they can arise. A number of methodologies are then outlined that may enable society to overcome the limiting factors. One of these, which is a technology that is already being widely researched and developed and which may provide the key to the technological progress that can potentially save our society as we know it, is artificial intelligence (AI). Consequently AI, and deep learning methods such as convolutional neural networks, are considered in some detail.

The above considerations are followed by Part 2, which addresses significant threats, both potential and real, that we face and what the most beneficial responses to them might be going forward. Examples of emerging threats range from viruses such as the coronavirus that has had such a profound effect on the lifestyle of everyone in 2020, through to less appreciated but equally real threats such as meteorites colliding with the Earth; but perhaps the most serious threat to modern society is from global warming. Despite the fact that it is beginning to dawn on humanity that these threats could dramatically transform society or even be potentially existential in nature, it seems that they are often not taken seriously. Politicians still seem reluctant to take minimal measures to address potential dangers to society in an effective way. Reasons for this will be considered, and potential responses outlined, which are consistent with continued scientific and technological development (rather than requiring humanity to revert to a primitive lifestyle) and which have the potential to offer long-term benefits for our lives that may well dwarf those we enjoy currently. Whatever the exact details of how we deal with threats and what developments our technologies will provide for our descendants, perhaps the most important consideration is that it really is possible and necessary to take a positive view on the future and the benefits that science can offer. This is not just an idealistic desire for positive thinking – but more of a realistic appraisal of the benefits that science has already provided to humanity in the modern era. These dramatic lifestyle improvements are too extensive to be listed here so we will just confine ourselves to a couple of examples – it is only in recent decades that everybody in Western societies has had enough food to eat, and medical breakthroughs in the same period have had a dramatic effect on the quality and duration of our lives.

Part 3 provides an antidote for the earlier parts of the book by highlighting some important scientific and technological developments that we might expect to occur in the future and the effects we may expect them to have on our society, along with a very rough timescale for them. This is followed by some reflections on the possible destiny of mankind. Finally, one or two concluding remarks are provided.

Many people are, I feel, very interested in the potential achievements of science and technology and in gaining answers to such questions as: why are scientific/technological achievements today not as great as had been expected in the past, what exciting developments might we expect to see in the future and how might cutting edge science and technology help protect us from the various threats humankind faces going forward? I don't think these are esoteric concerns for a rarefied scientific elite; rather, they seem like important questions that it is very reasonable for members of the general public to be asking.

Finally, I must make a note on style. It has been my aspiration to make this book as accessible as possible. Consequently, I make no apologies for adopting an informal style, including numerous quotes and making frequent allusions to well-known icons from popular culture. I have tried to relate the discussions to well-loved characters and concepts that you, gentle reader, are likely to be able to relate to. This will, I trust, improve the chances of communicating a fuller appreciation of the current situation regarding science and technology, its effects on society (good and bad) and the advanced capabilities it could provide us with in the future. I also hope you will be entertained while reading it.

Part I.

Where we are with science and technology

In this part of the book we consider where we are with science and technology and to do this, we start by considering the wonderful engineering achievements of the 'gentleman engineers' of yesteryear. Of these Victorian characters, none were more inspirational than Isambard Kingdom Brunel – and particularly his engineering achievements in and around Bristol. One of the most famous of these is the Clifton Suspension Bridge. In the above oil painting by the author, of the river Avon at Bristol, the bridge and the Avon Gorge are shown in the background – very much as they would have appeared in Brunel's day.

Why can't you catch a rocket to Mars?

"Wait a minute... Ah... Are you telling me that you built a time machine... out of a DeLorean?"

— Marty McFly

Have you ever wondered why you can't catch a rocket to Mars? In a similar vein, you know that there is currently nobody living in 'Moonbase-Alpha' as Martin Landau was due to in 1999. On October 21, 2015, some of my students told me that it was the day Marty McFly was due to appear. Apparently, that is the date when McFly travels back in time to the 1980s in the film *Back to the Future: Part II*. I have not seen it but was told that in the movie we learn that in 2015 there are technologically advanced devices and that people travel around on hover-boards (looking rather like surf boards but able to hover in the mid-air). I said to the students: "well, Marty must be bloody disappointed since we are still travelling around on old technology diesel buses" and they laughed. Not only do we not have hover-boards, we don't even have a lightweight, clean low-cost power source to power a car (as I write this electric cars are finally becoming available, but they remain expensive and with limited range). By the way, as you no doubt know, as mentioned in the quote above, *Back to the Future* features a time machine in the form of a DeLorean. Now, to anyone who says the DeLorean is a useless car, all I can say is that I won't have that; and they will eat their words the next time they find themselves having to work out some aesthetic styling for a new time machine!

The DeLorean; perhaps not much of a car, but a great looking time machine! (Pen and ink drawing by the author.)

A couple of years ago, I was in conversation with a company scientist who remarked that he was impressed, even bemused, by the technological advances we are seeing. I couldn't help saying that I was bemused by the apparent lack of significant technological progress and gave the example of the car which has hardly advanced in its fundamental design and operating principles in the last one hundred years – only having become somewhat more reliable and efficient. He was forced to concur. As the American technologist, Peter Thiel, expressed it: 'We wanted flying cars, we got 140 characters.' Also, I must point out that there was not an expedition to the planet Jupiter in 2001 and there has been little progress towards being able to fly around the Galaxy in a spacecraft visiting various exo-planets, as Kirk and Picard do in the seminal TV series *Star Trek*.

James T. Kirk and Jean-Luc Picard; starship captains from *Star Trek*. (Drawings by the author.)

In short, technological progress in the last one hundred (and particularly the last fifty) years, has been, it has to be said, less than we had expected or might have hoped for. And this means that the challenge of getting to Mars is currently a relatively formidable one. It's not that a Martian round trip is impossible with current day technology – it's just that, up to now, the challenge of doing it has not really been focused on or taken seriously. But recently, and excitingly, that has all changed. In 2033 the relative position of the Earth and Mars will be favourable for making the journey and so NASA plans to go there during that year. Meanwhile,

Elon Musk's space travel company SpaceX, which so far has been very successful in its endeavours, is even more ambitious, and is planning a mission for 2024. But what would be involved in getting humans to Mars (and returning them) in an affordable and safe way?

First of all, we need a rocket. SpaceX is developing a 'Starship' spacecraft and Super Heavy rocket (collectively referred to as 'Starship'). This will be a reusable transportation system with the following planned characteristics: height 120 m, diameter 9 m and ability to carry in excess of 100 metric tonnes to Earth orbit. Impressive, eh? Once the Starship is in orbit the plan is to refill it with fuel from a tanker which then returns to Earth. The refuelled Starship will then break out of orbit, travel around the Sun and on to Mars – which will take about 6 months (it takes a while since although Mars will be relatively close to Earth in 2033, it will still be at a distance of about 35 million miles). After arriving at Mars, Starship will achieve a soft landing and then use local reserves of H_2O and CO_2 to re-fuel. After being fully re-fuelled it will make its Mars assent and then return directly to Earth. Does this sound too straightforward to be plausible? Sometimes the simplest plans are the best. But we can't assume it will be cheap – the cost of a mission to Mars might come in at the better part of a trillion dollars.

What will it be like when we get there? Mars is about one and a half times as far from the Sun as the Earth, so the sun will still be bright and will rise in the morning (days are about the same length as for the Earth). But since it is father from the Sun than the Earth and with a thinner atmosphere, it will be a bit chilly. Its atmosphere is primarily CO_2 with some nitrogen and argon and a few other trace elements, which will allow us to grow plants on Mars (a bit like in the film *The Martian*). Gravity on Mars is less than half of that of Earth, so I would be able to lift heavy things and my backache would be cured without the need for me to go on a diet. (The latter being the most important consideration as far as I am concerned.) Speaking of food, we would need to take a good deal of it with us and this may also be one of the rare occasions when being somewhat overweight would provide an advantage – more natural personal reserves would mean a better chance of survival if supplies ran low and/or that less food would be required for the voyage. It's sounding better suited to me all the time – I am more or less ready to go!

If you think all of this sounds a bit far-fetched, then think again. SpaceX has already launched the 'Falcon Heavy' rocket three times. This is by far the most powerful operational rocket in the world and is able to lift nearly 64 metric tons of payload into orbit. And their plan for the near future is to have the test flight of the Falcon Heavy that will demonstrate SpaceX's ability to send spacecraft beyond Earth's orbit. You might be asking if there will be any associated hazards for astronauts on a voyage to Mars and the answer is of course yes. Apart from the boredom or even mental health issues associated with being confined in a relatively small rocket for such a long period, there will also be dangers associated with cosmic and solar radiation that can damage the vision, and even cause dementia and/or cancer. Just getting to Mars would expose one to more than 15 times the recommended annual radiation exposure limit – although some limited protection may be provided by extra metallic shielding.

So, what can we conclude from these considerations? To summarise, even with today's technology, it is possible for mankind to make a journey to Mars, albeit a relatively hazardous and time-consuming one, and it is quite likely that such an expedition will occur around the year 2033. But it would be much less hazardous and time-consuming if we could significantly increase the speed of our rockets. And in fact, increasing the speed of rockets well beyond the current record of 20,000 mph would not be as difficult to achieve as you might imagine. We just need to burn the rocket motors for a considerably longer period – which naturally necessitates more fuel. This could be facilitated by getting a rocket into orbit that has an extremely large (empty) fuel tank attached, and then filling the tank with multiple visits from space tankers.

So, we can get to Mars and back, even with the limitations of current technologies. But although our title refers to catching a rocket to Mars, which is something we can do with currently available equipment, this book is not intended to specifically address current technology. Rather, its main focus is on what future technological achievements might be possible if we could unshackle and focus our research and development efforts, and the exciting outcomes that could ensue. These would certainly include quicker, easier and safer travel to Mars than is currently possible. However, perhaps the most astounding possibility would be the prospect of exploration well beyond the Red Planet to the nearest star, and perhaps even beyond...

But let's preface our considerations of the future by first reflecting on some of the achievements of previous centuries, to see if we can draw inspiration from the scientists and engineers of the past. We will discuss science in some detail a little later, but first I would like to consider engineering.

Marvels of engineering

"Engineering is not merely knowing and being knowledgeable, like a walking encyclopaedia; engineering is not merely analysis; engineering is not merely the possession of the capacity to get elegant solutions to non-existent engineering problems; engineering is practicing the art of the organizing forces of technological change ... Engineers operate at the interface between science and society."

- Gordon S. Brown

I don't know if you are aware of the location of the world's first iron bridge. Given that it is the first, you might expect it to be some modest affair passing at a low height over some remote backwater. But no, the first bridge to be made entirely of cast iron (which was opened in 1781), is a vast dramatic and impressive (and even ornate) metal structure that passes at a good height over the wide Severn Valley and River Severn in Shropshire. The bridge is near a village entitled, not surprisingly, Ironbridge, and there is something very special about this location – it is the birthplace of industry. To summarise, a man named Abraham Derby had invented 'coke ovens' which removed impurities from coal, thereby making it suitable for iron production. This was very significant since it meant iron could be produced without the need for charcoal – the production of the latter having required deforestation of vast areas. So now, cast iron could be made relatively cheaply and easily – thereby leading to an explosion in its applications. In a nutshell, this facilitated the industrial revolution and the myriad technological developments that enabled all of the benefits we enjoy today.

Another illustrious bridge example is provided by the impressive Clifton Suspension Bridge – a creation of the legendary engineer Isambard Kingdom Brunel (a man whose vision, ambition and achievement were so great that a whole book would be needed to do him justice – and indeed, numerous biographies have been written). The Clifton Suspension Bridge is a brilliant, majestic, and inspiring structure that spans the mighty Avon gorge, and does so at a prodigious height, at the famous maritime city of Bristol – in South West England. (This bridge, which links Clifton in Bristol to Leigh Woods in North Somerset, is only one of Brunel's legendary projects at Bristol. Others include the world's first iron ship - the SS Great Britain - and the futuristic wide gauge railway that links Bristol with London.)

What do these two bridges, and many other engineering projects of the same era, have in common? Their builders were visionaries with an enthusiasm for technology and its facility for generating advanced services for future generations. The two bridges mentioned were also highly practical, so much so that they are still in service today, without needing alterations and with only very basic maintenance. This is a result of taking a long-term view - they believed in building on a substantial and forward-looking scale rather than being concerned with cost cutting and bean counting (which are modern obsessions).

Engineers such as Derby and Brunel were romantic visionaries dreaming of the future – so we can certainly draw inspiration from them. When Brunel died in 1859, his friend Daniel Gooch wrote: "Great things are not done by those who sit down and count the cost of every thought and act." But if Brunel achieved greatness, and most people believe that he did, it was surely facilitated by science; in other words, he, rather like Newton, 'stood on the shoulders of giants'.

Isambard Kingdom Brunel, who built the broad-gauge railway between Bristol and London, and who was responsible for many impressive engineering projects in Bristol and the South West of England. Brunel is perhaps the most famous of the Victorian gentleman engineers, effectively personifying the romanticism associated with Victorian engineering. (Pen and ink drawing by the author.)

The majestic Clifton Suspension Bridge, which spans the Avon Gorge at Bristol. It was designed by Isambard Kingdom Brunel and opened after his death, in 1864. (Illustration by the author.)

The promise of science

Science really is the most powerful tool we have to attempt to make sense of the very complex, varied and constantly changing world in which we live. Personally, I have a strong affection for it, since just about the only thing we can say with certitude is that the universe is constantly subject to change and our knowledge of it is very much incomplete – our understandings are constantly improving and old theories are continuously being modified or discarded in favour of new ones. The reason it is so powerful is that it is based on objective observation and experiment, as well as theories that are always subject to change - but the theory must always accommodate the data and not the other way around. Sherlock Holmes, the most famous detective the world has ever seen (who was, apparently, not real), had something to say about this last point: "It is a capital mistake to theorize before one has data. Insensibly one begins to twist facts to suit theories, instead of theories to suit facts." (For those interested, this is from his short story 'A Scandal in Bohemia'.)

Sherlock Holmes – the greatest detective, that never was. (Drawing by the author.)

Isaac Newton was possibly the greatest scientist of all time, having effectively invented physics as a subject and formulated laws and made discoveries upon which the whole of our modern world depends. Physics is the mother of the sciences and Newton addressed many aspects of physics with a level of insight that could only be described as astonishing. The story of the apple falling onto his head is probably apocryphal but, nevertheless, illustrates just one of his genius insights – that the force that causes the apple to fall is the same one that keeps the planets in their motions, i.e. gravity. Newton did in fact establish many important branches of physics such as mechanics and optics and consequently great progress was made.

Sir Isaac Newton – perhaps the greatest scientist there ever was. (Drawing by the author.)

His three laws of motion are the basis of the whole of mechanics and govern the operation of machines from your car through to rockets (his gravitational and mechanical laws have been employed to calculate rocket trajectories with sufficient accuracies to land men on the Moon and return them safely to Earth). Having said all this, what important physics discoveries have been made in the last one hundred years that could enable the invention of a new type of lightweight power source?

Ideally, the latter would have a power to weight ratio similar to or better than that of petrol and could be made commonly available to power cars in the future. Such discoveries and developments are rather overdue and are also badly needed if we are to address global warming with any degree of effectiveness. I think many people would agree that recent developments in physics have been rather less dramatic than they were in the past – and this may explain why consequent developments in, for example, machines have been relatively limited (which brings me back to cars hardly having changed in 100 years, my local car dealer trying to sell me a diesel-powered vehicle, and the fact that I can't catch the Martian rocket). I would say that there are four main factors contributing to this deficiency:

1. Physics (and hard science in general) is a difficult subject in which to make dramatic leaps of understanding, unless you are a genius like Newton or Einstein; the world is highly complex and difficult to understand – there is not much we can do about that.

2. There is a general lack of appreciation of the importance of scientific research and its potential for providing societal benefits. This results in less investment in research, particularly when a short-term return is not clear (even though the long-term benefits may be enormous).

3. I would say that science is becoming increasingly dogmatic; that is to say there is resistance to any challenge, or even modification, of the currently accepted theory and approach to the subject. Rigorous mathematical treatments are also often viewed as more essential or important than relevant scientific arguments.

4. There is a general lack of collaboration between university research departments and companies who are in a position to further develop and market new devices/systems – this is a particular problem in the UK.

The first factor has more to do with science than society's attitude towards science. Life is hard and physics is hard; the Universe does not give up its precious truths easily (or, as Neil deGrasse Tyson put it: "The Universe is under no obligation to make sense to you.") The next three factors are important, and it may be possible for society to address them in the future to a greater or lesser extent – therefore each will be considered in some detail.

The importance of scientific research

"If we knew what it was we were doing, it would not be called research, would it?"

— Albert Einstein

Scientific research is all about discovering or inventing something new. It is not the same as market research – which just involves finding out what others think about various things (an example of this is product reviews that can be undertaken using questionnaires). Scientific research also has to involve more than just copying what someone else has done – even if their work is rather state-of-the-art. The problem here may be that humans have a tendency, and perhaps a need, to copy each other. Psychologists might say this has something to do with crowd mentality or 'safety in numbers' – if you believe in something that many others also believe you would naturally think it would be harder for some third party to shoot you down. Unfortunately, it is quite possible, and even fairly common for many people, sometimes even the clear majority, to believe something that is completely wrong. Consider, for example, diesel engines in cars. In 1994, only 7.4% of the cars on Britain's roads employed diesel engines. As the years progressed, people became aware of the threat from global warming and that diesel engines are slightly more efficient than petrol and therefore can achieve a few more m.p.g. resulting in slightly less CO_2 emission (if driven carefully). Consequently, the UK Government encouraged people to buy and run diesels by introducing big subsidies on diesel car road tax, so that by 2011 the number of UK diesel cars rose to 31%.

What they apparently did not realise is that diesel engines produce much larger quantities of seriously dangerous pollutants such as nitrous oxides and very small particles. The pollution released by the increased use of diesel cars has caused NO_2 levels to rise above legal limits in many cities. Legislators eventually started to appreciate the mistake that had been made and began to reverse the tax benefit for diesels and/or restrict their use – particularly in cities; for example, Bristol is now planning to ban all diesel cars (but not petrol ones) from the city. This, and other similar initiatives, introduced doubt into the minds of motorists as to the wisdom of a diesel purchase, resulting in a fall in sales - the proportion of diesel cars on Britain's roads fell from a record share of 39.6% in 2017, to 39.3% in 2018 and 38.5% in 2019. This is a trend that may be expected to continue and, in fact, is likely to be accelerated by the Volkswagen Emissions Scandal (Dieselgate – more on this later) and the UK Government statement that a ban on sales of new diesel (and in fact also petrol) vehicles may be in place as early as 2032 in a bid to meet carbon reduction targets. **Stop press!** This date has just been brought forward to 2030; the situation is clearly fluid – it may occur even sooner.

The whole 'switch to diesel' debacle is a good example of how politicians and lawmakers make mistakes as a consequence of their limited understanding and incomplete knowledge of science. Unfortunately, the political class (and the media) is pretty much dominated by humanities graduates, with their ranks containing relatively few scientists/engineers.

Martin Winterkorn, former CEO of Volkswagen. Shortly after the Dieselgate scandal broke Mr Winterkorn resigned as VW CEO and since then an arrest warrant has been issued for him in the USA, and he has been charged with fraud in Germany. Therefore, I am not surprised that he is not looking very chuffed in the picture! (Drawing by the author.)

Consequently, they have a limited knowledge of the threats some technologies can pose - as illustrated by the serious and dangerous pollution created by various technologies including diesel engines and nuclear power. Their general lack of appreciation of the advanced capabilities that science can bring, and the long-term benefits and life-changing potential of new technologies, also leads to less investment in research. In reality, scientific research can offer long-term commercial potential; so, it is ironic that governments may imagine that cutting research budgets will save money when in the long term it will reduce G.D.P. The lack of appreciation of the importance of scientific research actually occurs at many different levels: it can be international (an example here is the EC thinking the future of the EU involves focusing on subsidising potato production or funding Framework/Horizon projects that really aim to increase EU political/social cohesion rather than to fund research with impact), through to staff at the institutional levels. At many UK universities (although not all), there is a deficiency in the appreciation of the importance of scientific research. Sometimes assertions can take the form of "the teaching funds the research" or "research is a hobby", but such an attitude misses the point that research is enabling in the long term, both for providing societal benefits and for allowing any institution to realistically refer to itself as a university. Another manifestation of the lack of research appreciation is the desire to appoint managers (i.e. non-subject specialists or well-known academics) to university executives. The assumption here seems to be that academics lack the managerial skills needed to assume leading university roles. However, this flies in the face of actual research data (this is discussed in more detail later). As a scientist would say, rather than believing what we would (for various reasons) like to believe, we need to accept what the data are telling us – again the scientific method must have precedence over the common misconception. In response to all of this, I am sure that Holmes would simply say: "Data!" However, perhaps my attitude would be a bit similar to Jim Barksdale's: "If we have data, let's look at data. If all we have are opinions, let's go with mine."

Sherlock Holmes' top hat. (Drawing by the author.)

The dogma of science

"Somewhere, something incredible is waiting to be known."

— Carl Sagan

Science and religion have in common the fact that they represent methodologies, or systems, for interpreting and understanding or making sense of the world around us; but that is about all they have in common. The religious way is based on a fixed belief system where the holy books do not change. In contrast, science seeks to establish knowledge about our world that is informed by observations and experiments that can be used to establish various models that constitute universal laws or theories. In a hard science such as physics, these models should be, whenever possible, quantitative rather than just qualitative. Measurements can often provide more precision than descriptions. For example, if you go online and buy a garment of a certain waist size, it is more likely to fit you than if it just has a description such as 'Large' — since, in my experience, the description means different things for different retailers - either that, or I am getting fatter!

The important thing about scientific models is that they are always subject to alteration and refinement depending upon the level of understanding at any given time. For example, at one time it was thought that the Sun orbited the Earth, then it was realised that, in fact, the planets orbit the Sun and finally, observations showed that each planet actually follows an elliptical path around the Sun. While we are on this subject, did you know that Holmes was, or claimed to be, unaware that the Earth revolves around the Sun? Not only this, but once he was informed of the fact, he said: "Now that I do know it, I shall do my best to forget it." His explanation for this was as follows: ""You see," he explained, "I consider that a man's brain originally is like a little empty attic, and you have to stock it with such furniture as you choose. A fool takes in all the lumber of every sort that he comes across, so that the knowledge which might be useful to him gets crowded out, or at best is jumbled up with a lot of other things, so that he has a difficulty in laying his hands upon it. Now the skilful workman is very careful indeed as to what he takes into his brain-attic. He will have nothing but the tools which may help him in doing his work, but of these he has a large assortment, and all in the most perfect order. It is a mistake to think that that little room has elastic walls and can distend to any extent. Depend upon it, there comes a time when for every addition of knowledge you forget something that you knew before. It is of the highest importance, therefore, not to have useless facts elbowing out the useful ones.""
Some people ask whether Holmes could have been jesting when he said he was ignorant of the Copernican theory and of the composition of the Solar System, but I don't think so. He simply did not wish to remember something that he didn't consider to be useful either to himself or to his work. So even though he was given

to highfalutin abstract inference and flights of deductive reasoning, he was also the ultimate pragmatist.

Sherlock Holmes' violin; was it a Stradivarius or an Amati? (Drawing by the author.)

But what of the dogma of science? Well, it does seem that there is a modern trend towards a dogmatic attitude in the existing scientific establishment. Since a dogma is defined as a set of principles laid down by an authority as incontrovertibly true, this scientific dogma may well be viewed as a religion, which cherishes a set of models that are considered immutable. Even the scientific establishment itself seems to approve of this approach. An example that may help to illustrate this concerns Rupert Sheldrake, the English biologist and author, who proposed the concept of 'morphic resonance'. This phenomenon may or may not be real, but it certainly does not fit in with the modern mechanistic approach to science. After Sheldrake claimed to have data to support his theory, the editor of the famous journal *Nature* described him as a 'heretic'. Interestingly then, the editor has cast himself in the role of the high priest for a form of religion that can also be called scientific dogma. The truly scientific approach, of course, is not to reject a concept simply because we feel it might be categorised as parapsychology or that it does not seem to fit conveniently within the current structures of modern science; but instead to analyse the data and, if they can be shown to be significant, objective, and so convincing, to admit that our existing theories may need some modification or addition. Other examples of data being ignored in the favour of accepted current belief are provided by intravenous vitamin C – there is considerable evidence that this can be beneficial in fighting cancer – even for patients in the late stages of the disease; however, it is not available as a treatment option for cancer sufferers. Even more surprising is that, the last time I checked, there were no funded research studies being conducted in the UK into the beneficial effects of intravenous vitamin C for cancer sufferers. It is also true that there is considerable experimental evidence that taking aspirin can provide significant benefits in fighting cancer, but again it is not prescribed for the purpose nor is it being investigated as an anti-cancer drug (treatments for cancer, including the effects of intravenous vitamin C and aspirin, are discussed in more detail in a later section). It is, in fact, a remarkable drug with few serious side effects, in contrast to many other drugs. An example of the latter is the painkiller ibuprofen which has been linked to heart attacks in a number of scientific studies, but which is still widely prescribed and even commonly available on supermarket shelves. In case you are interested in this, in one study researchers analysed data from 446,763 people and found evidence that linked ibuprofen use to increased risk of heart attack, and that the risk rises in the first week of use, being highest with higher doses. The work was funded by McGill University and undertaken by researchers from McGill University and the Centre Hospitalier de l'Université de Montreal, both in Canada, the Hospital District of Helsinki in Finland, and the Leibniz Institute for Prevention Research and Epidemiology in Germany. The increased risk of heart attack for any dose of ibuprofen in the first week of use, compared to no use in the past year, was 48%. It is important to note that the risk increased *by* 48% not *to* 48% - there is an important difference. Suppose you were unfortunate enough to have a 40% chance of a heart attack – for you taking the drug would increase this likelihood to 59% - not good. However, if you only had a 1% chance then it would only increase this to around 1.5% - which some might consider acceptable. Not me, however - I would not take ibuprofen unless I was in real agony. I would normally advise anyone who has concerns about any drug to consult a doctor but having actually done so it seems to me that doctors are generally overly keen on Ibuprofen. So, my strictly non-medical opinion is that it's best not to take Ibuprofen if you for any reason believe you have a raised risk of heart attack. If you want to read more about the study, you can find out more for free by searching for it online in the peer-reviewed British Medical Journal (BMJ).

Another more historical example of the medical profession being biased against a simple solution is that of Ignaz Semmelweis, the Hungarian physician whose work demonstrated that handwashing could drastically reduce the number of women dying after childbirth. Despite his evidence, he was largely ignored by other doctors which led to the unnecessary deaths of thousands of women over a number of years. The lesson that modern science can draw from these and other cases is that data are always paramount, and if we have data that are not consistent with current theory, we need to consider modifications/additions to that theory. In contrast to this, however, modern dogmatic science tends to simply ignore data that do not fit in with current or traditional scientific approaches. But worse than this is the often-observed tendency to vilify and insult those who suggest that accepted approaches may be wrong. Such ill treatment of colleagues has now reached the point where people who may have a dissenting view will not publish for fear of their careers being ruined. It is almost as if science has transgressed from a free-thinking, data-driven progressive analysis of our world to a dogmatic, hyper-conservative construct where accepted theory cannot be challenged. Therefore, to some extent science does seem to have transmorphed into a religion; and if so, it is not surprising that scientific dissenters are now branded heretics. Having said this, there is still less dogma in science than in other areas of life; as that champion of science Carl Sagan observed: "In science it often happens that scientists say, 'You know that's a really good argument; my position is mistaken,' and then they would actually change their minds and you never hear that old view from them again. They really do it. It doesn't happen as often as it should, because scientists are human, and change is sometimes painful. But it happens every day. I cannot recall the last time something like that happened in politics or religion." And I think Carl was right (as usual) – particularly about the 'doesn't happen as often as it should' bit!

The mathematics

"It is the merest truism, evident at once to unsophisticated observation, that mathematics is a human invention."

- Percy Williams Bridgman

The other dogma associated with modern science is its singular obsession with presenting rigorous mathematical treatments and having them take precedence over rigorous scientific argument; thereby greatly reducing the likely applicability and accessibility of the science itself. Lord Kelvin once said: "Until you can measure something and express it in numbers, you have only the beginning of understanding." There is little doubt he was right; mathematics is a very powerful tool that is the key to the quantitative understanding that is generally applied in physics to an initial qualitative appreciation, and which is usually more useful. (I must point out, however, that Kelvin was not always correct – he apparently said "X-rays will prove to be a hoax." which was, I fancy, an error. But I would agree with him regarding the benefits of the metric system of measurement and his recommendation for its widespread adoption.) It is also not surprising that the great man who invented physics also invented the powerful mathematical tool that can be used to quantify and analyse so many phenomena – *the calculus* (and I don't mean the calculus dentists talk about). It does, however, have to be admitted that

Newton was somewhat eccentric – or prone at times to neuroses that would today be classified as mental illness. It seems he was subject at times to some degree of paranoia and that this tended to make him wish not to publish his findings or to do so in a relatively inaccessible way. This may explain why, although he invented calculus he did not publish it for twelve years (but did in that time discuss his invention with others, conversations that other mathematicians may have heard of – thereby giving them an opportunity to claim the invention for themselves). Regarding the slight inaccessibility of his papers, this may have been increased by his tendency to write them in Latin (although to be fair this was usual for scientists/natural philosophers of his time), but it also appears that in presenting his mathematics he avoided the use of algebra (which we employ today) in favour of the more traditional ratios and proportions – which would have made his mathematical proofs less accessible. It is, however, worth making a point in relation to this which illustrates the astonishing apparent prescience of Newton. In mechanics we think of his famous second law as $F = ma$, but Newton preferred to denote the force in terms of a change in momentum divided by the time taken: $F = (m_2v_2 - m_1v_1)/t$. If we are considering very high velocities near to c, then according to accepted modern physics the mass of the body will increase – this effect is accommodated in $F = (m_2v_2 - m_1v_1)/t$, but not in $F = ma$; so that in the 1600s Newton seems to have anticipated relativistic time dilation! I will in fact have much more to say on relativity and time dilation, later on.

Looking back over the long period since Newton, it is difficult to fully appreciate the influence he has had on physics (and science in general) and on all the technologies (e.g. engineering) that have been facilitated by it over the years. I do not think it is unreasonable to say that the whole of the scientific method, and its subsequent publication, have been and still are, heavily influenced by his approach. Consequently, the eccentricities mentioned above may be a capital cause of the criticisms that could be levelled at modern science (particularly physics) practice and subsequent reporting. The mechanistic approach to science that Newton pioneered, and which has proved so useful in our development of machines (e.g. trains and cars) over recent centuries, may not in fact be appropriate to revealing fundamental knowledge on the universe. More specifically, the tendency in physics to try to analyse particles/fields on an ever-smaller scale in the hope that this will reveal some 'general truths' of physics seems to be failing to generate useful outcomes, i.e. outcomes with high impact. Reasons for this may be, firstly, that there is no guarantee that looking at an increasingly small scale is producing more fundamental knowledge; instead, in reality all that seems to be happening is that more complex structures and behaviours are becoming apparent. If progress towards fundamental understanding were being made, instead of this we would expect to discover simplification that would indicate unification of our understanding of physics – rather like Einstein was seeking in his unsuccessful quest for a unified field theory. The second reason for the deficiency of the current 'bottom up' approach to physics is that observing behaviour on the scale of quantum dynamics does not imply that the behaviour can be directly translated to our macroscopic man-size scale. For example, quantum mechanics shows that *superposition* can occur at the quantum scale - an elementary particle such as a photon can be in two different positions at the same time - but this is certainly not something we observe on our human scale. Again, more on this later.

But if a mechanistic 'bottom up' approach is not working, what other methodologies should we apply in modern physics? We already have an answer to this in the form of a rigorous analysis of the physics involved in example physics scenarios – or, in other words, using our knowledge of physics to solve various 'thought experiments'. Yes, Albert Einstein made good use of the visualized thought experiment (which he called *Gedankenexperiment*) as a means for understanding physical issues and for explaining his concepts to others. And that is quite a recommendation when you consider that he developed the theory of general relativity that describes how matter and energy interact with time and space, which has been checked experimentally. With Einstein, the physics ideas and logical reasoning came first and then the mathematical framework followed. But if you were to write a paper based on your carefully reasoned thought experiments, in order to shed light on an important question of physics, it is very likely publishers would refuse to print it if it did not contain a rigorous mathematical treatment. In fact, it is quite possible that they would be more likely to publish it if it contained the rigorous maths, even if it were not to make really significant points about physics. Freeman Dyson made some interesting comments somewhat relevant to this, when he described first meeting Richard Feynman. He said that prior to meeting Feynman he had been publishing papers that essentially comprised presentation of some 'pretty maths', but when they met he realised that Feynman was actually trying to understand the physics of what was going on. Dyson has also said: "Dick Feynman, who was my mentor as a physicist, had very little math. He never really thought in terms of mathematics; he had a very concrete imagination. He drew pictures instead of making calculations, and somehow got the right answers."

There is a tendency for authors and publishers to prefer publication of technical papers that display a good deal of relatively abstruse, and so quite inaccessible, mathematics. One reason for this is that it helps to build a mystique around the subject which authors and publishers often believe boosts the impressiveness and gravitas of the work in question (this is, I believe, what Freeman Dyson was referring to when he mentioned pretty maths and is similar to the aversion that some clinicians have to simple solutions to medical problems, which is discussed later). Another reason for preferring the inclusion of relatively esoteric maths is simply a tendency to follow in the tradition established by Newton, which was discussed earlier – this is perhaps somewhat understandable given the giant of modern science that he was.

Therefore, to summarize this aspect of the dogma associated with modern science, we can say that maths is an extremely powerful tool in physics, but it is a *facilitating* tool – not an end in itself. The maths we employ in Newtonian mechanics, which is based on Euclidian geometry, does not have an inherent preternatural quality, but instead has great value because it is extremely useful for solving mechanics problems. If we developed another type of maths, based on non-Euclidian geometry, we might find this to be of no use in solving practical problems or describing the universe, and hence it would have no inherent value for us. But maths as we know it *is* useful; if we use an analogy of building a road, if we did not have maths available in physics it would be like trying to build the road using a teaspoon. What maths is to physics is what a JCB is to roadbuilding; but detailed analysis/endless variations on the JCB will provide very limited information on the nature of the road.

Another way of expressing the idea of the maths not having intrinsic general applicability to our world, but instead only being suitable to abstract calculations was put forward by Poe in his short story 'The Purloined Letter': "I dispute the availability, and thus the value, of that reason which is cultivated in any especial form other than the abstractly logical. I dispute, in particular, the reason educed by mathematical study. The mathematics are the science of form and quantity; mathematical reasoning is merely logic applied to observation upon form and quantity. The great error lies in supposing that even the truths of what is called pure algebra are abstract or general truths. And this error is so egregious that I am confounded at the universality with which it has been received. Mathematical axioms are not axioms of general truth..." Of course, Poe is best known for his gothic horror stories, such as 'The Cask of Amontillado' and 'The Fall of the House of Usher' (the latter being somewhat metaphysical and comprising what may be his most important story); and who can forget the pieces of doggerel that he penned, such as 'The Raven': "Once upon a midnight dreary, While I pondered, weak and weary..." (I seem to remember from *Star Trek*, that at one stage even the unemotional Mr Spock found this famous rhyme upon his lips – I believe it was the episode 'Charlie X'. But Charlie was forcing him to say the words – as well as the first two lines from Blake's 'The Tyger'. I was entertained.) By the way, one of Poe's perhaps less well known works is his essay *Eureka*, where he starts off by saying that: "I design to speak of the *Physical, Metaphysical and Mathematical – of the Material and Spiritual Universe: of its Essence, its Origin, its Creation, its Present Condition and its Destiny*". A pretty tall order you might think; but then, he was a genius. He is said to have considered it his greatest work and to claim it was more important than the discovery of gravity. That might be over-stating things a little I fancy, but I do find Eureka to be rather astonishing.

Edgar Allan Poe, creator of the modern detective story and poet, who had some doubts about the general applicability of 'the mathematics'. (Drawing by the author.)

Sometimes of course, a rigorous mathematical treatment is appropriate and needed, but it is often found that this occurs when trying to solve problems in relatively simple situations. When the situation becomes more complex (as is usually the case in the real world), the closed form solution becomes too complicated or limiting and we need to look for other solutions. An example of this is provided by the calculation of strain distributions in engineering components that are exposed to mechanical stresses (forces). In the past there were attempts to employ classical stress strain calculations, based on closed form geometrical analyses, to calculate the strain distributions within components. However, it turns out that, other than for very simple geometries, such analyses lead to highly complex equations. For parts with geometries similar to those needed to be useful in practice, it is unlikely that closed-form solutions would be available. The 'other solution' in this case is simply to employ Finite Element Analysis (FEA), which is a commonly used iterative computer technique that has been shown to enable useful stress/strain analyses of a wide range of complex component geometries. It is necessary to mention that some maths is employed in FEA, but it is not complex, abstruse, or impenetrable. Each element in the FEA mesh is linked to its neighbour by means of an equation (for simple elastic simulations it would be the linear equation of a spring – for simulations of plastic deformations a more complex equation would be needed). However, the important point is that the 'cleverness' and so power of the technique does not lie with any particular complex equation, or set of equations; but instead is associated with the patterns formed when all of the elements combine and are iteratively calculated by the FEA programme.

A similar situation arises with the new computer modelling that is demonstrating an ability to automatically facilitate the undertaking of complex tasks in the real world, specifically *deep learning* and in particular *convolutional neural networks*. This is a large subject, but to summarise, it can provide a very powerful method for classification or solution of real-world problems (e.g. face recognition), by employing relatively crude simulations of the functions of the human eye (convolution) and brain (neural network). Deep learning comprises a genuinely impressive development in artificial intelligence that has demonstrated pattern recognition capabilities well above any competing methods; and is thereby opening up possibilities for automating a wide range of tasks which, up to now, have been considered too difficult to automate. The resulting systems may well prove to be lucrative for the inventors and their companies, but perhaps more importantly, they offer potential for liberating human workers from the labour and dangers associated with a large number of difficult, dangerous, and/or dirty jobs.

It is worth noting that this facility is being provided to us not by developments in classical mathematics that have a preternatural inherent knowledge of the world somehow associated with them, but rather by employing relatively simple mathematical algorithms, but utilising them in large numbers in highly inter-connected networks – where the model is in the network. The only drawback to such an approach is that it does require access to prodigious amounts of computing power. But now, fortuitously, we find such power to be commonly available to us all and at relatively low cost – through breakthroughs in the performance of graphics processor units (GPU); and the affordability of modern GPU technology which has been driven by none other than the demands of the computer gaming market. Wasn't it Feynman who said that to get the best out of people at work you must also let them play? (I seem to remember that one of his ways of playing at work was to spin plates on long sticks – which is not something I have tried as of yet and am not sure that such an activity would be appreciated by Hospitality Services.)

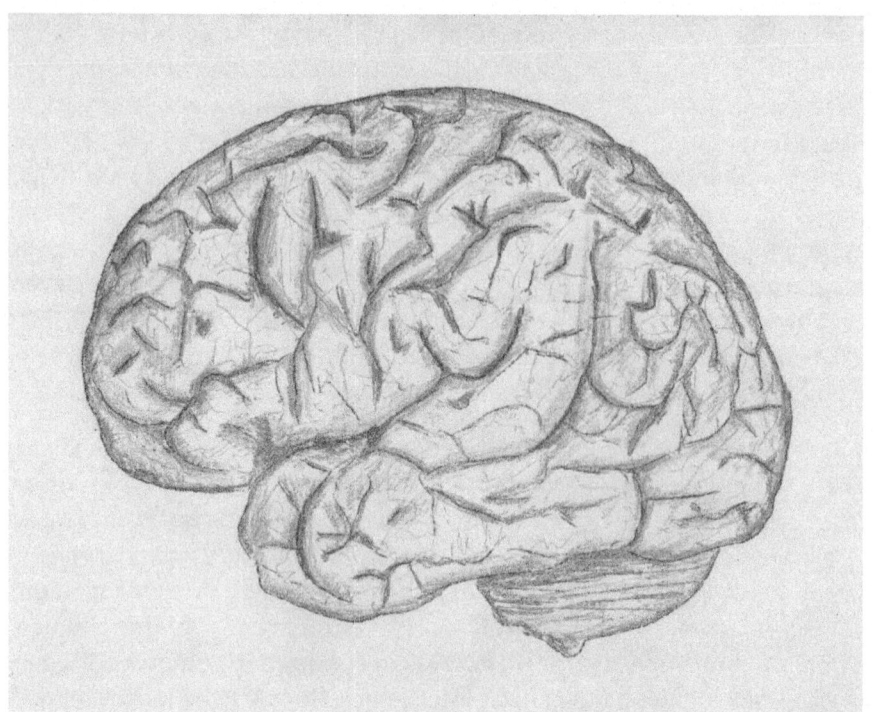

Deep learning: a method for pattern recognition that is inspired by the human brain. (Drawing by the author.)

It may have been that for many years the obsession with the perceived need for a classical mathematical equation for every significant piece of work, has resulted in much research (and its subsequent publications) while having relatively little impact on the development of science and technology. However, this situation has now changed, and conferences and journals are full of research into the use of deep learning for solving a wide range of tasks that had been considered intractable.

Unfortunately, the same situation does not occur in industry, where much of the time models are considered to be impractical – this may have to do with the fact that often industrialists seem to be preoccupied with some of the maths issues just discussed (e.g. the Newtonian requirement for everything to be reducible to an equation or equations). Can these two points of view be reconciled for everyone's benefit?

Never the twain shall meet

"There is no adequate defence, except stupidity, against the impact of a new idea."

- Percy Williams Bridgman

University science and engineering department academic staff and students are certainly good at coming up with new ideas. Evidence of this comes from the large number of PhD theses and technical publications that are produced. UK universities are, in fact, particularly good at research. This may be due to the streak of creativity and individualism that tends to be part of the British character. We do have a tendency to want to do our own thing – which explains why the UK publishes more books per capita than any other country and why UK universities are surprisingly good at 'research on a shoestring' - producing some pretty good research outputs and at a relatively low cost. 'Punching above our weight' in research may also be helped by the UK habit of often employing unusual methods or creative solutions for minimising expenses in research. In some sectors (e.g. motorway building), working on a shoestring and doing things in a piecemeal fashion is perhaps not a good approach and can lead to higher long-term costs, but for scientific research it can often pay dividends – particularly if the researchers have apparatus that may be somewhat simple or less advanced technologically, but for which they fully appreciate the intricacies and can really make 'sing'. So, one thing we can say is that the British are good at scientific research – in fact, they have a bit of a flair for it.

But are we as good at applying the research; in other words, can UK universities demonstrate exceedingly strong research impact? In order to do so, we need to get over the *Valley of Death*. But you may ask, what is the Valley of Death? I mean, we know what *Death Valley* is – a large national park in California where, in 1913, the highest ever ambient air temperature of 56.7 °C (134 °F) was recorded at Furnace Creek.

Death Valley: a desert valley located in Eastern California, in the northern Mojave Desert. (Photograph by the author.)

37

I really like Death Valley, by the way. It has a particularly unworldly atmosphere; Martian-like I would say. If you, like me, are a fan of the original *Twilight Zone* TV series, then it is fun to seek out the exact locations in Death Valley where various episodes were filmed. The last time I was there, in 2018, the temperature was 52 °C. They call it a 'dry heat' but, believe me, 52 degrees is hot, dry or not; and I don't know if it wasn't some kind of record – if it's not it should be.

Again, apologies for the digression; let's get back to the Valley of Death – which refers to the difficulties people have in taking a new concept/product, that may be quite developed, and turning it into a saleable item. Thinking again about the British character, I believe it may have one aspect to it that is not particularly helpful here – I refer to the British tendency to be reserved. When one first goes to America, one can be struck by how *forward* and *loud* people are. In fact, this can be so extreme that the persons concerned can often seem to be being aggressive, although nearly always they are not trying to be so. There is little doubt that, generally speaking, the British are quieter and more reserved than most dudes from, say, the West Coast. And while being thoughtful and cautious may be commendable characteristics for a science researcher, they are probably not such great virtues for a salesman. In order to set up a small company and launch an entirely new product, one not only has to be convinced of the utility of it, but it also helps to exude perhaps sometimes almost irrational levels of enthusiasm and righteous confidence in the product and oneself (as you can imagine, such qualities are less useful for objectively quantifying scientific truths).

Another problem in the UK is that there seems to be less willingness to take a punt on something new; and, particularly, there is noticeably less of a tradition for universities to form genuinely close and useful collaborations with companies. The blame for this cannot, though, all be laid at the feet of the universities concerned. For example, in my job as a professor at a university, I often say that companies seem to think that the university is a charity (i.e. that we can do things with no, or very little, resourcing), but although it is technically a charity, it's not a *charity* (if you know what I mean). There also appear to be fewer examples in the UK of academics launching successful spin out companies (perhaps with the exception of one or two universities). Reasons for this, I believe, range from the natural reserve mentioned above, coupled with a general conservatism, as well as the way that most UK universities are run. Unfortunately, most British universities suffer heavily from institutional navel-gazing, which is currently being accentuated by the levels of administration and middle management that they are increasingly being saddled with (with a large dose of political correctness and, often, Marxist ideology, thrown in). There are likely to be a number of reasons for the self-obsession prevalent at UK universities. Probably principal amongst them is the tradition for many UK institutions, and particularly ones that have public-sector origins, to be inward-looking (conspicuous examples of this include the BBC and the NHS). This, coupled with the fact that actually undertaking research is difficult, dealing with companies more difficult (particularly as a result of the 'culture shock' that can result, for reasons that are touched upon above), and securing money for resourcing more difficult still (and becoming increasingly so as purse-strings tighten and competition increases), means that many academics prefer to simply avoid research. A consequence of fewer academics undertaking research is that the idea of 'it's OK, someone else can do it' can start to prevail. This leads to a generally increased lack of research and consequently technological innovation and progress. In other words, it is part of the reason why I can't take the rocket to Mars. Much can be, and has been, written about this concept of 'someone else can do the actual work' and its implications for the economy – including a whole book – and as soon as I can remember the author and title of it I will give it a read...

Everyone, at heart, would prefer to give advice rather than to take it. Also, who wants to experience the emotional rollercoaster ride of trying to publish papers and win grant funding – especially when for most academics the ride seems to spend most of its time going down rather than up. In short, who wants to spend a lot of time screaming?!

The emotional roller coaster of publishing papers and winning grant funding. (Illustration by the author.)

Every research active academic, no matter how successful he or she may be, will have had plenty of experience of rejection by reviewers. (As I keep saying to my colleagues: 'The most successful researchers are the ones who have had the most rejections. And I keep quoting Churchill: 'Success consists of going from failure to failure without a loss of enthusiasm'; and I keep waking up in a cold sweat: 'Aaahhhhg...' Sorry about that.) At the same time, as outlined below, many university executives are staffed by middle managers, who naturally tend to find it difficult to relate to or trust academics and researchers. Considering these factors, it is no surprise that administration in many universities is expanding in size and reach. To some extent, this is useful in that it can provide support for academics in following the procedures and paperwork that are associated with any academic endeavour. It does, however, become less of a blessing when the rules and paperwork are exploding in volume and when the utility or need for much of the additional complexity is not clear. Also, it is difficult to avoid the conclusion that if I were to decide to devote my professional life to university administration activity (which I will refer to as admin), I would be likely to be pre-disposed to creating more of it at an increased level of complexity. The other great bane of the life of an academic is meetings, particularly meetings relating to university admin. My conviction, borne of experience, is that Elon Musk was right in telling his staff that if they are in a meeting which they do not feel to be making progress towards being useful then it is OK to leave. Holding a meeting is not an end in itself – it has to be moving towards a useful outcome. It really has. Talking is of limited use if it does not lead to a practical conclusion – there must be a genuinely useful discussion and it needs to make progress towards resolving one or more important/pressing issues. You might think this is so obvious as to not need stating, but in my experience of around 30 years of being involved with educators and attending their meetings, I have to say that it does need stating. And repeating. Notwithstanding all these comments about the managerial and admin culture in our universities, it has to be admitted that most universities do understand, to some extent, that academics and researchers need assistance in bringing the results of their research to market and commercial exploitation. This is indeed not easy to achieve, but the difficulty is compounded by the insular and parochial approach that the university is likely to take concerning technology transfer, simply by virtue of it being a public sector institution. For example, the university is likely to employ many staff to, in various ways, assist with technology transfer or exploitation, but because of the previously mentioned lack of trust in academics, they are unlikely to submerge/implant the majority of these support staff. Instead they will be in separate buildings, not understanding the real issues and problems the academics face and thereby not being able to provide effective support. Again, this may seem a matter of detail rather than a critical issue, but it goes to the heart of the reasons why UK universities find it so hard to commercialise their research and to compete in this respect with US universities.

Many academics, quite understandably, do not wish to experience the disappointment associated with rejection of their grant applications – each of which is likely to have absorbed a great deal of time and effort. But what options are there for such a person? One, of course, is to undertake only teaching, resulting in the attendant drawbacks discussed above. The other is for them to become heavily involved in university admin, of which there are two types: general admin and research admin. The former is necessary for the university to function; but a heavy emphasis on it has similar consequences to if the academic were to be fully immersed in teaching (however admin might offer more opportunity for promotion into senior roles for attaining significant salary increases). Research admin refers to administration activities related to undertaking research. Again, as mentioned, this is required to some degree (excuse the pun) – for example, academic regulations are needed for research, to ensure that candidates for degrees such as PhD do actually undertake research, and follow procedures appropriate for that level of research. However, perhaps one of the main threats to the quality and quantity of research being undertaken is the explosion in the volume of research admin that has been occurring for some years in British universities and which is currently accelerating. Why is this happening? Well, as outlined above, research is difficult to do. Everybody knows that it is easier to critique what others are doing rather than undertake anything especially useful or creative yourself. It's easier to give advice than to take it and act effectively upon it. Then, once an academic has decided upon a career in research admin, what could be more natural than that they should wish to make as much of it as he or she is able? A kind observer would say that they are endeavouring to cover the increasing requirements of modern research governance, while a less-kind one would say that they are justifying their job. In any case, as the amount of research admin increases dramatically, the chances for those who wish to actually undertake research, of getting some high-impact work done, diminish. The expanding research admin can take the form of increased numbers and complexities of forms that need to be filled out (some of which may never actually be used for anything), an astronomical increase in the number and length of meetings that are held (which often seem to be effectively duplicating each other), and an increase in the number and complexity of online research admin information systems (e.g. for research governance). Such systems can often involve duplication as well as delving into complex subjects that they do not need to address. For example, research governance information systems are increasingly asking researchers about the details of their research methodology, but often such information is not needed within the scope of the system. An example would be a project in science and engineering that models data using deep learning, where the question of why the modelling is being done may have ethical questions associated with it, but the exact detail of the techniques used is not needed and also would require a very complex and detailed explanation (as would be the case if a convolutional neural network were to be employed).

Therefore, there are two main aspects to the concept of *never the twain shall* meet when it comes to research in UK universities. The first has to do with the culture difference between the way the organisations themselves operate – specifically the public-sector universities vs. private sector companies. This aspect results in UK research having much less impact than it ought to and is capable of having. The second aspect relates specifically to university academics and involves formation of two groups – those who are research active and those who are not. A pronounced differentiation in this regard has implications for the reputation of the university and the priorities of one group can influence the other, as mentioned above. However, this differentiation also has other effects that may be more noticeable in the shorter term and which can have on-going influences on very large sections of society.

Newly graduated university students. (Pixabay Pexels photograph by Andrea Piacquadio, used with permission of Pexels.)

Nowadays more than fifty per cent of young people are going to university (twenty years after Tony Blair set the target as Labour policy), and so university education is becoming a subject of more importance for society. In the UK, people are very keen on pigeonholing others and also, in fact, themselves. This perhaps results from the still influential idea of the class system. People tend to wish to identify with a particular class - it makes the world easier to understand and particularly one's place in it. Or maybe it is a hangover from the feudal system that was so dominant years ago and which, to some extent, still survives today – witness the apparent popularity of the monarchy in Britain. However, in the case of universities, the pigeonholing of staff into research and teaching means that many universities are missing out on all the research opportunities that could arise from identifying and nurturing research-able students and encouraging them to undertake PhDs. The pigeonholing is thus intrinsically detrimental to the university concerned, and for the learning experience of the students. For example, the less research that a university undertakes, the less right it has, in truth, to the appellation 'university'. The research-reduction situation can form into a vicious circle, with less academics being research active, and when they are senior this naturally means there is less incentive for others to undertake significant research. If such a university is not careful, it will consequentially transform into a glorified teaching college; and having spoken to professors from various UK universities I believe this is already occurring at a number of institutions. Research can also inform teaching and improve the quality of the learning experience. I have witnessed the interest sparked amongst students when they see products being marketed that are based upon the state-of-the-art methods that they are learning. Also, lecturers being able to share and discuss their journal papers and conference presentations gives students an assurance that they are learning about the latest research developments. In contrast to this, if a more 'teaching college' approach is dominant, where lecturers tend not to be research active, then students can become aware that the teaching is employing more of a 'from a book' methodology and this can limit their inspiration and desire to explore a career in the subject area. So, to summarise, having a large proportion of university teachers who are not research active does not benefit the student experience. But what is the situation in the universities that are more research active? They can certainly enjoy the symbiotic benefits of the cross-fertilisation between research and teaching, but how good is the teaching, really, at these institutions? Actually, it turns out that it is not that good on average and many departments in such universities struggle to get awarded 'gold' standards for teaching (or in some cases, even silver). But why is this? I have quite a long experience of being a student, researcher, lecturer, and professor at a range of universities in the UK. My belief, stemming from this experience, is that the problem with quality of teaching in the highly research active (or 'top 50' or 'red brick') universities is, surprisingly, that they are perhaps too research active! By this I mean that many academics are keen to do research but quite often wish to avoid teaching. When they do condescend to lecture, they often wish to talk mainly about their own research. This would be fine if it were not for the unfortunate human tendency to wish to 'big oneself up' – often at the expense of student understanding. Such a mean sentiment can take many forms, such as explaining the simplest concepts in a complex way, or the tendency, as discussed above, of couching ideas in complex mathematics and placing this in front of a straightforward explanation of the ideas involved. All this can make lectures at many 'top' universities pretty inaccessible and of limited utility for many of the students. And when combined with a tendency to be rather too 'up on oneself' to spend much time on teaching, or to answer too many questions, you have a recipe for a less than ideal learning experience. So, what is the answer to all these possible problems? Well the solution is perhaps relatively simple to express but perhaps less easy to implement. Certainly, the way forward seems to be to have greater percentages of academics being research active across a wider range of universities in the UK. But equally importantly, these academics need to be quite integrated with the teaching experience rather than isolated; and the importance of accessibility and practical utility concerning the way in which their research should be brought into their teaching to inform it, in a symbiotic way, cannot be over-stated.

Having digressed into this discussion of issues surrounding the quality of the learning experience at various UK universities, let's return to the earlier subject of why UK industry is not benefiting as much from UK university research as would be expected (especially considering the fact that, overall, UK universities do a good deal of research on relatively modest budgets). As mentioned above, there are various cultural and traditional management-related issues that may be making it difficult for many universities to produce high impact from their research. Perhaps many of these considerations can, to some extent, be summarised by the concept of academics still being somewhat in their 'ivory towers'. However, I believe this is only part of the overall picture. There is, after all, a good deal of quality applied research being undertaken in UK universities – it would not be right to say it all comprises window-dressing. What is stopping this research from creating new products/systems that can be launched in the marketplace? I believe it is the result of a combination of all the effects discussed above with a phenomenon that seems to dominate much of modern life in the West – specifically, political correctness.

The academic ivory tower: "a metaphorical place—or an atmosphere—where people are happily cut off from the rest of the world in favour of their own pursuits, usually mental and esoteric ones" (Wikipedia). (Illustration by the author.)

Science: politically incorrect?

"We're led to believe everybody opposes it and disagrees with political correctness, yet everybody's scared to death of it. So, who is it? Well, it's the power structure wherever you happen to be."

- Rush Limbaugh

What is political correctness (PC)? A good question. According to Wikipedia: "Political correctness is a term used to describe language, policies, or measures that are intended to avoid offense or disadvantage to members of particular groups in society." I would say that in terms of common usage, i.e. what most people understand it to mean when they use the term, this definition is quite wrong. You know, I actually wrote most of this chapter before seeing the above quote, but Rush Limbaugh is about right – political correctness is "the power structure wherever you happen to be". If you happen to be in the UK, or USA, you will find that being PC has got such a stranglehold that one can't even discuss the subject without being considered politically incorrect. So, this chapter is highly likely to be politically incorrect; so perhaps I should not have written it and if you wish to skip to the next chapter, I'll understand.

Congratulations, you don't mind reading something that might be a little politically incorrect – that's an important first step in combatting the PC threat.

If you live in the West, are a white male, and work in one of the professions (I would hesitate to say middle class since it seems to be unclear as to how this term is currently defined in the UK and it appears to have a different meaning in the USA), and you say *anything* about race, gender, religion, or sexuality, it will be almost certainly considered politically incorrect and it is also likely that you will be considered to be prejudiced; so that even if you are not so, just by speaking you may find your career under threat. That's another reason I should not have written this chapter.

In science, 2 + 2 always equals 4. In a PC world, 2 + 2 might equal 3, or it could equal 5; depending upon the race, gender, religion, or sexuality of the 2s. This is why I believe the Wikipedia definition of PC is wrong – being PC, as it is commonly practiced, is not just a matter of language or presentation – it's more than semantics. Being politically correct can involve treating people fairly and not being prejudiced, and when this occurs it is undoubtably a good thing. However, in practice, political correctness is often about asserting that reality is different than what it actually is, as a consequence of the value framework that makes up one's PC world. Science is (or should be) about describing things exactly as they are. To quote Sherlock Holmes: "My dear Watson, I cannot agree with those who rank modesty among the virtues. To the logician, all things should be seen exactly as they are, and to underestimate one's self is as much a departure from truth as to exaggerate one's own powers." By the way, you might protest that Sherlock Holmes was not a real person and perhaps that's right, but in that case how can you explain the fact that there are (rather impressive) statues of him in London, Meiringen, and other places around the world? (I have to wonder: if a future woke mob decides Holmes was not PC, will they attempt to pull these statues down? Perish the thought!) And if he is fictional, how can he have more common sense and his feet more soundly on the ground than his famous creator? All respect to Sir Arthur Conan Doyle, but I have to wonder about what he was playing at in believing in the Cottingley Fairies. (By the way, speaking of Meiringen, the Sherlock Holmes Museum is excellent; if you have any interest in Sherlock Holmes do visit it.)

The Statue of Holmes in London. (Photograph by the author.)

Apologies for that digression, getting back to political correctness; as I mentioned, the problem with it is that it often attempts to make false claims about reality, depending upon the nature of its value system. This makes it the enemy of science, which is instead concerned with objective and dispassionate observation of the world as it actually is. If situations cannot be observed and evaluated objectively, then it becomes impossible to accurately identify problems; and if you don't clearly understand a problem, you stand around 0% chance of being able to solve it.

Another problem with it is that it has a tendency to upset people on a large scale, which can lead to reactions that can seem extreme. A convincing argument can, for example, be made that Brexit and the election of Donald Trump in 2016 can be put down to reactions of large sections of society to the PC nature of the media and the politicians in the UK, Europe, and the USA – but discussion of that could itself form the subject of an entire book.

Also, it seems that it would not be right to have a section on PC without mentioning the BBC. I have always loved the BBC – or should I say *Auntie Beeb*. From dramas with excellent production values, through to incisive documentaries and news (the BBC has more embedded/foreign based journalists than any other news organisations); from unrivalled natural history programmes to excellent coverage of sports and important public events, the BBC seems to offer everything, or at least it used to. Over recent years, the BBC has become more and more PC, so much so that its presentation style and selection of news stories seems to be moving farther and farther into a kind of PC wilderness that threatens to leave it isolated and in danger. Couple this with what seems, in our modern multi-technology internet age, to be an archaic 'broadcasting poll tax' and the Corporation appears to be entering an existential crisis.

Since I still love the BBC, I hope someone there will wake up and 'cut the crap' (as Greg Dyke used to say before he was forced to resign as Director General, following publication of a critical independent report – which was another sign of crisis at the Beeb). Yes, at the world's most respected broadcasting organisation, someone needs to cut the PC crap; otherwise its famous tendency to navel gaze may turn into a painful disappearing up its you-know-what. By the way, since this book is supposed to be about science, I would just like to make one observation about the BBC – its science programmes seem to be about the only ones that do not currently appear to be highly biased by PC considerations – but it may not be long until they change that. I mean, even John Humphries – stalwart of Radio 4's Today programme and veteran BBC broadcaster, has written a book where he lambasts the BBC for its PC culture.

The BBC: always an icon of British culture – now also an icon of PC culture? (Pen and ink drawing by the author.)

So, what then is the chief problem with political correctness? Well, I would say it's that it tries to tell you what to think and say. You know – 1984 and the *Thought Police*; first communism, then fascism, and finally political correctness. But to be honest, most of us have been around a bit and we know a thing or two and have a reasonable ability to think for ourselves – we don't need or want to be told what to think – unless of course science is telling us, and even then we need to be sure that the science is not getting mixed up in any way with PC considerations. The latter has, to some extent, already occurred, but analysis of that would again be the subject of a whole book. Perhaps the saddest thing about political correctness is the way it eventually ends up attacking and attempting to discredit members of the very groups it purports to support – and these are respected members of these groups who are often role models. For example, consider Germaine Greer, who for years was a hero of the women's movement/feminists. Today she is apparently under attack from the PC brigade for saying that it is not possible for a woman to change into a man, despite most people tending to agree with her and her views being grounded in scientific fact. And internationally, there are many other examples relating to race, gender, religion, or sexuality. Such attitudes can be explained if political correctness is not viewed as an attempt to achieve social justice for the groups concerned, or an effort to bring scientific truths to bear on society; but instead is a political movement that has an hyper-liberal and radically

48

social liberal viewpoint, with little regard for scientific or general truths. In fact, scientific truth and quality of life are increasingly being sacrificed for the multitude, on the altar of politically correct ideology. And this is not just happening in the UK and USA – it is spreading across the globe.

OK, you may say, perhaps some of that is true, but why would that mean that PC is holding back science, and why, in particular, would it prevent science from having good impact and resulting in new technologies and products? Perhaps the first part of the answer to this question would be that if you put much of your time and effort into a subject such as analysing society in relation to PC questions, there is little time or resources left for actually establishing the new knowledge needed for implementing the advanced technologies of the new products. However, the more fundamental problems are the limitations or distortions, or actual fallacies that a PC culture introduces. The most common manifestation of this is the commonly encountered PC tendency, mentioned above, of refusing to admit, for PC reasons, that certain situations or problems exist, with all the attendant long-term societal disadvantages and limitations. However, serious issues also arise when PC attitudes become entangled with administration (as touched on above) and particularly, management.

The march of the managers

"Being a manager is easy. It's like riding a bike except the bike is on fire and you are on fire and everything is on fire and you're in hell."

- Anonymous

I remember having a discussion some years ago with a (very senior) university administrator. The situation was that we were preparing to interview for a new lecturer post. After there was much talk of race and ethnicity considerations, I proposed that race should not be an issue, and the senior administrator's response was 'What about unconscious bias?', and this was followed by a discussion of all the processes and determinations that might be occurring in the unconscious part of our minds. I knew I had lost him at that moment and that he was submerged in that PC-laden value system that has pervaded so many of our institutions. The chief problem with buying into this PC agenda is that it wastes time and effort on explorations of imaginary/unreal landscapes such as my (or anyone else's) subconscious. This talk of the subconscious reminds me of the film *Awakenings*, in which Robert De Niro plays psychiatric patient Leonard Lowe. At one point in the film, a psychiatrist asks Lowe if he is aware of all the unconscious hostility he's exhibiting. His reply was to ask, not unreasonably, how, if it's subconscious, he could be aware of it.

Robert De Niro as Leonard Lowe in the film *Awakenings*; De Niro received his fifth Oscar nomination for his portrayal. (Drawing by the author.)

As mentioned above, there is a tendency, particularly at many of the post-1991 universities, for academics to not be engaged in research. As discussed, I believe that this is detrimental to the institutions concerned. There is also a tendency for departments, faculties, and even institutions to be run by managers rather than academics – I refer to this phenomenon as the march of the managers. I have had direct experience with how academics tend to run pre-1991 universities while managers are more prevalent at other institutions. Having been puzzled as to why this was the case, I asked a member of (non-academic) staff at one of the universities why she thought this was occurring. She said that she thought managers were being employed in senior roles at her university because there was a belief that academics would not have the skills needed to run the institution successfully. However, this comprises another example of how certain people hold beliefs that are not supported by a shred of evidence. In fact, in this case there is considerable evidence to the contrary. A 'well-researched, detailed, and comprehensive scientific study of research universities (i.e. institutions that aim to do research as well as teaching) in the USA and UK has shown that those that are led by academics perform better than those that are not (see *Socrates in the*

Boardroom by Amanda Goodall). Despite this, universities continue to appoint middle managers instead of senior academics to their executive roles, since they prefer to follow their hunches rather than being directed by what the available data indicate. Having said all this about managers, I should also say that management is, of course, a challenging and important task and a very necessary one. Certainly, in my university career I have appreciated that there is a tremendous amount of management and administration required just to maintain one of the important activities, such as teaching, and I am very glad and appreciative of the fact that there are people around who are capable of it and willing to do it. One of these people has a sticker on his desk where I saw the above quote: ""Being a manager is easy. It's like riding a bike except the bike is on fire and you are on fire and everything is on fire and you're in hell." I had to chuckle. And so much for middle managers in higher education, but what about managers in industry?

The UK has, sorry to say, a problem with management. Simply stated, many managers in the UK are not particularly competent technically and do not have a good understanding of the technologies their companies are supposed to be employing/developing. In fact, it might even be that this applies to the majority of managers in the UK – and possibly also the USA. Why is this the case? I suggest that it has to do with the concept popular in the UK/USA that management is a discipline in and of itself. Many years ago, while I was doing a masters' degree in manufacturing at Cranfield University (back in the 1980's – now I'm feeling old!), I noticed that on the campus there was a school of management offering degrees in the subject. A couple of years later, I mentioned this establishment to a colleague who suggested that I probably had never met a company manager with a degree from such an institution – my response was to say that I had never met such a manager with a degree from *any* institution! At a different time, I met a manager of a company who asserted that he 'had a degree from the university of life'. Don't we all? I couldn't help thinking that he also needed a degree in the subject related to the products his company was producing. The arguments that can be made here are similar to the ones expressed earlier in relation to university leadership; specifically, it would be best if those leading a company were experts in an area closely related to the product or service their company is marketing. I don't think we all have to be geniuses to understand this – those with an in depth knowledge in an area highly relevant to a company are in the better position to anticipate and deal with issues that the company may face, than those who do not have such knowledge. It's common sense really. This managerial problem may also go a long way to explain why short termism is so often observed in the way British companies operate, with all the attendant lost opportunities for market dominance and long-term profitability. Consider how many brilliant ideas for new products British inventors have come up with over the years; here I will name just a few that come immediately to mind: jet airliners, programmable computers and the World Wide Web, military tanks, vacuum cleaners, the jet engine, and milk chocolate (with the latter being by far the most important, in my view). In most of these (and many other) cases, the invention was British, but most of the commercial development and consequent long-term profitability, was generated, or is now located, in another country. Often this is the result of a British company being set up to commercialise the invention and then, once some sort of success is demonstrated, being immediately sold to investors in another country (usually the USA). What I am suggesting is that this short-termism and inability to appreciate or at least fully realise the long-term commercial potential (which is where the bulk of return on investment usually lies), is a consequence of the companies concerned being led by executives who do not have a real passion for their products and determination to be involved in the products reaching their full potential. And what is the reason for this? It may in part be due to a tradition of wishing to see short-term returns on investment, but I believe a major factor is that if the executive concerned does not have an in-depth knowledge relevant to the product then it is not easy for them to fully appreciate the potential scale of its long-term development and exploitation, as well as making it less likely for them to have the passion and belief in the product that is so necessary for success in an increasingly competitive and global marketplace.

Schools and teaching, or 'just because some thing is new/different/fashionable, that doesn't mean it's better'

"The art of teaching is the art of assisting discovery."

– Mark Van Doren

A passionate belief in something is not only relevant to commercial exploitation of products in the marketplace, but also the subject of a wide range of vocational pursuits. One such subject is education in, for example, secondary schools. Wasn't it Tony Blair who said he had three priorities – education, education, and education? He may have been right about this since we are talking about sending the next generation forward with the skills needed to complete in such sectors as high-tech information technology – which is becoming more complex, fast moving, and competitive by the day, on an international basis. This is why I am concerned that the march of the managers seems to currently be impacting schools in the UK. To summarise, schools need to employ teachers; consequently, we need positions such as headmasters to be filled by teachers who are effective at both leading their schools forward and teaching. We do not need head teachers to be managers who are more interested in making an impression and introducing a 'corporate' approach, than the finer points of the prerequisite skills for effective teaching.

Unfortunately, I have seen this management approach in schools and must say that its application does not tend to end well. Rather, it can often lead to terrible consequences such as a drop in staff and student morale, discipline, and engagement issues, and a reduction in the long-term performance of the school, particularly in relation to important measures such as the GCSE and A level grades of the students and the percentage of them entering university. And yet the manager-teachers concerned don't seem to acknowledge this and tend to carry on looking good with their 'corporate style' as though nothing were wrong. Even when parents say to them that they are unhappy with the school/department performance, they don't seem particularly concerned. All I can say is that some teachers/managers do appear to have a very thick skin. In my view, there is much more that can be said about schools in relation to the modern fashions they seem to be falling victim to and the likely consequences for us all. And since this book is principally concerned with the influence societal factors can have on scientific and technological accomplishment, I feel that it is worth examining what is going on in our schools and what its implications may be for both science and society.

(Pexels photograph by Andrea Piacquadio, used with permission of Pexels.)

Political correctness, which was discussed above, is, unfortunately, infiltrating many aspects of society and, naturally, education has not escaped (in fact it was on American campuses that the dread philosophy was invented). The media is, of course, obsessed with PC issues and hardly a day passes when we are not bombarded with stories about LBGTQ issues and often these concern schools in relation to such issues as children being enabled to question their gender and, for example, the provision of 'gender neutral' toilets. While much of this kind of socio-

53

political mumbo-jumbo has, in certain sections of the media, received the derision it deserves (which is perhaps one of Piers Morgan's more useful functions as a journalist), I am more concerned with the subtler manifestations of fashion in education. There is, for example, in many levels of education, a worrying tendency towards multiple choice questions; again originating, I fancy, from that great republic on the other side of the pond (I need hardy point out that while our American cousins have spread one or two fashions/ideas that we could do without, they have also, like the UK, given the world a multitude of useful things – far too many to start listing here). The proponents of this pedagogic abomination claim that it tests the more subtle nuances of the student's understanding. In reality, it is hard to avoid the conclusion that it is popular because it means the marker/examiner does not have to think – all they have to do is apply a 'stencil' to see how many questions were answered correctly. There are, in my view, many reasons why multiple-choice questions are a bad fashion. The principal factor is the apparent dumbing down of education that they constitute. Firstly, it is hard to see what represents insufficient (or indeed impressive) knowledge in a system where just marking random answers down would result on average in a student scoring 25% (if there were four potential answers). Secondly, multiple choice goes against the aspirations we have, or should have, to be creative and inspirational in education. By telling a student that the correct answer is there, and you just must select it is immediately limiting them – preventing the student from thinking just because the marker themselves can't be bothered to. Thirdly, presenting a set of answers that are similar to the 'correct' one but yet not actually deemed correct may be a recipe for confusion. Multiple choice questions are a shortcut to thinking (as Jim Morrison used to say – but I think he was talking about people likening him to a Barbie doll - fair enough). To summarize, the multiple-choice approach does seem to be emerging as a student appraisal tool in pedagogy, but perhaps not for the right reasons. But are there problems with other new approaches/fashionable methods? The answer, I fear, is yes. Teaching is an estimable profession, and it's great that teachers devote their lives to helping others (and understand that in doing so they are themselves benefitting), in return for what can only be described as modest remuneration. There are many inspirational teachers – I know because I have met many of them. Teaching is definitely a profession that requires intellect; but at the same time, it has to be admitted that, if you will excuse me for saying so, there can be something of an issue with some teachers confusing their role with that of an *intellectual* (with a definition for the latter from the web being: "An individual who is deeply involved in abstract erudite ideas and theories.") A desire to fulfil this role is, I believe, the root cause of much of the over-complication of, for example, A level curricula in many subjects. It may be that there is a tendency towards delusions of grandeur (something that is discussed in more detail below), that compels some teachers to wish to adopt the role of an intellectual. Thereby, in maths, for example, focussing heavily on calculus, and in science on quantum theory and methodological reductionism. In my view, it would be more valuable to teach students about basic theories and commonly employed approaches for quantitative problem-solving, with a generous provision of illuminating examples of their application, rather than trying to immerse them in mathematical complexity or scientific minutiae. Or to put it another way, we need a *back to basics* campaign in maths and science (which will have nothing, I hasten to add, in common with John Major's lamentable back to basics political campaign in the 1990s!) In pre-GCE O level maths lessons, I remember being taught about topology and set theory, but I don't remember being taught about algebra. Likewise, in English lessons we covered *The Old Wives' Tale* in all of its over-the-top minutiae (if you will excuse a slight digression, when someone was asked to read aloud from this book to our class, they made a mistake when reading the following passage from chapter 3: "She knew him simply as an organism on a bed" – there was general laughter!); but I don't remember being taught about spelling or grammar. Perhaps there was an assumption that we already knew it? At the levels taught in schools, the rules of maths and English have not changed for many years and it is perfectly correct (if you will excuse a possible pluralism – that, by the way, is something they may have taught us, along with the alleged incorrectness of the split infinitive...), to teach the basics – we don't always have to endeavour to appear clever. Science (and English) has, and will always have, a critical role to play in society; and so, *due to its nature*, it remains highly relevant through the years – there is no need for us to try to big it up – it already has more than enough gravitas.

"Looking back, I realize that nurturing curiosity and the instinct to seek solutions are perhaps the most important contributions education can make."

- Paul Berg

Science and society

"Novel technologies and ideas that impinge on human biology and their perceived impact on human values have renewed strains in the relationship between science and society."

- Paul Berg

In the 19th century, many people thought the 20th century would see the rise of science as the dominant force in society, instead of religion. I wouldn't exactly say that actually happened. In many societies, and particularly in the Third World, religion has grown tremendously in the last 100 years. In some developed countries, it is true that organised religion seems to be less popular than it was in the 19th century; as is evidenced by shrinking congregations in many English churches. However, I feel that this is perhaps somewhat due to religion falling somehow out of fashion, rather than due to a strong belief or interest in the nature or promise of science. Why aren't people more interested in science? Perhaps it is because it does not seem to be able to answer many of the huge questions in life that children ask when they first become aware of their place in the Universe. You know the kinds of questions – things like: what is the meaning or purpose of life, how did we get here, what will happen to us after we die? I live in central Somerset and, despite the fact that many of the villages are not large, their churches are usually extensive, detailed, and generally impressive; so it is clear that years ago people did have a strong interest in religion.

Mark: a village in Somerset with a population of less than 1500, but the church is, I feel, rather grand - and beautiful. (Photographs by the author.)

Humans are, as far as we know, the only animals able to imagine themselves in dangerous situations or dying in the future. Since clearly nobody alive has experienced death (excepting, perhaps, those who say they have had 'near-death experiences'), dying represents a passage into the unknown and it is natural to fear what we do not know. This is surely why religion exists – to give a form of meaning to things we will experience, such as death, that are absolute as well as unknown, but which we can imagine and so are frightened of. And we assume that science is not able to answer the fundamental questions of the type mentioned above; but is this necessarily true? Is science capable of answering the fundamental questions of existence? Perhaps the reason we think not is because the accomplishments of science seem so modest in contrast to the enormity of the questions we face but have yet to answer, or even to formalise a methodology by which we might try to start answering them. One factor contributing to this situation may be the preference that exists in modern science for applying methodological reductionism, which is defined in the *Oxford Companion to Philosophy* as: 'the scientific attempt to provide explanation in terms of ever smaller entities'. This holds that the best scientific approach involves attempting to reduce explanations to the smallest possible constituents.

In physics, methodological reductionism takes the form of always trying to look on smaller and smaller scales to identify ever more 'fundamental' particles. The way this is done is to study particle collisions in ever-more powerful particle accelerators. Such an approach does, in fact, have quite a strong pedigree. Every A-Level physics student is familiar with the experiments of Rutherford with alpha particles and thin gold foil. He was amazed to find that a small number of such particles were sent back by the foil (it was "as if you had fired a 15-inch [artillery] shell at a piece of tissue paper and it came back and hit you") – an observation that led him to the discovery of the atomic nucleus. This was one of the most important discoveries in nuclear physics and one which led to significant (if potentially harmful or controversial) new capabilities such as nuclear weapons and nuclear power. But do modern experiments in particle accelerators offer such potentials? The techniques here, in contrast to Rutherford, seem rather crude – just fire the particles into each other with as much power as we can muster and hope the result will be significant. And the results are … what? Endlessly increased complexity involving phenomena that are so small or devoid of mass that they are more like mathematical formations in field patterns than *physical* particles. If I were trying to solve a difficult mathematical or scientific problem and experienced continuously increased complexity, I would tend to start thinking that my methodology may be in error. Further, as mentioned above, the aim of science should really be to reduce complexity as much as possible and to simplify and unify one's findings. Consider, for example, a fractal; depending upon how you approach it this can appear as a couple of simple equations with numbers substituted into them, or a series of endless and increasingly complex patterns. Also, the scale upon which these particles are colliding and being studied is the quantum scale, where many complex and curious phenomena are often observed.

So, are the current experiments in nuclear physics likely to result in any really useful outcomes? Who knows? The jury is out and for the above reasons I have some doubts; but if not, we would have to conclude that a tremendous amount of resources and effort have been wasted on equipment such as the Large Hadron Collider at CERN (to be more exact, about a decade of work, at a total cost of about $4.75 billion).

In the context of biology, methodological reductionism involves attempting to explain all biological phenomena in terms of their underlying biochemical and molecular processes. The problem here is that there seem to be severe limits to what can be explained using conventional biochemistry. As mentioned above, much emphasis is placed today on genetics and there is a common perception that nearly everything can be explained through study of the cell DNA; with attendant expectations that most diseases can be cured through genetic technologies. It is no doubt true that genetic engineering offers many possibilities for the treatments of various conditions, and that gene therapy may be expected to assist in finding cures for a range of diseases.

CERN's \$4.5 billion particle accelerator; Large Hadron Collider or Large White Elephant? (Pen and ink drawing by the author.)

One related high-profile endeavour, the Human Genome Project, was launched amid much fanfare 30 years ago, with promises that it would yield untold health benefits for us all. But *Scientific American* have reported that Francis Collins, who is a geneticist who once led the Human Genome Project, has said that: "The genetic architecture of common diseases is turning out to be more elaborate than we might have guessed". In addition, *Scientific American* is of the opinion that genetics has not been able to offer the sorts of health benefits that had been envisioned and that COVID-19 has laid bare the need to: "reconsider the hope and money we invest in genetics". However, they do acknowledge that The Human Genome Project has produced profound health benefits for some individuals, in relation to testing for, and treating, inherited cancers. It also must be acknowledged that the current generation of vaccines, upon which the world places so much hope in its fight against COVID-19, have benefitted in many ways from genetic related technologies and understanding.

Although there is a general perception that genetics can explain most of our highly significant questions relating to cell and animal behaviours, in reality the situation may be somewhat different. For example, two questions that genetics apparently cannot currently answer are: how cells are able to specialise (we know that cells in different organs, such as the skin or liver, have different genes expressed, but how this comes to be is unclear), as well as how animals know instinctively how to do things which are often rather complicated tasks (e.g. a spider spinning a web). To be honest, it might be best to say that genetics gives insights into how various characteristics (e.g. hair or eye colour) are inherited by animals, but currently it fails to answer many of the more profound questions in relation to animal structures and behaviours – whether it will be able to do so in the future remains to be seen. Another example is evolution. Much has been made of the implications of Darwin's ideas of natural selection and it is likely that this process has, over the years, caused numerous species to adapt to various environments as well as leading to the extinction of those that could not adapt. So, it is certainly a significant contribution, but surely it is wholly inadequate for explaining the extreme diversity in characteristics of plants and animals that are found to exist and thrive in the same environmental conditions. How did such fantastic diversity come to be? I don't believe that it can be explained by evolution, even when combined with the outcomes of occasional mutations; obviously something else is going on... Finally, I cannot agree with those who suggest that the existence of the theory of evolution somehow shows that God does not exist. If God's existence were to be disproved by the fact that humans evolved from primates, one would have to ask where the primates came from, or going back in time, how the amino acids and proteins in the first primordial soups produced life. If this was sparked by lightning, who created that? Going back far enough would lead us to the question of what caused the Big Bang and, unfortunately, I don't think Darwin can help us here. By the way, despite this I do think that Darwin was a genius and do consider his contribution to biology to be astonishing.

Why there is still no cure for cancer

"If we can put a man on the Moon, we should have cured cancer by now."

- A commonly-made statement, but finding the cure for cancer is proving to be more complex than mastering the engineering and physics required for spaceflight – or, at least spaceflight to the Moon

In September 1961, US president John F. Kennedy set a goal for America to "... put a man on the moon and return him safely to Earth before the end of the 1960s..."

Many people thought this an unrealistic goal and yet, through a massive programme of research and development, it was achieved in July 1969. This must comprise a significant step towards being able to 'catch a rocket to Mars'. At the same time, there was also much discussion of finding a cure for cancer; but here, unfortunately, success has been more elusive. What are the reasons for this? While it is undoubtedly true that curing cancer is a more complex and involved problem than was thought in the early 1960s, are there also other methodological/ideological factors that are also holding medicine back? It is often assumed, for example, that a complex problem necessarily requires a complex solution; but is this really the case?

Consider, for example, the previously mentioned case of the introduction of handwashing saving the lives of many women in childbed, or the money spent on complicated lotions for application to the skin before a nurse discovered that bed sores can be eliminated through the simple expedient of moving the patient at regular intervals (and hence the invention of inflatable mattresses that automatically change pressure slightly over time thereby altering the pressure distribution of the patient on the mattress and so avoiding the prolonged pressure spots that lead to bed sores). Can we also fight cancer by the application of simple and low-cost remedies? While the answer to this question depends entirely on the data associated with scientific ('blind') testing of the proposed cures, the unfortunate fact remains that we may never get the answer since the data may never be collected – perhaps in part due to a bias in traditional medicine towards complex solutions (in the tradition of scientific reductionism).

This reminds me of a Sherlock Holmes short story. There are surely few aspects of our lives (and certainly little to do with the great city of London) that a study of Holmes cannot shed some degree of light on. It is, of course, in 'The Adventure of The Abbey Grange', that Holmes makes the famous quote: "The game is afoot!" However, Abbey Grange is also the story in which it seems like the crime has been committed by 'common rogues' and Watson goes so far as to say: "An abstruse and learned specialist who finds that he has been called in for a case of measles would experience something of the annoyance which I read in my friend's eyes." John Watson and Sir Arthur Conan Doyle were both medical doctors and would have understood this sentiment.

The disappointment of the abstruse and learned specialist in being confronted with a common condition may be analogous to the disappointment/denial that a very experienced cancer specialist might experience when confronted by the possibility that a simple remedy might be able to cure cancer. For example, there is considerable evidence that injection of vitamin C directly into the bloodstream can significantly reduce the progress of cancer. Having noticed publications indicating this, I contacted a well-known cancer charity and asked if any trials of intravenous vitamin C as a cancer treatment were being undertaken in the UK.

"Come, Watson, come!" he cried. "The game is afoot..." (Drawing by the author.)

I was told that no such trials were underway, and a reason given for this was that previous trials of intravenous vitamin C for cancer treatment have showed 'mixed results'. Since I had done quite exhaustive searches of databases such as MedTech in relation to this treatment for cancer and seen no indication of negative results, I was forced to question the assertion. Subsequently, I was told that they were referring to a study that involved the use of chemotherapy. Chemotherapy is a type of cancer treatment that uses drugs to kill cancer cells. Traditional chemotherapeutic agents are toxic to cells by means of interfering with cell division (mitosis), but cancer cells vary widely in their susceptibility to these agents. To a large extent, chemotherapy can be thought of as a way to damage or stress cells, which may then lead to cell death; but unfortunately, healthy as well as cancer cells can be affected and being powerful enough to kill the tumours can often mean they have adverse side effects for the patient. It is hardly surprising then that studies which employ chemotherapy can sometimes produce mixed results. (By the way, this is in no way a criticism of the cancer charity involved, which, like many other charities and organisations, undertakes excellent work that has, and continues, to alleviate suffering and save lives.) Another example is the common-or-garden drug aspirin. You may think of aspirin as something to take when you have a cold or a headache of a night and want to reduce your aches and pains to get a good night's sleep. But aspirin is a wonder drug! Yes indeed, you name it, aspirin is good for it and has precious few side effects (except in larger amounts a slight tendency for stomach/internal bleeding which makes it unsuitable for certain people such as haemophiliacs, as well as the fact that it is unsuitable for children under 16). Yes, study after study has shown aspirin to be beneficial in the fight against cancer, heart attacks, strokes, and more. And yet there are precious few randomised trials investigating the beneficial effects of aspirin for cancer sufferers – as I write this, I am not aware of any being conducted in the UK. The reasons for this are, I believe, due to both the abstruse expert issue mentioned above as well as the tendency to hyper-conservatism in the medical profession. In other words, vitamin C is a vitamin (i.e. food supplement) and aspirin is a painkiller – and so these things cannot also constitute drugs that might help fight cancer. Also, they are cheap and readily available – what drug company is going to be able to make money out of aspirin as an anti-cancer drug when you can buy a box of aspirin tablets in Tesco's for 30p? Another factor is the fact that the medical profession is biased away from solutions that don't build upon the accepted practice and body of work that constitutes *Western Medicine*. To some extent I can understand this – traditional medicine constitutes a vast body of knowledge that is constantly drawn upon all over the Earth and used to cure a multitude of illnesses, thereby saving endless lives. But there needs to be a limit to the attitude and when a simple and effective treatment or cure for a serious medical condition is staring you in the face, really I think it's best to acknowledge it. Otherwise we end up in a crazy situation where a medical doctor tells you he does not want to know about 'alternative' cures and if they worked he would still not want to know - I actually saw a (respected) medical doctor saying this on TV in the 1980's – on the late night Channel 4 discussion show called *After Dark*. As you probably know, this was a late-night live discussion programme that was broadcast on Channel 4 from 1987 to 1997 (and in 2003 on the BBC). Apparently Roly Keating of the BBC said it was: "one of the great television talk formats of all time", so I can't imagine why they cancelled it. Maybe it was a consequence of the complaints about that episode in which Ollie Reed ran amok; or perhaps it was just to do with TV executives' tendency to cancel shows that are strong on ideas/intellectual content in favour of focusing on the lowest common denominator, in an effort to get a bigger audience. This happens quite often in the world of TV; it could be argued that examples of this happening in US TV include the shows: *Star Trek*, *Nero Wolfe* and *Ellery Queen*. I must make a note here for those interested in television – please skip it if you are not. In 1969 *Star Trek* was usurped by the comedy chat show *Rowan and Martin's Laugh-in*, while the 1980

Nero Wolfe series lost out to the lightweight show *The Dukes of Hazzard*. Regarding *Ellery Queen*, this series ran for one season on NBC in 1975 and 1976. Its titular sleuth was played by Jim Hutton, who was the father of Timothy Hutton, with the latter playing Wolfe's wise-cracking leg-man Archie Goodwin in the A&E drama series *A Nero Wolfe Mystery*, which ran from 2000 to 2003. Many viewers were disappointed when the network cancelled the show. Perhaps the cancellation had to do with a move away from 'the arts' toward 'reality' (they even changed their name from 'Arts and Entertainment' to simply 'A&E'). I have spoken to people in the States who say that the quality of A&E programs went downhill as a result of it getting more into 'reality television' and the last time I was stateside I was of the same opinion after watching TV for a while. This in fact brings us back to Channel 4, since the same charge has been levelled against that network, after it started to focus more on its own reality TV show – *Big Brother* (the first time I heard someone mention that show I thought they were talking about Orwell's novel *1984*).

But let us return forthwith to the situation regarding finding a cure for cancer. It may be surprising to learn that the cure is ... nothing ... or nothing but the human body! There are many anecdotal cases of people being diagnosed with serious malignant tumours that doctors say will be fatal if not treated by conventional methods such as surgery, who have gone on a fast and the tumour has shrunken and effectively disappeared. In fact, this actually happened to a friend of mine – for an extended period the person concerned took only water. It is not that water was the cure - it was, he believes, more of a case of the extreme regime he underwent removing toxins from his body, stimulating the immune system, and helping his body fight off the disease. Likewise, the intravenous vitamin C and aspirin treatments mentioned above might not represent a cure for cancer, but due to their antioxidant and anti-inflammatory characteristics they may strengthen the body and thereby help in the fight against the disease. This approach of encouraging the body in fighting cancer is, in fact, also the basic philosophy of one of the most promising treatments that might even result in a cure – I refer to immunotherapy. The latter is a type of cancer treatment that helps the immune system (white blood cells and organs and tissues of the lymph system), to fight cancer. It does this by treating cancer with a type of biological therapy – which is a treatment that uses substances made from living organisms. This technique makes use of the natural function of the immune system to detect and destroy abnormal cells in order to prevent or minimize the growth of many cancers. Several types of immunotherapy are used to treat cancer. These include:

- Immune checkpoint inhibitors, which are drugs that block immune checkpoints, thereby allowing immune cells to respond more strongly to cancer.

- Immune cell therapy - a treatment that boosts the natural ability of your T cells to fight cancer.

- Monoclonal (or therapeutic) antibodies, which mark cancer cells so that they will be better seen and destroyed by the immune system.

- Cancer treatment vaccines, which work against the disease by boosting your immune system's response to cancer cells.

- Immune system modulators that enhance the body's immune response against cancer. Some of these agents affect specific parts of the immune system, whereas others affect the immune system in a more general way.

Immunotherapy technology is, though, still an emerging treatment, albeit a very promising one. Not all cancers can currently be treated in this way, side effects can occur, and in practice we are still largely dependent on conventional treatments such as surgery, chemotherapy, or radiation therapy. However, the number of cancers treatable by immunotherapy is constantly increasing, thereby providing hope that this terrible disease will one day be conquered. So, although we may not yet be at the stage where we can say we have a cure for cancer, we are on the way.

Delusions of grandeur

"Delusions of grandeur make me feel a lot better about myself."

- Jane Wagner

When you were a bright-eyed young schoolchild, did you ever say that when you grew up you wanted to be a popular singer, or a top racing driver, or a brain surgeon, or an admiral of the fleet? And why not? What's wrong with having a dream, aspirations - something you hope to work towards? Surely being inspired and trying to make your dreams come true is something that we would wish for everyone. Yes indeed. But then our dreams become tempered by the long experience of many years of trying, hopefully having some success and surely also some disappointments. Such is life – this is the experience that nearly all of us are familiar with. But the delusions of grandeur I am thinking of in this chapter are not those of the naive and beautifully innocent schoolchild. No sir. Rather, they are those of the adult who, shall we say, is keen to 'accentuate the positive' (as Bing Crosby used to say) and perhaps to accentuate it rather too much.

I very much like going to the Greek Islands for holidays. If you will excuse a digression, the Greek Islands are a rather splendid place to vacation. Corfu is a particularly lovely island – the 'Garden of the Gods' as Gerald Durrell named it; and in fact there is a beautiful garden in Corfu town that contains a bronze relief of Gerry (and his brother Larry, also very much a man of letters).

The bronze memorial in Corfu Town of Gerald Durrell - the author who wrote numerous books that immortalised life on the island. (Illustration by the author.)

I also like the historical connection between the British and the Greeks; Corfu was, for some years, administered by the British with cricket still being played on the green in front of the Durrell's garden. And, in Crete, who can forget the impressive ruin of 'Europe's Oldest City': Sir Arthur Evans began excavations in Knossos in 1900, and they continued for 35 years! Dedication to the cause, I call that. Eventually, he gave the whole site to the Greeks and they showed their appreciation by allowing British archaeologists to visit and study the site at any time – something that continues to this day... And who can forget how keen Lord Byron was on Greece and how much the Greeks took him to their hearts – there is even a statue of him in Athens! So, I go to the Greek islands quite often – mainly Corfu, Crete, and Rhodes. And regarding the latter, Lindos must be my favourite place in Greece.

"Fair Greece! sad relic of departed worth! Immortal, though no more! though fallen, great!"

- Lord Byron

The beautiful and interesting village of Lindos, on the island of Rhodes. (Photograph by the author.)

But nearly every time I go to a Greek restaurant and start chatting with a waiter, he tells me how he is a 'major investor in the hotel'. How then, one wonders, did he find himself under the necessity to undertake such relatively low paid employment as waiting on tables? Similarly, I had a relative who once gave advice to another relative: "L-, if you don't have money, always make out that you have…" (It turns out that L- was in fact quite well off, so I guess the advice was hardly necessary). Another example concerns someone I know well who now works for his own company but used to, for a while, work for a university. I have been advised, by someone at the university who would know, that my friend was on the senior lecturer pay-scale. Despite this, the latter assures me, in all sincerity, that he was on the professorial pay-scale, presumably for reasons of image maintenance. What, you may ask, has all this to do with science and society or Martian rockets? Well, I am convinced that delusions of grandeur (amongst adults) are one of the main reasons why I can't catch a rocket to Mars; and I will briefly try to explain below why this is the case.

I can understand why a person running a small business, such as the friend mentioned above, may need to 'big themselves up'. It is, after all, a very competitive world – it's a 'dog eat dog' marketplace where to survive a businessman needs a 'can do' attitude just to keep his head above water. But away from the commercial world, in the academic and research world, surely we should be more objective and straight-forward i.e. 'call a spade a spade' as my mother used to say (who was, you might not be surprised to learn, from Yorkshire). In

66

science, a spade is in fact always a spade; it is not for example, a spade 60% of the time and an 'agricultural implement' 40% of the time. By the way, this is, if I may say so without being accused of being politically incorrect, one reason why English is so well suited to describing scientific research – and hence why it is the language that nearly all scientific papers are published in. English is a remarkably simple language in its grammar and, importantly, does not employ all the colourful imagery and metaphor that is seen in the Latin-based languages. I am not a philologist, but I believe that the reason for this has to do with the fact that English is a relatively modern language compared to, for example, French. Consequently, English has mercifully dispensed with such archaic complexities as continuous colourful metaphor, changing grammar depending upon whom or what one is addressing or referring to, and the (apparently random) assigning of gender to inanimate objects. Yes, when you call a spade a spade in English you are also doing it using a language that inherently, in its style and structure, calls a spade a spade – particularly in the American usage of English.

But why does any of this mean that I can't catch the rocket? The answer is that not calling a spade a spade, or 'bigging oneself up' or 'trying to cut a good figure', or whatever you want to call it – perhaps it could simply be called vanity, is not a characteristic that particularly accelerates or encourages scientific or technological progress. For example, since I have mentioned scientific papers, it is worth pointing out that an emphasis on the presentation of 'pretty maths' (something that was mentioned above in relation to Dyson and Feynman), rather than on real novelty or genuinely useful new approaches, will tend to lead to stale/unprofitable avenues of publication. Another way of expressing this is to say that 95% of all journal papers are of very limited use and do not demonstrate good impact or have a strong influence on scientific thought or technological progress. The reasons for this include the widespread obsession with involved mathematical presentation as well as the modern tendency towards dogma in science, which was also discussed above. However, 'cutting a good figure' by those involved in science has its most conspicuous effect on society through education, since education, particularly in schools, is where the majority of the public have contact with scientific concepts. We covered education/teaching above in some detail, but I would like to return to the subject, since I do feel it is quite relevant to the subject of this chapter.

Science education is an extensive field that could easily fill a book by itself and there is not room here to discuss it in detail. I would, however, like to say how much respect I have in general for teachers (or in fact for members of any caring profession). They work long hours and often take great pains to ensure that they help their students as much as possible. I am sure the pay they receive is hardly in proportion to the work they do and the contribution they make to society. Interestingly though, I believe that most teachers understand that helping others is one of the most effective ways of helping oneself and that the satisfaction they glean from their pastoral roles is one of the things that compensates a relatively meagre pay packet. Having said all that, I do believe that some of the major problems in science education result from teachers, and others associated with the education process, trying to adopt the role of intellectual or, again, trying to big themselves up. Take, for example, A levels, where the decision of what subjects you choose usually has a strong influence on one's entire career choice. We often hear that there are insufficient trained engineers (particularly female engineers) – what might be the reasons for this? One conspicuous reason may be the scaring off (for want of a better phrase) of potential science students by an unnecessarily complex and esoteric treatment of the subject at the advanced level in schools and colleges. Open, for example, a modern A level physics textbook and you will find, possibly on the first pages, much coverage of quarks and many of the esoteric characteristics associated with such (relatively non-physical) phenomena. What is the likelihood that the A level student opening such a book will be employed in a post that will necessitate knowledge of the characteristics of quarks? Virtually zero! What does the presentation of such material as the first thing in a physics textbook achieve? Possibly it disorientates the reader, who may feel that the subject is one they cannot relate to, is difficult, esoteric, and will be of little practical use to them in their careers. While this may be true of studying quarks, it has never been, and should never be, generally true of studying physics. In fact, I can't think of a subject that would be more practical and useful to anyone who wants a technical education and/or career than physics! I can't help thinking that the other thing it may achieve is to enable the book's author and various physics educators to go on something of an ego trip at the expense of physics education in the UK. To summarise, I feel that the curriculum of A level physics is becoming too involved and has gone beyond what is required or would be essential for entering a technical degree course. There are too many equations and there is too much coverage, both in terms of breadth and depth – which I suspect is putting students off studying the subject and thereby reducing the UK's technical skills base. Rather than expecting students to appreciate esoteric physics and multitudes of equations it would, I believe, be more beneficial to test the student's understanding of the various concepts involved and the application of physics to various real technologies that they can relate to. This was an approach adopted by the *Nuffield A Level Physics* course that I remember being taught back in the early 1980's. It seemed enlightened to me then and it still does now – I don't know why the modern A Level examination boards (or at least the ones I have dealt with recently) appear to have abandoned the Nuffield Physics curriculum.

The other sciences also suffer from similar problems, manifested in terms of the A level biology memory game and in A level chemistry, legions of organic reactions. Are students embarking on, say, engineering degrees likely to find knowledge of these organic reactions useful in their studies and careers? I think not; and this provides a strong indicator that the traditional grounding in maths, physics, and chemistry may not be the best way to prepare for a degree course and career in engineering.

Having again mentioned maths, following the earlier lengthy discussion I would just like to add that this is an extremely powerful tool for a person such as an engineer, but unfortunately I don't think it is generally taught as such. Is the traditional massive emphasis on calculus really justified? Is an engineering student, in truth, likely to find they need to recall how to perform 'proof by induction', or to employ the binomial theorem? I think not. When I was studying A level maths, the course covered such subjects but provided no coverage of statistical analysis - which is very important in, for example, medicine and a range of industries. Consequently, when undertaking my PhD, I had to teach myself statistical techniques such as multiple regression (with appropriate non-linear transforms), effectively from scratch.

Many students take A level maths, and according to media report graduates and non-graduates who took maths A-level earn on average 10 per cent more than those of similar ability and background who did not; however, in current maths A level courses there is little emphasis on applications and real-world needs. (Pexels photograph by Andrea Piacquadio, used with permission of Pexels.)

To summarise, I feel there should be a move away from the wide-range of involved closed-form maths techniques that are currently being taught in schools and colleges, towards approaches that are very powerful and likely to be useful to the students later in their careers. Such techniques definitely include statistical analysis and are likely to include numerical methods that have proved so powerful in solving problems in disciplines such as engineering. But perhaps the most important new form of modelling/analysis that promises to change our lives in innumerable ways is artificial intelligence (AI) and specifically deep learning. Surely it is time to dispense with our delusions of grandeur and instead embrace the possibilities of existing new AI technologies by introducing our students to them.

A great deal of funding, but just a little bit of impact

"Research is creating new knowledge."

- Neil Armstrong

University researchers and professors are, not surprisingly, experts at undertaking research; but they are, generally speaking, rather less expert at generating impact from their research. What, you may ask, is the difference between research and impact? Well, research, at least in the hard sciences such as physics and engineering, consists of generating new knowledge (as Neil Armstrong very astutely pointed out). This definition is important because research, as is being discussed here, does need to be differentiated from research as is commonly undertaken in, for example, the social sciences, where the activity is more about finding out what some people think about something. For example, a social scientist might go to a shopping centre and ask people there what they think about a given product or service, perhaps also asking them to fill out a questionnaire about it. Such activities are really information gathering, and will be referred to here not as research, but as market research.

To return to research, it is an activity where the researcher is establishing something novel, and then usually going on to describe it in one or more journal papers, which are appraised by the researcher's peers and, if accepted, published for access by the research community (and general public). (By the way, in order to facilitate the undertaking of the research, the researcher or professor is likely to have had to win a grant from a funding body – this is something that will be discussed in more detail below.) However, such publication does not represent impact. The latter is more concerned with the impact or influence of the research on society. For example, in engineering the paper could describe a new approach to the solution of an engineering problem that will allow development of a machine or system able to undertake tasks that had previously been deemed too difficult for automation, thereby saving labour or perhaps, in the case of dangerous tasks, even saving lives. Fine and dandy you might say; what is wrong with any of that? Nothing, in fact, but at the same time, it is true that most research that is reported in journal papers leads to very little, if any, impact. Why is this? One reason is that, as mentioned above, academics are, as a general rule, not very skilled in generating impact. The reasons for this are quite obvious – they have spent much of their lives studying in a corner, trying to master various difficult subjects in order to pass exams and thereby demonstrate their competency in their chosen field. Following this, they may have undertaken a PhD which, at least in technical subjects, is also certain to require much more time to be spent in that corner. They will need to capture data, appraise it, process it, model it, use it for generating knowledge about their subject, and then employ that knowledge in a form that progresses scientific understanding. They may have had to teach themselves how to undertake rigorous statistical analysis, or even more involved methods of system analysis and prediction, such as machine learning.

"The only limit to your impact is your imagination and commitment."

- Tony Robbins

What then, are the skills needed for generating strong impact? These may be characterised as being more similar to the ability to operate in the commercial world – to have a can-do attitude and to be a good salesman. Chalk and cheese, I think you will agree. Another significant factor may be the competitive system that is used for most allocation of research funding and the Full Economic Costing (FEC) method that is employed to cost the research proposals. Once an academic has decided to try to gain funding for a piece of work, they will generally need to do the following:

- Find a relevant funding source.

- Look for a currently open call.

- Fulfil the funding conditions – for example, often an industrial partner is required – therefore they will need to identify and approach a company and get them to agree to participate, with all the complex associated procedures, such as arranging for non-disclosure agreements, and agreeing to costs distributions, IP sharing and, if the application is successful, a contract between the university and the company.

- Write the application and get the FEC completed – which will need to include a time allocation for the academic and for the researcher concerned.

- Get the university to agree to the costing and to submit the application for funding.

- Deal with all relevant ethical or risk assessment considerations.

- Submit the application and, if required, provide strong technical responses to assessors' comments or criticisms.

Due to the modern academic/university/funding environment, there is a good deal of pressure for academics to submit applications and to win funding. Consequently,

71

many academics find themselves spending most of their time undertaking the above tasks. It is also a fact of modern academic life that funding competitions tend to be over-subscribed, so that even if a very good proposal is submitted there may not be enough money available to fund it. Consequently, the success rates for many competitions are often very poor – at perhaps around 20% or less. Therefore, the academic has to submit around five or more good quality applications before being relatively sure of winning funding. (By the way, this is one reason why the FEC is not a terribly realistic calculation for the cost of a project, since if it were it would have to take into account the enormous amount of time and money spent on the multiple unsuccessful applications – which is something that is just about never accounted for.) If the poor old academic is lucky enough to be awarded the money, they may not have any energy left to actually undertake the work; and in any case the grant probably only covers a year or two so their main priority may be to think about another grant to cover the period from the end of the first one. This is now beginning to illustrate the main problem associated with all of this; specifically, the way funding is allocated tends to provide motivation for able academics to undertake all the multitudinous tasks associated with winning research funding, but relatively little motivation for actually undertaking the associated research and generating a useful outcome. There is likely to be even less motivation for taking the research outcomes and using them to generate strong impact since this, at least in the short term, is not likely to generate money for the university – in contrast, it is more likely to require significant investment by the university. Such investment is not very likely to be forthcoming, both because of the traditional tendency in the UK towards short-term reward, and the tradition of the university to instead invest heavily in the teaching resources. The latter will tend to be the preferred option for the university for at least two reasons: they can see a very good chance of an immediate return on this investment in terms of student fees, and like most institutions they have a natural conservatism – they tend to wish to fund the kinds of things they have funded before.

Considering high-impact research undertaken in the UK, most of it tends to be funded by companies, sometimes supplemented by government money through schemes such as Innovate UK (which used to be called the TSB and before that the DTI). Then, of course, there are also the research councils such as the Engineering and Physical Sciences Research Council, the dear old NHS and, dare I say it, the European Commission. I would like to cover these all at some stage and to a greater or lesser extent, but let's start with the mighty (but perhaps somewhat less mighty than it used to be) European Union (EU). I apologise for not being overly diplomatic regarding my EU research comments, but to be honest it's such a nebulous and overreaching subject that, due to a lack of time and space, I must be succinct. The EU does not fund research. If you get some money for research as a consequence of its operations/programmes, then that is nice, but the EU is not interested in funding research. What it does want to fund is social engineering aimed at improving European cohesiveness. I know this is true because I heard it from the horse's mouth - I was told it many years ago during my attendance at a presentation that was given by an organisation that I will not name, but which is a British organisation based in Brussels that aims to maximise UK engagement in EU-funded research, innovation, and higher education activities. So, if they don't know what EU research is about, nobody does. Or is it that nobody does? I must point out that I have nothing against the organisation concerned – a lovely group of people I am sure – and trying to help other groups that really need help, i.e. persons considering applying for EU funding. I must also point out that I do know something about EU funding – having applied for and received it on a substantial scale for a major EU ('Framework') research project. At the same time, there are some home truths about EU research that one must point out: EU funded research has notoriously low impact and EU research seems to be more about interesting foreign travel and dinner parties than about undertaking useful research. Why does it have such low impact? One reason is surely the overly complex project requirements, such as projects requiring participation of three European companies/universities, with two from the EU and one from Eastern Europe, and complicated costing methods with everyone following different rules. I remember that in one application that I wrote I had to complete about a dozen pages on exploitation plans (which of itself represented over-complication). No doubt they were asking for all those pages because they realised that the impact of their projects is amazingly low, while at the same time not understanding that the reason for this was that all their complex (politically motivated) requirements were diminishing the likelihood of anyone running an effective project and producing a useful outcome. I remember trying to put down significant time and funding for actually undertaking the research, but meeting with resistance from a European commissioner who was anxious for it to be spent on 'networking' (remember the travel and dining?) She was Spanish; which is a country and people that I have nothing against - having good Spanish friends for many years and, like the next man, having been on Spanish holidays and drunk the wine. Despite the plonk that was sent our way for many years, while visiting Spain during the project I found that Spanish wine (and food/hotels) can actually be very fine indeed! But the commissioner was hostile - I might even say anti-British - I know it sounds ridiculous but there we are. I was told by a Portuguese friend of mine that she was saying things like: "These British, they always want all the money" (despite the fact that we were undertaking most of the actual work and being paid less than some of the other project partners). I think it would have been rude to point out that for many, many years the UK had been the second largest net contributor to the EU, making massive contributions each year, and that for all those years much of that money had been going to Spain. But, after many years of experience of collaborative research projects, the last thing I would have wanted to do would be to start squabbling over project cost breakdowns. In any case, unlike Clarkson, in Spain I would not have asked people coming from ATMs to give me money or have refused to pay the tolls on their roads.

Motivations for technological progress - private versus public funding

"Every hour a scientist spends trying to raise funds is an hour lost from important thought and research."

— Isaac Asimov

Anyone interested in research and particularly research with high impact, is at some stage likely to consider the question of what funding mechanism produces the best outcomes. One of the first questions to be asked is which tends to be more productive: private or public funding? After studying the subject of impact, it is hard not to come to the conclusion that in recent years most impact has been generated by private companies rather than publicly-funded organisations. Consider, for example, modern personal computers (PCs). The majority of commonly utilised hardware and software for PCs has been generated, standardised, and made popular by private companies, nearly all of which are based in the USA (e.g. IBM and Microsoft). So why is the private sector so dominant? The reason is perhaps associated with the nature of private companies and in particular their structure and patterns of operations. A private company is, essentially, a group of (often very talented) private individuals who have effectively clubbed together with the aim of doing something well; so well that they hope to make money and, if possible, achieve long-term dominance in their chosen area (something that, for example, Microsoft has dramatically demonstrated for the sector of office and home software). In order to do this, they have to work hard; they need to apply an intensive effort, meet goals and deadlines and be highly efficient in their operations. To increase productivity, they have avoided many of the distractions that most of today's organisations often seem to be obsessed with; an example is political correctness (or at least they used to be able to avoid it). So, what is the situation in the public sector? We have to be honest and say that there is less pressure to be efficient and highly productive – which is undoubtedly due to the lack of a pressing need to 'get the product out the door'. Whereas private companies always seem to want something done yesterday, an organisation such as a university will be looking towards the next semester – which is likely to be in several months' time. Regarding political correctness, while private companies do not generally have the time to indulge the subtler aspects of PC culture (at least in most of their internal operations), public organisations such as universities and the dear old BBC are, as was observed previously, pretty much obsessed with PC issues. By the time public bodies such as universities have completed their PC selfflagellations, they hardly have any time or energy left for undertaking productive research. The other important factor is, of course, competition. Where there is very strong competition, technological progress is often markedly pronounced. Perhaps the most intense form of competition is that of a total war between powerful nations. If countries fear for their survival in such a war then the effect is even more intense, and a good example of a conflict where this occurred is World War Two (WWII). As most people know, in the summer of 1940 Britain did fear for its survival. Nazi Germany had invaded nearly all of Europe, had an air force twice the size of the RAF and was planning an invasion of merry olde England (Operation *Sea Lion*). About the only thing that would make Britain safe would be a victory by the RAF over the Luftwaffe. And so, what happened? Sure enough, the British put enormous amounts of ingenuity and effort into invention and development of a radio-based early warning system all around the south and east coast that would detect enemy aircraft many miles away (giving both direction, range, and number of aircraft). This new system was known as RDF - *Radio Direction Finding* (later designated as *Radio Detection and Ranging* or RADAR). This meant that the RAF were ready for the invading planes and could often intercept them well before they reached English soil.

A Supermarine Spitfire; the Battle of Britain was a pivotal moment in WWII and one of the most significant parts of Britain's long history. (Pen and ink drawing by the author.)

The result was that RADAR (along with critical and breath-taking bravery and dedication to duty from the Hurricane and Spitfire pilots and support staff) enabled the RAF to win the Battle of Britain. A small country on the western edge of Europe had halted the apparently insurmountable wave of conquest of an aggressive, efficient, powerful, and politically anachronistic Nazi Germany (which modelled itself on the Roman Empire - 2000 years after the fall of the latter). The consequences of this first blow for freedom by Britain, for the future progress of WWII and hence the future destiny of the civilised world, can hardly be overestimated. And what of German technological progress in WWII? I think you would have to call it impressive, in fact, very impressive (in stark contrast to their politics of the time).

Consider, for example, the Panzer Tank, or the Messerschmitt Me 262 (the world's first operational jet-powered fighter aircraft), or (most amazingly) Hitler's 'vengeance' weapons – in particular the V2 rocket. These three instruments of war were developed in chronological order as the war progressed. When it started to look as though the Axis was losing, Germany naturally started to fear for its survival and so the technological inventiveness and rates of development became correspondingly accelerated. The V2 rocket is indeed a technological marvel and was so technologically advanced that the Allies were studying and launching them years after the war ended. Hitler launched V2s (and V1s) to exact vengeance on the UK for the heavy bombing of Germany by the Allies towards the end of WWII (which was actually quite catastrophic for the German cities and civilians). What he was really trying to do was to terrorise the British public with these weapons. To be honest, a V2 hurtling towards you is indeed quite a terrifying prospect, since it was the first weapon to have the dubious characteristic of being able to kill you without you even realising it was approaching, travelling as it does at velocities greater than that of sound (which is something that also made them extremely difficult to shoot down). A V2 loaded with 1000kg of high explosive is certainly something that could terrify and also kill quite a number of people, but it is not a weapon that could win a world war (at least not when manufactured in the limited quantities that Germany could manage towards the end of WWII). Nevertheless, V2s loaded with nuclear warheads do represent a weapon that could have enabled the Nazis to capture the world, even in conditions of limited production. Chillingly, during the war the Germans were working on a nuclear weapons project (with heavy water production via hydroelectric plants in Norway) and the world owes a debt of gratitude to the Norwegian commandos and Allied bombers who sabotaged these operations.

After the war, America employed the V2 creator, Wernher von Braun, as the chief architect of the Saturn V super heavy-lift launch vehicle that propelled the Apollo spacecraft to the Moon. Speaking of the Apollo project, it was again competition that spurred this project on – specifically competition with the Soviet Union to be the first to land a man on the moon. I think that anyone who is a baby boomer and who has any kind of interest in science/technology feels the enormous influence on their childhood learning and experience that Apollo and the Saturn V rocket had (or at least it had on me). I can remember seeing Neil Armstrong making his 'enormous leap for mankind' and I still have the science encyclopaedias that my parents bought my brother and myself for Christmas – which featured articles on the great Saturn V rocket.

Apollo 11 mission commander Neil Armstrong on the lunar surface in 1969. (Photograph courtesy of NASA.)

By the way, if the Nazis had won the war it would almost have certainly led to widespread and on-going political unrest and continued fighting, to such an extent that it is very unlikely that manned space flight would have been developed or a moon shot undertaken. In fact, it would have led to such chaos that I am not sure that much in the way of electronics technology such as personal computers would have been developed – so I would not be here now enjoying the luxury of gently tapping keys on my PC. Such reflections lead me to think of the famous gonzo journalist Hunter S. Thompson - specifically his comments in *Fear and Loathing in Las Vegas* on the Circus Circus casino in Las Vegas: "The Circus Circus is what the whole hep world would be doing Saturday night if the Nazis had won the war. This is the sixth Reich. The ground floor is full of gambling tables, like all the other casinos ... but the place is about four stories high, in the style of a circus tent, and all manner of strange County Fair/Polish Carnival madness is going on up in this space."

A typical Las Vegas street scene - the Circus Circus is by no means the most outlandish or surreal hotel/casino in town. (Photograph by the author.)

There does not, however, have to be a war raging or space race in full swing, for us to be able to see the benefits of competition. Consider, for example, how good the operations are of the four major UK grocery retailers: Tesco, Sainsbury's, Asda, and Morrisons. Long gone are the days of the old rogue food outlets that used to adulterate food with the consequent need for the trusty old Cooperative Retail Society to give us good food at an honest price. In fact, the big four are so efficient that the Co-op has a job competing with them – but the good old Co-op still, in many communities, provides a local shopping experience and community feel – which is invaluable for those who are unable, or who cannot afford, to drive.

So the British are very good at shops and selling (Napoleon did, after all, call us a 'nation of shopkeepers' – he meant it as an insult but I believe it was largely taken as a complement!), but are they equally good at, for example, secondary education? To judge by the crises that seem to regularly engulf schools around the country, perhaps not. If so, has the reason to do with the fact that state education is not something for which it is very easy to introduce competition? And what about healthcare in the UK?

I, like many people, love the NHS and consider it a cornerstone of British culture. There is something tremendously civilised about the concept of everyone paying into a fund that provides help to fellow citizens when they fall ill and, critically, provides it on the basis of clinical need rather than the ability to pay. This is a great thing, and it needs to be maintained and continuously enshrined in our culture. However, in my view, this does not mean that the NHS cannot make use of provision from the private sector to care for or treat some of its patients. Although I have not, thank God, suffered much ill health or needed much medical treatment, I have occasionally had treatments on the NHS and on one such occasion at a private hospital near Bath. I was very impressed with the whole experience and believe that such quality experiences should be available to other NHS patients. Also, while maintaining and funding the NHS, something does need to be done to tackle organisational cultures that result in poor quality food, dreary hospital buildings, and interiors which, I believe, without the effects of some injection of new thinking and competition, would forever remain sub-standard, no matter how much funding were applied.

So much for NHS practice; but what about NHS research and technological developments? Unfortunately, despite high levels of funding (£billions per year) these are often, particularly outside of London and the 'Golden Triangle' (Cambridge, Oxford, and London), relatively limited in terms of their accomplishments and impact. There are many reasons for this – one is undoubtedly the effects of lack of competition in public sector organisations – but another has to do with the way clinical careers are structured within the NHS. Put simply, there are insufficient incentives for leading clinicians, particularly those with extensive/demanding practices, to undertake research. Or, to express it another way, leading NHS surgeons or senior clinicians are often so busy with their medical practices, i.e. treating patients in need in the NHS, that they simply do not have time for research. This can limit research outcomes/impact since, from personal experience, I can confirm that it is impractical to undertake research and development of medical devices without the close involvement of clinicians.

Another circumstance that the NHS finds itself in is that of extreme conservativism, perhaps resulting from the natural and understandable conservatism of the medical profession, as well as the tendency of British public institutions to be inward looking and relatively resistant to change (a good example being the BBC). This can result in slower adoption of improved procedures and/or devices than would be desirable. Therefore, no matter how much funding is available, as long as the proportions of NHS clinicians who cannot (or do not wish to) undertake research remain at their current levels, it will be difficult for the NHS to attain the levels of research with impact that would perhaps be expected of so substantial and admirable an organisation.

Re-inventing the wheel

"In the old days, you would chastise people for reinventing the wheel. Now we beg, 'Oh, please, please reinvent the wheel."

- Alan Kay

I am an engineer, from a family of engineers. My wife is an engineer, as was her father. My brother is an engineer, as was our father, and his father, and his father... Being an engineer has a meaning of itself and anyone who wants to understand the significance of the role can learn a good deal from popular culture – I mean just study Scotty from *Star Trek*.

The *Star Trek* engineer Montgomery "Scotty" Scott in a Jefferies Tube (with Chief Medical Officer Leonard H. "Bones" McCoy in the background). (Pen and ink drawing by the author.)

In fact, an engineering transport technology features in one of the most famous quotes in popular culture: "Beam me up Scotty!" While we are talking about Jimmy Dohan's portrayal of Scotty, I have got to say that some of his reflections on being an engineer that I enjoyed most were in the episode 'Relics' of *Star Trek: The Next Generation*.

Scotty in the episode Relics of *Star Trek: The Next Generation*. (Drawing by the author.)

For many years, I lived in the Great Western Railway city of Bristol – that jewel of the South West. Most Bristolians are not slow to tell you about Brunel – perhaps the most famous engineer of them all. If you don't know about Brunel's broad-gauge railway that joined Bristol Temple Meads to London Paddington, then you need to learn about it as soon as possible. In a nutshell, the great engineer created a masterpiece of a railway that helped to transform our lives and our country by linking two great cities in the south of England by a railway that had a gauge of 7 feet! And this was in 1844! Today, most of the world is still toddling around on railways that employ George Stevenson's standard gauge of 4 feet 8-and a half inches, well over a century and a half after Brunel built his masterpiece. If we were using a 7-foot gauge today I expect that our trains could regularly travel at 200+ mph and if Brunel were alive now I have little doubt that he would be considering the engineering challenges associated with my mythical Martian rocket. While we are here, if you also have not walked across Brunel's world-famous Clifton Suspension Bridge (the one, in fact, that I mentioned earlier), then you need to do so – and *NOW!* By the way, about thirty years ago, I used to live on the far side of the suspension bridge – in Leigh Woods. At that time, I was working as a technology tutor at a training company in central Bristol. The idea was that the local authority would send people to us who had had health issues such as a heart attack or a nervous breakdown, which meant they could not do the jobs they were accustomed to, so we would re-train them to give them technical skills so that they could undertake new types of work. I used to enjoy talking to them and we had a few laughs, but they would wind me up from time to time. I remember saying to them that considering I had to come in to work and see them it was a wonder that I got across the bridge every day without throwing myself off it – they, quite earnestly, agreed. It's a wonder *I* didn't have a nervous breakdown!

Getting back to the romantic gentleman engineers of the nineteenth century; I have always been an admirer of them and have great interest in their work. Telford, Stevenson (and son), Brunel and the others; their feats of engineering are legendary and seem almost miraculous, particularly when you consider when they achieved them and the limited tools available – no JCB I'm afraid – this was the age of the navvy and the wheelbarrow. But although I admire the great romantic engineers of yesteryear, I am very much aware of the inefficiencies of engineering in the past. They say that before computers, around 20% of an engineer's time was spent just trying to find things such as data and drawings. Whereas nowadays, 90% of our time is usually spent trying to start up our computers in the morning. (That was a joke, but when you have a PC with a 'University Build' on it, simply starting it up is not a task to be taken lightly!) Seriously though, one of the great benefits of the age of computers is the capability they offer for sharing critical information and making materials such as engineering data, 'virtual models' and drawings/diagrams, available to those who need it, when they need it. This enables companies to implement what is called concurrent engineering, which essentially means staff can share important information and consequently numerous engineering tasks (e.g. design of various parts) can be undertaken at the same time – hence the term concurrent. Nowadays, companies have to employ these kinds of methods in order to remain competitive – products as complex as modern aircraft could certainly not be delivered with the lead times and price that they are without the use of concurrent engineering (or similar techniques). Back in the mid-1990s, my PhD was, in fact, related to concurrent engineering and I subsequently taught a master's course in this subject for many years. As you may have noticed, I like to think about historical examples of engineering. One day, when I was introducing concurrent engineering, I decided to talk about the Supermarine Spitfire and projected an image of it up onto the screen. This is an aircraft that I, like I think many British people, have a romance with. Many of us spent numerous evenings making and painting Airfix models of it when we were young – at least I did. So, I was musing away, showing the class a picture of the aircraft that seems to epitomise the spirit of the Battle of Britain in the imagination of the British, and I said: "Isn't this the most beautiful aircraft you have ever seen?" and there was a loud and abrupt reply from the centre of the room: 'No!' It turned out that this year, unbeknownst to me, there were a considerable number of German students in the class. I said, "well, what is then?" and the voice replied, "the Messerschmitt Me 262" and I said: "watch yourself!" and there was general laughter in the class. The student went on to choose the Messerschmitt Me 262 as a case study for the assignment that students undertake in the course. Of course, during WWII the term 'concurrent engineering' had not yet been coined, but many of the circumstances the Germans faced at that time were somewhat similar to what many manufacturing companies face today: limited resources and time available to get the product out, fierce competition and so on (although I fancy that the situation faced by Messerschmitt at that time was a tad more desperate than that faced by most engineering companies today). We also had an ongoing debate about whether the world's first jet fighter aircraft was the Gloucester Meteor or the Messerschmitt Me 262. He went on to do an excellent assignment – in which he was sufficiently diplomatic not to point out that the Me 262 was the first *operational* jet fighter. I am still connected to him on LinkedIn. By the way, another quip I used to come out with in the lectures of this course was: "In England we are of course going metric ... *inch by inch!*" I always enjoyed this and, honestly, it used to get quite a few laughs. The curious thing is that it is true (while of course in America most people are not even bothering with giving the impression of going metric).

Messerschmitt Me 262 - the first operational jet fighter. (Pen and ink drawing by the author.)

But what, you may ask, has all this to do with re-inventing the wheel? Well, one of the main concepts in concurrent engineering is that we should not re-invent the wheel. If we want to make excellent scientific and technological progress, we can't afford to waste time and effort on it. Take, for example, scientific papers and publication. The essential idea of publishing a journal paper is to communicate a new finding that you may have to your fellow subject specialists. Therefore, it is necessary for the paper to describe something *new* – it could be an observation of something new in, say, astronomy, or a description of a new technique for modelling or analysis in the physical sciences or in engineering. However, if we all start publishing papers that do not describe something novel, then we are effectively wasting our time and not making significant progress towards being able to offer the ticket to Mars. It may be that a technique has not been used in your profession/sector, and therefore you are not familiar with it, but that does not make it a new technique. This is illustrated by an example I remember in a medical journal. Such publications generally have high 'impact factors' (which is a measure of how much they are referenced in other papers – and so is related to how much interest they generate – or *impact*). This is, of course, quite understandable – it is natural that there should be great interest in clinical research into curing diseases such as cancer – and I am certainly glad that publications such as *A Cancer Journal for Clinicians* have high impact factors. However, the problem arises when a technique is presented in a clinical journal paper which is, in fact, not new, but the paper is published and referenced as though it were. I remember seeing this occur in an article in a well-known clinical journal (not *A Cancer Journal for Clinicians*, by the way) – a well-known mathematical data treatment was being discussed and referenced as though it were quite novel. The journal was of course peer-reviewed, but this may illustrate a problem that occurs for reviewing clinical papers – specifically that such reviewers are necessarily clinicians and so unlikely to have a specialisation in mathematics, making it more likely for them to accept such articles for publication.

I have, in fact, also had personal experience of techniques being presented as new when they are not. In 1997, I published a paper that described, I believe for the first time, a technique that involves overlapping spheres (typically a larger one at the centre surrounded by smaller ones), and then using the resulting construct in discrete-event simulations (which are numerical techniques that can simulate the movement and packing of particles). The idea was to simulate the morphology and packing behaviour of irregular shaped particles; and, in fact, the technique worked quite well – so much so that it was incorporated into commercial software for simulating the packing of irregular particles (powders comprising such particles are commonly used in industry and the packing densities of such powders are often of critical importance for the process outcomes.) That's all hunky dory, you might think. Then you can imagine my amazement to see the technique I have just described being presented as new in a journal paper published in 2012! This paper was published in a well-known journal relating to geotechnics, unlike my 1997 paper; so it may well be another case of journal referees not being aware of developments in other disciplines. By the way, I contacted the editor of the journal, who admitted to me in email communications that the method described in the paper in his journal was very similar to the 1997 paper and said he would be amenable to acknowledging this fact. Rather amazingly though, he refused to acknowledge the same in a notice or addendum in his journal. He claimed that he had contacted the referees who did not wish to acknowledge the problem. But who wants to acknowledge that they made a mistake and were not aware of prior art that effectively describes a technique that they have accepted to be presented as new – far better to keep quiet and/or pretend there isn't a problem. And I am not going to tell you what *Géotechnique* journal the paper in question appeared in.

I don't want to keep going on about this, because I don't want to play the victim; but I have got to mention one more thing. As late as 2016, I found that the technique was again being presented as new in a further journal article! And I am definitely not going to tell you what *Soft Matter* journal this last paper appeared in. Presumably, this can go on and on, with successive journal papers, over many years, making out that the given approach is new. Never going to get to Mars at this rate!

The media: the enemy of scientific understanding and progress?

"If media content didn't fascinate us, there would be no desire to engage with it; but if it didn't frustrate us on some level, there would be no drive to rewrite or remake it."

— Henry Jenkins

What is the role of the media in the public's appreciation, or otherwise, of science? If we look at how scientists are generally portrayed in films, for instance, we find that the usual image is that of the 'mad scientist' – a character, probably wearing a lab coat and with thick spectacles, who is almost certainly up to no good. Actually, one notable exception to this is *Star Trek*, where the scientific officer is Mr Spock – who is certainly not a villain – but is in fact a main hero/lead character of the series, along with Captain Kirk – and, as I am sure you know, the other two famous hero characters were Dr 'Bones' McCoy and engineer Montgomery Scott (who was discussed earlier) – both men of science. And, of course, there were also a couple of women of science – specifically nurse Chapel and Lieutenant Uhura, the communications officer. The fact that Gene Rodenberry was keen to cast women and actors from ethnic minorities (and in the case of Uhura both of these things together in one person), in important roles back in the 1960s, shows how fantastically ahead of his time he was. More than this, he was also responsible for what is commonly considered to be the first inter-racial kiss to appear on US television. In the November 1968 *Star Trek* episode entitled 'Plato's Stepchildren', Captain Kirk (William Shatner) is seen to kiss Lieutenant Uhura (Nichelle Nichols).

The first inter-racial kiss to appear on US television. In the November 1968 *Star Trek* episode entitled 'Plato's Stepchildren, Captain Kirk (William Shatner) is seen to kiss Lieutenant Uhura (Nichelle Nichols). (Drawing by the author.)

This was so progressive for the time that the series producers were concerned that such a scene would generate uproar in the conservative South, and so did not want the kiss to go ahead. Consequently, it was suggested that two versions of the kiss be filmed – one with an actual contact and one without – with the decision about which to include to be made later. There was only time for one take for each version of the scene; and they went ahead with the one featuring the contact kiss. This turns out to be a rather amusing story, since during the second (non-contact) kiss, Shatner crossed his eyes dramatically – thereby ensuring that the footage showing the contact kiss had to be used. It transpired that the episode, kiss included, was well received and there were none of the feared complaints. No doubt this was an agreeable piece of filming for Shatner, since most people would agree that the *Star*

86

Trek actress Nichelle Nichols is an attractive woman (even now, many years later, she is an elegant lady). At any rate, the story goes that he was a little taken aback at having to ask the permission of network executives to kiss her and was reported as saying: "I kiss women every day of the week!"

The *Enterprise* crew from the original *Star Trek* series. (Illustration by the author.)

But Roddenberry is very much the exception; most film/TV producers have tended to look somewhat askance at scientists. The apparent lack of interest of the film industry in science is perhaps reflected in the relatively limited number of science fiction (SF) films that tend to be produced compared to films of other genres. And even in the case of SF films, most are what could be characterised as 'soft' SF – in other words they are more like fantasy or adventure films with less emphasis on technology than is seen in 'hard' SF - consider the *Star Wars* franchise, for example. The lack of interest in science in Hollywood, in fact, often transgresses into an active dislike of it, or perception of it as a threat to the future of mankind. There are, in fact, many films that have this as the basis of their plot – far too many to mention here; but being something of a fan of the SF genre, I have some favourites even here – such as *Westworld, Logan's Run, Soylent Green* and *Silent Running* (OK, I'm an enthusiast for 1970s SF films). Well-known examples of dystopian SF films from the 1980s include *Blade Runner* and the *Terminator* franchise.

So much for films, but what about other forms of media such as TV and print? Well, I think we would have to conclude that there is generally a relative lack of coverage of science. There are, of course, some exceptions, such as on the BBC, *The Life Scientific* on Radio 4, and the BBC TV series *The Planets* on BBC4. These two series have the advantage of featuring presenters who know something about science, since they are (or were) professors at well-known universities. But these programs represent, I fear, very much a minority. The root of the problem with science coverage at the BBC may result from their apparent bias towards employing humanities graduates. Since the journalists consequently often know little about science, they spend a good deal of time talking to other BBC staff ('our science correspondent'), who may have more knowledge. However, it could be argued that they, and the viewers, would be better off talking to persons outside of the organisation who have in-depth knowledge, rather than interviewing other BBC staff, since one of the main criticisms laid against the corporation has been its propensity for talking to itself.

Considering printed media, there are a number of newspapers, or newspaper supplements that address education, including science education. One of the more considerable of these, which focuses on higher education, and therefore academic life, research, and technological developments, is the *Times Higher Education* (THE). This is, in fact, quite an interesting publication which contains articles relating to various aspects of the lives and careers of academics. Having said this, I would also have to point out that it suffers from the fault associated with journalism, as mentioned above in relation to the BBC – specifically that most journalists have relatively little background, knowledge, or real interest in science, despite its critical importance for the future of humanity. This can be illustrated by opening an edition of THE and reading the reviews of new books. If the book relates to the humanities, as most do (due to the journalistic orientation away from science being observed in nearly all branches of the media, including the bibliophilic ones), you can expect a very in-depth analysis from various socio-political viewpoints and with a good amount of literary and philosophical allusion. But in the unlikely event of the book relating to science, what can we expect? A rather less in-depth treatment I fancy. Perhaps THE and other similar publications need to get their feet rather more firmly on the ground in order to more comprehensively address the important issues facing our civilisation and the possible solutions that science and engineering may provide. Many years ago, I wrote an article that appeared in THE (back in those days it was called the *Times Higher Education Supplement* – THES). The subject of the article was: 'Why I believe the PhD is in danger of becoming a joke'. The essential thesis of the piece was that there are many pressures that may have the effect of 'dumbing down' the PhD and that we need to guard against this, with one of the suggested methods for doing so being to require a candidate to have published a number of papers – for example six papers, before being eligible to hold a defence (this is not such a crazy idea – when I started on my PhD back in the early 1990s, my supervisor calmly told me that he wanted me to publish ten papers!) The next week, I saw that there was a letter replying to my article which was written by a no doubt highly respected academic who I believe was an historian. He was essentially saying, as far as I can remember, that requiring a PhD candidate to publish six papers was a daft idea, since an eighteenth century Oxford don would only expect to publish a couple of papers in their career. Can you believe that? For me, this symbolised many of the problems with academia in the UK. We are not living in a time bubble in Oxford; we are living in the 20th and now 21st century in a very competitive academic and industrial environment where we have to compete with the best academics and industrialists in the world. We don't have time to sit around musing about Oxford dons hundreds of years ago – instead we have to focus on the here and now, look to the future, and undertake the best research we can, which is reported in as many high-quality journal papers as we can manage and which generates as much impact as possible. With all due respect to THE and similar publications, I feel that they need to reflect more on this and not be afraid to deal with difficult issues that are associated with academic integrity and the value of publication. I am thinking of, for example, issues of plagiarism and the constant 'reinventing the wheel' mentioned earlier, where existing techniques are constantly presented in journal papers as being new. I did, in fact, contact THE about the latter but they did not seem interested; I submit that considering such issues would be more important to the future of British academic quality and integrity than continuously publishing tables of 'The Top Universities', although I appreciate that addressing contentious issues may be more difficult and not guaranteed to increase circulation.

I would like to make one more point in relation to studying the humanities and also studying science. Considering, for example, history; there is of course nothing wrong with studying it – in fact I myself enjoy watching documentaries and films about, for example, World War II. However, I don't think we should try to big the subject up or employ gimmicks in an attempt to make it more relevant or dramatic. Consider, for example, the *historic present tense;* this term must represent an oxymoron, since clearly an event cannot be occurring in the present as well as being historical. It seems completely reasonable to me that things that are happening in the present should be referred to in the present tense with events of the past being discussed in the past tense. Consequently, I found it irksome to turn on to the *Today Programme* on BBC Radio Four one morning and hear something like 'Athens is in a great position of power' only to learn that the speaker (an historian) was talking about the situation of Athens during the first phase of the Peloponnesian War, which was fought between Athens and Sparta from 431 to 404 BC. The programme was hosted by John Humphries, who did deign to point out that this was the situation some thousands of years ago and would the speaker, to avoid misleading the listeners, mind speaking about it using the past tense. The speaker agreed, and then went on to continue to discuss the war as though it were presently in full swing! Apparently, Humphries dislikes the historic present tense as much as me, describing it as irritating and saying that it lends an entirely bogus sense of immediacy to what is being described – he is, of course, completely correct. Subsequently, I learned that Melvyn Bragg also dislikes the historic present tense, and all I can say is that he must really have suffered over the years since nearly every time I tune into *In Our Time* (which is a Radio Four Programme that I generally admire), I find a speaker employing it left, right, and centre. I have to admit that it often leads me to the off switch. Humphries and Bragg are right that it is irksome and dislikeable; but why? Simply because, of course, we don't like to listen to things being 'bigged up' – we don't want to have to deal with a salesman. We prefer not to listen to someone trying to make something sound more dramatic, relevant, or important than it really is. History is about events that happened in the past – this can be thoroughly engaging, but if you don't find the past interesting enough, or would rather think about current events, then you aren't interested in history and there is no point in someone pretending something isn't history in a lame effort to make it seem more interesting/relevant.

The Guardian writer David Shariatmadari thinks that Humphries and Bragg are wrong about historic present tense and says: "As part of the process of reading a story, one's mind's eye conjures the action as though it's happening right now. The same is true of history. Even when the past tense is used in a textbook, we "see" the events playing out before us – at least, that's what I experience. In that sense, there's nothing wrong with the historic present. In fact, it represents an instinctive response to narrative. It is neurologically truthful."

Melvin Bragg and John Humphries – both have said they dislike the use of 'historic present tense'. (Drawings by the author.)

If this is the case, then there is nothing wrong with using the correct past tense, since we will, in any case, be able to enjoy seeing the events 'playing out before us'. This is far better than having historic present tense forced upon us, since the latter is likely to result in the playful images of the imagination being blocked out by the thought of 'why is this guy trying to big this up?' For similar reasons, I also find the Radio Four programme *The Long View* hard to listen to and feel it could be subtitled: 'Historic present tense: the deluxe version'. In short, I can't see how contrivances such as the historic present tense will help us get to Mars.

"Avoid the use of the historical present unless the narrative is sufficiently vivid to make the use spontaneous. The historical present is one of the boldest of figures and, as is the case with all figures, its overuse makes a style cheap and ridiculous."

- Royster, James Finch and Stith Thompson, Guide to Composition, 1919

To move on to slightly more controversial or less trivial ground, let me ask the following question: 'is a technical/science/technological PhD more valuable than a humanities PhD?' Here I must dispense with political correctness; the answer to this question, as far as I am concerned, is: YES. Why? Well, here are a few reasons:

- Science and technology can offer the potential, in many situations, to save your life.
- Science is objective, while the arts are subjective.
- Science can be proven to have real value, whereas the arts cannot; here is an example: I live in the Somerset countryside, many miles from any shop. I can use my car (a product of science and technology) to drive to the shops and get the food that will enable me to survive. At the same time, I like the paintings of John Constable - so much so, that I went as far as to dabble in oils to endeavour to paint my own versions of them, (an example being *A View On The Stour Near Dedham*). And I'm determined to have a go at painting *The Hay Wain*, as soon as I can find the time. So, I like Constable's pictures, but I cannot prove that they have real (objective) value.
- Modern Art. Consider the Turner Prize, about which we could ask: 'we know it's art, but is it rubbish?' The kinds of emperor's new clothes submissions that regularly win this prize are lampooned annually by the parody of the Turner Prize known as the Turnip Prize; and in regards to the latter the organisers ask: 'we know it's rubbish, but is it art?' Sorry, but I had to put that Somerset reference in, since they award the Turnip Prize each November (on the same night as the Turner Prize) in our local village pub. Competitors submit entries of very commonplace objects posing as contemporary art, generally titled with spoofs or puns. The prize is a turnip impaled on a rusty six-inch nail. I am really keen to enter something for this high-profile prize, later this year.

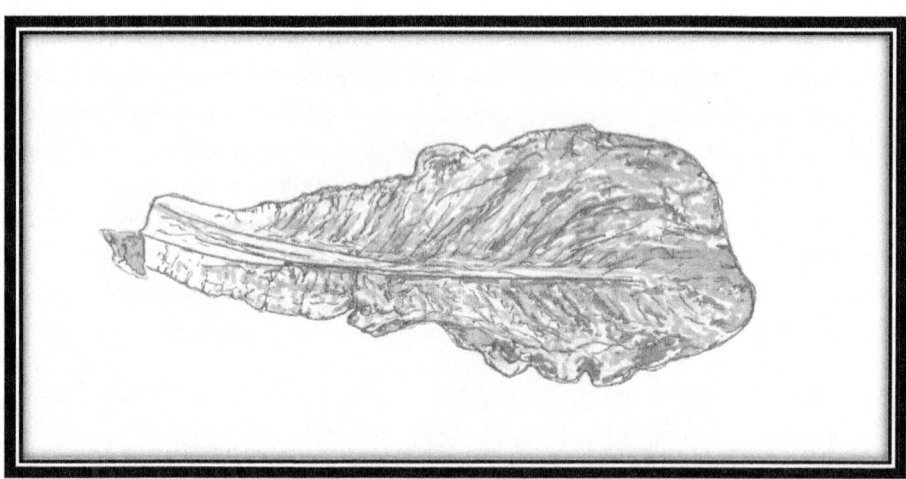

A View On The Stour Near Dedham, by John Constable. (Oil painting by the author.)

2019 Turnip Prize runner-up: 'Lettuce Leaf or Romaine' by Will Ted Gutful. This piece features a clever play on words relating to Brexit and also benefits from requiring an impressively low level of effort from its creator. (Illustration by the author.)

- Science and technology can help me get to Mars, I fancy; but the humanities cannot.

Before moving on I must say a few more words about *The Hay Wain*, since I have just mentioned it. This is surely one of the most famous of all British paintings; in fact, an icon of British art. Doing justice to this great picture is beyond what I have space for here. It is, of course, a masterpiece – wonderfully evocative of the English countryside. Ironic then, that the great impression and excitement that it generated, at least at first, was in the Louvre, at the French Royal Academy Exhibition in 1824. But did you know that the painting includes a couple of 'ghosts'? The next time you get a chance to study it, have a look in front of the dog – you can see an outline of a barrel and near this there are also traces of a human outline. The latter was a horse and rider which Constable decided to paint over. He then painted over this with the barrel, before deciding to paint over both to give the final composition we see today – over the years the underlying painting has emerged somewhat, as a ghostly presence.

Although I have just said that I feel science and technology are more important than the humanities, I don't consider myself to be a complete philistine; for example, I like visiting art galleries and appreciate the plays of William Shakespeare. Also, I enjoy music, watching selected films and dramatic plays (before COVID-19 I used to go on occasion to the theatre), reading books, and studying history. On a much more serious note, I have personal experience of the flooding here in Somerset – as mentioned, global warming seems to be leading to extreme weather. The point I am making is that the artistic/humanities pursuits mentioned in this paragraph are not going to save the planet – for that we need science and technology.

So much for the problems; what are the solutions?

"There are no problems, only solutions."

— John Lennon

No doubt John Lennon had a very positive attitude and I generally prefer to be around people who are looking for solutions rather than problems; but can we be certain there will be attainable solutions to all the myriad complex problems that have been outlined above? Perhaps not all... Many of the issues touched on above are associated with social questions that are influenced by historical and cultural factors to an extent that reliable modelling of them for predictive or corrective purposes is not realistic. At the same time, the 'Black Swan' syndrome can always be potentially present and is often very far-reaching and influential economically, politically, and socially (examples include 9/11 and the coronavirus). Having said this, some of the issues most germane to the theme of this book surely can be addressed more effectively than is occurring at present – good examples are provided by scientific and medical research that can lead to accelerated technological progress. But how can this be done? The answer, I believe, is unexpectedly simple and emerges when we consider the approaches taken in relation to many of the limiting factors discussed above. Put simply, all these considerations lead to the conclusion that identifying and implementing effective solutions to significant problems is enabled by dispassionate and objective analysis of reliable data, rather than the adoption of a prescriptive approach. The best implementation of a scientific method *requires* the analysis of the problem and the generation of the solution to be data driven – there is no place for dogma. Data is everything; knowledge cannot be *a priori* but must be based on analysis of observations. The problem, of course, is that many of the problems requiring solution in science/technology and medicine are so complex and multi-factored that modelling or analysing existing data for generation of new solutions is a non-trivial task that has, at least up to now, been considered too complex for effective and reliable modelling. However, in recent years this has all changed – principally through the exciting developments that have occurred in artificial intelligence (AI) and specifically convolutional neural networks (CNNs).

In science fiction, it is quite common for computers to gain an ability to think for themselves – perhaps one of the most famous of such computers is 'HAL 9000' in the epic 1960s sci-fi movie *2001 A Space Odyssey*. HAL is a fictional artificial intelligence character created by Arthur C. Clarke in the book from which the film is adapted. But in reality, artificial intelligence capable of independent thought is beyond what could be claimed for even the most powerful of today's CNNs. To judge from the film, this may be just as well, since later in *2001 A Space Odyssey* HAL starts behaving eccentrically, causing astronauts to discuss plans for turning 'him' off. HAL discovers their plan and, faced with the prospect of disconnection, the computer decides to kill the astronauts in order to protect itself and continue its programmed directives. A famous line from the film is when HAL responds to an astronaut's command by saying: "I'm sorry Dave, I'm afraid I can't do that".

Despite the fact that current artificial intelligence can't match HAL's apparent capabilities, CNNs *do* operate in ways that can be considered similar to (vastly simplified) versions of the human eye and brain. The architectures and methods of operation of CNNs will be described in more detail later, but to give a very brief summary, a CNN is a form of artificial 'neural network' that simulates the human brain in the form of a network of interconnected neurons, which are analogous to the synapses in the human brain. In conventional artificial neural networks (of the kind that have been commonly employed in computer vision research since the 1980s), the networks are relatively limited in the number of neurons and layers of neurons that they employ. Each neuron simply relates its input to an output (following a standard function known as a 'transfer function'), and the model is stored in the weights (multipliers) that are associated with each link between two neurons. The difference in CNNs is that the number of neurons and layers of neurons tends to be much larger (hence use of CNNs is often called 'deep learning'). Further, in a CNN the neurons in the initial layers of the network consist of kernels (i.e. a small mask), used in convolution (where the mask is passed over the whole image, changing it), in order to filter the image and produce 'feature maps'. These layers are followed by other layers (principally for data reduction) and these by still more – the 'fully connected layers'. The latter do, in fact, rather more closely resemble the layers that appear in a conventional artificial neural network and are employed for classification. As can be imagined, having so many layers and neurons, many of which operate in convolution operations over the whole image, requires huge amounts of calculation and data generation. It is therefore fortuitous that another computer-related industry (which is in fact quite significant commercially) that has emerged recently also requires high performance computation – specifically computer gaming. Therefore, in deep learning we employ the high-performance graphical processing units (GPUs) and high-end computers (with large amounts of random-access memory (RAM) and data storage capacities), that have been mass-produced for gaming at relatively low cost.

But why should we go to such lengths in terms of the software complexity of deep CNNs and all the associated required computation? The answer is that CNNs are very powerful pattern-recognition devices that can be used to identify features of interest in complicated sets of images and thereby solve complex problems that have previously been considered too difficult for anything but human solution. How are they able to do this? The answer, in a nutshell, is that they are entirely data-driven and are not prescriptive. They employ data that are representative of objects that we are interested in detecting - for example, dogs. If enough images of dogs are available, they can *automatically learn* what a dog looks like. This is the important point – humans don't have to tell the CNN what a dog looks like – it can work it out for itself! This provides two strong advantages: firstly the vast amount of work that used to be needed to 'hand craft features' of dogs is no longer required since this is now automated, and secondly since the computer generates its 'dog' feature purely based on images it has been given of dogs, it is more reliable than if we had 'told' it what a dog should look like.

So, it is doing what we wanted – it is solving problems in an objective and data-driven way, rather than relying on prescriptive inputs. The result is that the CNN is robust and remarkably reliable in recognising various objects – even when the training and test data it has been given for those objects contains a good deal of variation (such as shadows or changes in light levels).

Convolutional neural networks can automatically, and reliably, detect various objects in images. (Pen and ink drawing by the author.)

CNNs are, of course, able to solve all manner of problems beyond simply detecting the presence of dogs in images, which means they have great potential for solving a wide range of formidable problems that may be critical for advancing science and technology. Although one characteristic that is often associated with CNNs, and which is mentioned above, is the need for extensive training data, there have been developments in recent years which can be used to very much reduce the amount of data a CNN needs before it can start producing useful outcomes. This is likely to dramatically increase the rate of uptake of CNNs, since many companies, particularly smaller ones, tend to find it difficult to spend the time and money required for capture of large numbers of images in the field. These data reduction methods are, in fact, surprisingly simple in terms of what they involve and how they are implemented, but before going into what they are called and how they work, it is worth giving a slightly more in-depth background to machine learning in general and CNNs in particular.

Machine learning

"Machine learning will automate jobs that most people thought could only be done by people."

- Dave Waters

So, what exactly is machine learning? According to a definition given on the Web, machine learning is: "...an application of artificial intelligence (AI) that provides systems the ability to automatically learn and improve from experience without being explicitly programmed. Machine learning focuses on the development of computer programs that can access data and use it to learn for themselves." In other words, machine learning is an AI technique that allows us to solve problems that cannot be solved with explicit programming or conventional mathematical techniques. It may, therefore, be no surprise that it effectively provides solutions to many of the problems outlined above that are consequences of a reductionist view of the world and a desire to reduce every problem to a few equations. The solutions of the vast majority of real-world problems are far too complicated for such a simple approach. As discussed, if we try to apply a closed-form mathematical solution to problems we wish to solve in, say, engineering, we quickly find the mathematics becomes hideously complex for the solution of all but the simplest of problems. In contrast to this, machine learning takes ideas from the fields of artificial intelligence, computer science, and computational statistics; it uses algorithms that can learn from data through a process of self-improvement. Not that machine learning always has to involve use of CNNs; other approaches that have been used for many years include 'Local Binary Patterns' and 'Support Vector Machine'. Going into the details of how these work is beyond the scope of this book – suffice it to say that the former recognises patterns by analysing local 'textures' in the patterns, while the latter employs lines or planes for classification. The resulting models can then be used to make predictions on similar, domain-specific data – and by that we simply mean solving various useful tasks in a range of application areas. This is reasonably straightforward when we are talking indoor situations or 'structured' environments. However, when it comes to outdoor environments or 'unstructured' indoor situations, things get a bit more tricky. Here, dramatic changes in lighting often occur as well as relatively random variations in object position and/or orientation. Since such apparent disorder cannot be modelled explicitly, conventional machine learning methods can struggle to maintain good performance. This calls upon investigations and comparisons of different methods that can automatically obtain reliable features regardless of the complexity of data available. One such method is neural networks which, as mentioned above, is a class of machine learning algorithm/model based loosely on neuronal processes in the biological brain, where a number of neurons are connected together by 'weights' (where the model is stored).

A very brief history of neural networks

While the initial studies involving artificial 'neurons' were in the 1940s, the first paper to receive widespread interest was when Frank Rosenblatt introduced the Perceptron in 1958, as an electronic device constructed in accordance with biological principles and able to learn.

Frank Rosenblatt who described the Perceptron, which was an early type of neural network; despite his comments in the *New York Times*, so far Perceptrons have not been able to walk, talk, see, write, reproduce, or be conscious of their existence – but he had a wide range of interests and was a forward-thinker who built his own observatory to search for extra-terrestrial intelligence! (Drawing by the author.)

Unfortunately, this led to an article in the New York Times which you could categorise as hopelessly hubristic (if you were being kind): "The Navy revealed the embryo of an electronic computer today that it expects will be able to walk, talk, see, write, reproduce itself, and be conscious of its existence ... Dr Frank Rosenblatt, a research psychologist at the Cornell Aeronautical Laboratory, Buffalo, said Perceptrons might be fired to the planets as mechanical space explorers."

It's the old story of claims being made for technology which are based more on wild conjecture than actual useful achievements in the real world; and when the real situation becomes clear there is disappointment with a resultant backlash. In this case, it took the form of a perception that the approach was not suitable for solving non-linear problems, which led to a long period of limited research in this area. By the way, there was a similar backlash against robotics when in the late 1980s, all the hype surrounding the subject was replaced by understanding of what robots were actually currently capable of doing (i.e. very little outside of highly structured environments). We have to hope that the current apparent strong enthusiasm for robotics will not suffer a similar fate – perhaps CNNs will save it this time around!

It turns out that most things you observe in the real world behave non-linearly. Consider, for example, the rate at which water flows out of your bath; when the bath is full and you pull the plug the flow rate is high but when it is nearly empty the rate is much lower. To be more specific, in this example the flow rate varies exponentially, as is the case with all things that are caused by something which they are themselves reducing (in this case the height of water in the bath). Saying something changes *exponentially* is an often overused or incorrectly applied expression, but in physics it does occur quite often and is certainly non-linear. In fact, it has a mathematical implication that the level, in theory at least, will never reach zero (or will only do so at infinity). All I can say is that in the case of a bath I have some experimental data to back up this claim, since when I drain my bath no matter how long I wait the level never actually goes to zero – there is always a bit of water hanging around at the bottom! So, getting back to neural networks, there was a desire to model non-linearity.

Following the above hiatus, a big resurgence of interest in artificial neurons occurred in the 1980s, when there was wide realisation and exploitation of the capabilities of multi-layer neural networks to model any relationship between inputs and outputs, whether linear or non-linear, (as long as you have enough data). Unfortunately, this came too late for Frank Rosenblatt, who died on his 43rd birthday in a boating accident in Chesapeake Bay in July 1971. Let's just mention a few more things about him – his scientific interests were exceptionally broad. For example, he was a psychology academic – publishing a good deal on rat behaviour. Behavioural psychology became big in the 20th century – presumably because it enables experiments to be conducted and thereby generates data that can be analysed, but the extent to which these data are useful or can be extrapolated from, say, rats to humans, is a matter of debate; and many have indeed debated it at some length (one such who comes to mind is Arthur Kostler). Rosenblatt was also interested in areas of science that relate to other parts of this book - he had a serious research interest in astronomy and went so far as to propose a new technique to detect the presence of satellites orbiting stars. He also did the kind of thing I would like to do - building an observatory on a hilltop behind his house! Once he had completed this, he used it to start an intensive study in the Search for Extra-terrestrial Intelligence (SETI). In short, I would say he was a forward thinker and perhaps also something of a Renaissance man – something which, if you ask me, is a good thing; but somewhat out of fashion nowadays, when everyone is expected to specialise and eyebrows can be raised if he/she takes an interest in subjects somewhat outside of their narrow field of expertise. His Mark 1 Perceptron, which is surely a landmark in machine learning, can be found in the Smithsonian Institution in Washington D.C.

Considering the great potential that has been realised in recent years for applying machine learning to image processing, Fukushima was on the ball when, in 1980, he proposed an architecture inspired by the human visual receptive fields that he named the 'Neocognitron'. It described alternating layers that convolved and sub-sampled an input image – so he was also on the money regarding the great potential offered by combining neural networks with convolution – more on this below.

Despite all these developments, the usefulness of neural networks was severely limited without a robust approach to learning the weights (which are multipliers in the links between the neurons - where the model is stored). A significant advance was made in 1986 by David Rumelhart, Geoffrey E. Hinton, and Ronald J. Williams, who presented a paper that described a method of weight optimization called 'backpropagation' that allowed several layers of neurons to be stacked together to form a multi-layered network. Backpropagation uses the 'chain rule' to propagate the error signal at the output back through each layer of the network, for calculation of weights that tend to minimize the error. The paper was influential, and its adoption helped dramatically increase the ability of neural networks to be trained and hence moved the field forward by greatly improving their pattern recognition capabilities.

To summarise, the work of Fukushima, Rumelhart, Hinton, and colleagues, effectively inspired and enabled the development of the powerful machine learning technique that we have been talking about and which is known as the convolutional neural network (CNN).

Convolutional neural networks for deep learning

"Take any old classification problem where you have a lot of data, and it's going to be solved by deep learning. There's going to be thousands of applications of deep learning."

- Geoffrey Hinton

The CNN is a method that was developed for image recognition tasks by taking inspiration from the biological brain, in particular the connective topology of neurons in the visual cortex. The achievements of Geoffrey Hinton in the field of AI include his role in popularising backpropagation as described above, as well as the pattern-recognition capabilities of the influential 'AlexNet' system, which he conceived and was built by his student Alex Krizhevsky for the ImageNet challenge 2012 (where objects are recognised from a database of 14 million images).

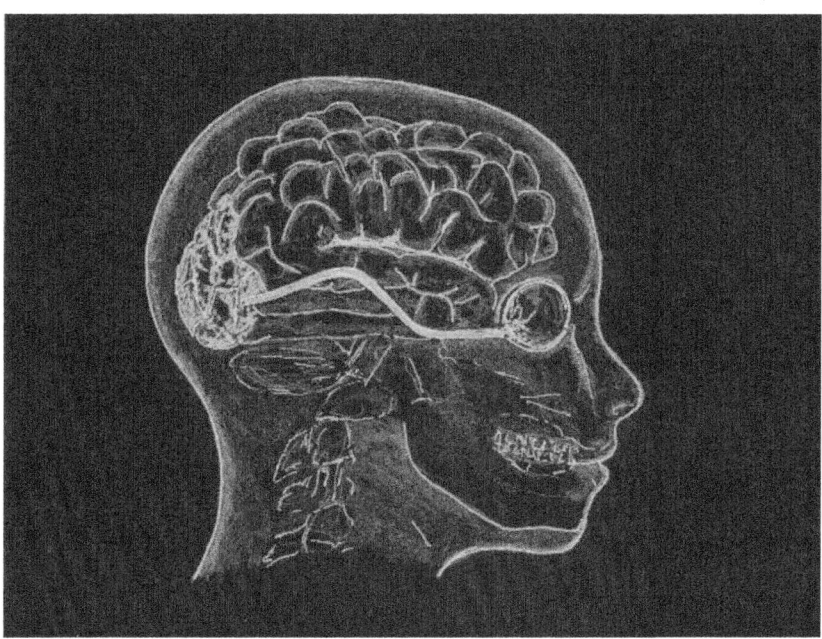

The convolutional neural network (CNN) is a neural network that employs deep learning, and which is inspired by the visual cortex of the human brain. (Illustration by the author.)

When analysing ImageNet, AlexNet outperformed all other approaches by a wide margin: 15.3% error versus the next best of 26.2% error. Subsequently this method was universally accepted and largely adopted by the machine vision community. Such accomplishments have resulted in him being viewed as a leading figure in deep learning, who has helped to revolutionize the field of computer vision. Although Hinton may be the most important figure in the history of deep learning, he was not the only one to make significant contributions. In fact, one person he advised was the AI researcher Yann LeCun who, back in 1999, described 'Le-Net-5', a 7-layer CNN that recognized handwritten digits; and the power of the new approach was proven when it was used for an automated cheque reading system that has been used by banks ever since.

Three Godfathers of Deep Learning: Geoferry Hinton (top left), Yann LeCun (top right), and Yoshua Bengio (bottom left); as well as one Godfather of the street: Vito Corleone AKA Marlon Brando/Robert De Niro (you recognise *The* Godfather – and better show some respect!) (Drawings by the author.)

Mention should also be made of Yoshua Bengio, who established a laboratory called 'LISA' that has done much AI theoretical work – resulting in extensive publication and high-profile international conferences on deep learning (in collaboration with Yann LeCun). As a result of all this, Hinton, Bengio, and LeCun are sometimes referred to as the 'Godfathers of AI' or the 'Godfathers of Deep Learning'. Godfathers indeed. But presumably the difference between these three Godfathers and *The* Godfather, is that they: "...have not learned more in the streets than in any classroom". The latter, of course, refers to Don Vito Corleone (born Vito Andolini).

In 2018 Hinton was awarded the Turing Award alongside Bengio and LeCun, in recognition of their work on deep learning. We should also not forget to mention Andrew Ng, who created Google Brain – a pioneering large-scale distributed system for Deep Learning, which brought the ImageNet competition to an entirely new level.

But what, in simple terms, *is* convolution? A useful/intuitive way to think of convolution is as an operation that takes as input two functions: an input signal, and a filter; and outputs a third function that is a modified or 'filtered' version of the input. This idea has been used for some time in image processing, where specialized 'filters', also called convolutional kernels, have been designed to modify images. Most of us have used some form of image processing programmes in the form of software that might have been supplied with a digital camera bought for taking holiday snaps – or perhaps in the form of well-known packages that we have installed on our computer – such as, say, Photoshop® or PaintShop® Pro. When we use such software to perform operations such as image smoothing, sharpening and edge detection, what we are really doing is getting the programs to perform convolution, or filtering if you prefer, to generate the effects we desire. Of course, when using such packages we generally don't need to be concerned with the maths behind the convolution – or, say, the exact configuration of the masks employed in the filtering operations. But to give a very brief summary, what the program is doing in convolution, is applying a small mask (or 'kernel') iteratively across the image, and each time the image pixel in the location of the centre of the mask is changed – depending upon the values in the kernel and the pixel values in the image. Another way of explaining this is to say that in convolution, or image filtering, the value of each of the pixels is modified slightly, depending upon the filter being employed, and the values of the pixels surrounding the pixel being modified.

In the case of CNNs, the kernels are known as 'feature detectors'. The output from the convolution operation is often called a 'feature map' and can be used as the input to traditional machine learning/classification algorithms for feature detection - to enhance the performance of the model. So, in comparison to 'traditional' neural networks, the CNN is a new type of neural network that is trained using backpropagation and which has a new architecture. It consists of several 'convolutional layers', each containing several separate convolutional filters that each output a feature map from the layer's input image. These are then stacked together and sent to the next layer. Also, the network has several 'fully connected layers', similar to those traditionally found in neural networks. This creates a powerful image classification model that combines the feature detection properties of convolutional filters with the versatility of neural networks. I hope that is clear. Any further questions can be directed towards one of the three Godfathers of Deep Learning. And as long as you don't subsequently find a horse's head in your bed, all should be OK.

In the film *The Godfather*, Jack Woltz was not 100% happy to wake up and find a horse's head in his bed. (Pen and ink drawing by the author.)

That was a joke – you are not going to find a horse's head in your bed. But I was just reading about that scene in the film *The Godfather*: "This is an iconic moment. Jack Woltz wakes up with a horse head in his bed, showing him that the Corleones mean business. Apparently, this forces Woltz to give Johnny Fontane (cough Frank Sinatra cough) a part in a movie that will make him a star, despite his personal distaste for Fontane." Either that or it was seriously poor housekeeping/carelessness on the part of the maid. On another web page, someone goes on to ask whether the horse head that appears in *The Godfather* is real and they are answered thus: "While a fake head was used during rehearsals, Coppola swapped it with a real one for the actual shot, meaning the screams you hear from actor John Marley were absolutely genuine." Wow, I guess that actor was really suffering for his art – after shooting that kind of scene it's a wonder he can get any sleep. In any case, putting horse heads into people's beds is not the *modus operandi* of the Godfathers of Deep Learning. They would be more likely to want to put some extra memory into their computers.

While we are on the subject of computer upgrades, the final development, in 2009, was to employ graphical processing units (GPUs) as general-purpose processors for training large machine learning models. So, finally, all of the development money and effort that has been poured into gaming development in recent years has found a useful application – and one that does not involve having to shoot as many Nazis per minute as possible (or whatever the hell else is going on in video games nowadays). Use of GPUs in deep learning enables great reductions in training times, so that a network that would previously take months to train can now be trained in days. This means that the use of exceptionally large networks is possible – which has led to a period of rapid development of CNN architectures. The result has been a dramatic increase in the performance of vision systems, and the subsequent research into the application of CNNs across a wide range of sectors that we see today. As mentioned above, there has been only one significant drawback to the CNN approach – traditionally very large amounts of training data have been required to train networks that are sufficiently complex to accurately and reliably perform useful tasks in the real world. We can now introduce two techniques that have been developed to address this: transfer learning and data augmentation.

Transfer learning

The method known as 'transfer learning' is based on a pretty simple concept: first take a CNN that has already been trained with some data (perhaps obtained from the internet) and then further train the CNN with a relatively small amount of data relating to your application. Would you expect this to work well? Probably not, but in fact it does work remarkably well. To reiterate, transfer learning involves combining a 'pre-trained' network with a limited amount of application specific data. The result is a CNN that has a performance comparable to that of a conventionally fully trained CNN, but a much smaller requirement for training data. Bingo! This offers potential to dramatically increase the number of useful applications of deep learning, since one of the biggest challenges for companies wanting to make use of this technology is that of getting all the large amounts of training data that used to be required. Not only this, but these data generally need to be 'annotated' – in other words, each image needs to have a note attached to it saying what is being shown. One application we worked on was using a CNN to automatically detect whether weeds are present in images. To do this, we took 6000 images of a field and for each one a person had a close look to see if weeds were present. This is not as easy as it sounds - even for humans deciding whether small amounts of weeds are present (e.g. 5 – 10%) is not that easy. And for 6000 images? It's a wonder we didn't go stir-crazy.

In transfer learning, the lower convolutional layers of the pre-trained network (with 'frozen' weights), are combined with several, untrained, 'fully connected' layers. The resulting model is then trained on an application specific dataset, resulting in the training of only the 'fully connected' layers. The pre-trained network can be generated by employing a dataset known as ImageNet, (as mentioned above this contains millions of images in thousands of classes, such as animals, types of vehicles, household objects and many more). In 2014, Ali Sharif Razavian et al. released a paper that explored the following idea: Since the ImageNet dataset is so diverse, the lower convolutional layers of a CNN, trained on this dataset, would contain very general feature detectors that could be used as the low-level feature detectors for a number of machine vision tasks. This theory proved to be true and ImageNet-trained CNNs have shown strong performance when compared to other more sophisticated methods. There are now a number of the best performing models, pre-trained on the ImageNet dataset, available to download and use freely. Implementing transfer learning in this way has become a very useful tool for creating high performing models without the large data and computational requirements that are often needed to train complex networks. As mentioned, this is important since, for large amounts of data, much effort is required for both the capturing and accurate labelling. Considering again the automatic weed detection application, suppose you are a farmer who wishes to detect weeds in grass so that he/she can selectively spray them with herbicide. This is shown in the figure below, where the dock weed has been 'segmented' making it a relatively simple matter to spray some herbicide at it – or even to zap it with a high-power laser!

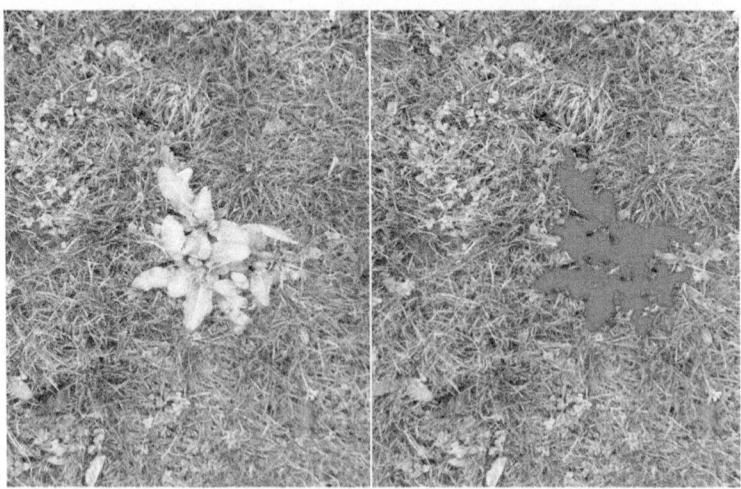

Using machine vision and deep learning, dock weed in grass has been 'segmented' (in the right image), making it a relatively simple matter to spray some herbicide at it. (Images by the author.)

106

It is, in fact, quite important to remove dock weed from grass, since ingestion of such a weed can be quite harmful to animals. A facility for automatically detecting the weeds and selectively spraying a small amount of herbicide at them clearly offers great potential for realising very significant cost and environmental benefits. It's only a matter of time until all farmers, at least in the West, employ such methods for weed control.

So, that's great. The farmer does not want to go around the field for days on end capturing vast amounts of weed images in order to train a CNN for this task, and by employing transfer learning he/she doesn't have to. So much for transfer learning, but what about data augmentation?

Data augmentation

Suppose you had a certain amount of image data for a given application – for example, images of weeds in grass for the weed detection task discussed above. Imagine if you used the data to train a CNN, then took part of the data, 'messed around' with it a bit, added the results to the original dataset and then used the new dataset to train a second CNN. How do you think the performances of the two CNNs would compare? This is data augmentation and as with transfer learning, you might expect that it would not provide a significant improvement in the learning and hence the network performance. But, you guessed it, it does. Data augmentation is often employed to artificially enlarge datasets being used by applying random transformations such as zooming or rotating the image. This can help to reduce the problems from overfitting that are often present when modelling small yet complex datasets. Commonly available software, such as Keras, TensorFlow, and Google Colab are free to access and provide useful tools for real-time image augmentation and CNN training. To give an example of how it is used, our weed-in-grass application mentioned above employed an augmentation regime that consists of the following: First the pixel values are scaled between zero and one; a process that yields slightly better training results. Next, the images are randomly rotated and shifted in both width and height. A random zoom is then applied. The final augmentation technique used is to randomly flip images horizontally and vertically. In the figure below, images are shown for just grass as well as grass with Rumex and grass with clover. Being able to differentiate between these plants being present in grass is, in fact, a very beneficial thing since, as mentioned, ingestion of dock is bad for animals, which is not the case for clover. The presence of clover in grass is certainly a good thing seeing that it is good for grazing animals as well as providing valuable nutrition for the soil. However, up to now the treatments farmers give grazing grass for killing docks have generally involved blanket spraying of herbicides or 'broadleaf' weed killers which will, of course, kill clover along with the dock, as well as being more expensive and bad for the environment. Also, there can be little doubt that at some time soon the Government will ban the use of commonly used weed killers such as glyphosates. So, I am sure this kind of technology is going to become more important and widespread in the near future. Rumex is another name for dock weed – and to give it it's full fancy name: *Rumex obtusifolius*.

Original and augmented images of grass with Rumex present and clover present. (Images by the author.)

By the way, giving plants common names and fancy names reminds me of *Logan's Run*. In the film, Logan and Jessica go to the ruins of Washington D.C., where they meet Peter Ustinov playing a slightly crazy old man who keeps legions of cats and talks about them at length. As he rambles on, he claims all cats have three names: a regular name, a fancy name, and a name only the cat itself knows. I am not sure if this is true of plants, but if so, the names for the weed above are: bitter dock, Rumex obtusifolius, and a name only the plant itself knows.

One thing I do know is that dock weeds are taking over my garden, and any kind of weed control, automatic or otherwise, would be most welcome. Also, I will swear that Rumex obtusifolius manages to grow to a much bigger size in Somerset than it does in Scotland (where the farmer we were working with on this was based). If you have enough data to train a CNN from scratch, that will still give you the best possible performance, and when training a 26-layer CNN from scratch (with data that incorporated augmentation), for detection of docks in grass, we obtained

95.6% accuracy – which seemed impressive. However, perhaps even more amazing is the fact that when employing transfer learning we achieved a classification accuracy of 83.5% using a dataset of just 50 samples!

Logan and Jessica: "Are you all alone here?"

Old Man: "Hardly, I've got all these cats."

Scenes from the film Logan's Run, with Michael York as Logan, Jenny Agutter as Jessica and Peter Ustinov as the old man they meet in a future Washington D.C. (Pen and ink drawing by the author.)

This represents higher accuracy results than previous non-deep learning techniques, while only requiring a training dataset that could be collected and processed by a single person in a day - clearly showing the advantages possible with these methods.

OK, that sounds great – but can you explain a bit more about how convolution actually works?

Sure, and let's keep this simple. As touched on earlier, convolution is a common image processing technique that changes the intensities of a pixel to reflect the intensities of the surrounding pixels. A common use of convolution is to create image filters. Using convolution, you can get popular image effects like blur, sharpen, and edge detection. Below, a well-known image that has been widely used in image processing is used to illustrate the effects of a slight blur. This image has in fact been employed since 1973 in the machine vision community, to illustrate image processing. Quite recently I was chatting with a researcher who told me they had just attended a conference where this image was shown, and they didn't like it – they thought it was sexist and they were considering complaining about it. Good Grief!

An example of image processing; softening or blurring. (Standard test image that has been widely employed in the field of image processing since 1973.)

To achieve effects such as the one shown above, convolution is performed using a grid-like mathematical construct called a *kernel*. The figure below represents a 3 x 3 kernel. The height and width of the kernel do not have to be the same, though they must both be odd numbers. The numbers inside the kernel dictate the overall effect of the convolution. The kernel (or more specifically, the values held within the kernel) is what determines how to transform the pixels from the original image into the pixels of the processed image.

2	2	0
2	6	0
0	0	0

A kernel for use in convolution. (Illustration by the author.)

Convolutions are 'per-pixel operations' - the same arithmetic is repeated for every pixel in the image. Bigger images, therefore, require more convolution arithmetic than the same operation on a smaller image. The numbers in the kernel represent the amount by which to multiply the number underneath it. The number underneath represents the intensity of the pixel over which the kernel element is hovering. The process multiplies each number in the kernel by the pixel intensity value directly underneath it. This should result in as many products as there are numbers in the kernel (per pixel). The figure below shows how a kernel with 9 pixels operates on one pixel.

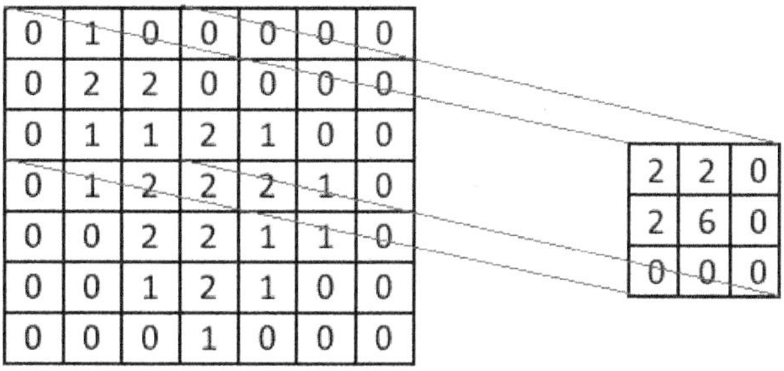

How image convolution works. The centre element the kernel is placed over is called the source pixel. The source pixel is replaced by the sum of the multiplied (weighted) values of itself and nearby pixels. In this case the source pixel originally has a value of 2, and this would be replaced by (0+1x2+0+0+2x6+0+0+0+0) = 14. (Illustration by the author.)

The final step of the process sums all the products together and this value becomes the new intensity of the pixel that was directly under the centre of the kernel. The blur effect shown on the last page for the image of the lady, can be produced by a filter that is known as the 'mean filter'. Here, all the values in the kernel are 1 and the sum of the products is divided by the amount of numbers in the kernel. The result is to soften or blur the image (with the extent of the blurring depending upon the size of the kernel used), as well as providing an additional benefit of removing any pixel (or 'speckle') noise in the image. The latter was made use of for the first images sent back from the Apollo voyages to the Moon – to reduce the noise in the images received on Earth as Neil Armstrong made his 'giant leap' for mankind by stepping down from the Lunar Module onto the surface of the Moon.

Now, I hope that is all clear and that you are now wised-up about convolution. That bloody well better be the case, since I can't go through it again.

Fine and dandy, but can you give a simple explanation for how CNNs make use of convolution for identifying objects?

No problemo. We will consider a simple example of how convolution helps with automatic feature identification. Let's say our first kernel (or filter) is 7 x 7 and is going to be a diagonal line detector. As a line detector, the filter will have a pixel structure in which there will be higher numerical values along the area that is in the shape of a diagonal line. This is shown below; and due to the fact that our lives in our house seem to be pretty much dominated by cats (with think we are the masters, but I can see from the expressions on their faces that they know better...), I have taken the liberty of using an image of a cat in this example.

0	0	0	0	0	0	0
0	0	0	0	0	0	40
0	0	0	0	0	40	0
0	0	0	0	40	0	0
0	0	0	40	0	0	0
0	0	40	0	0	0	0
0	40	0	0	0	0	0

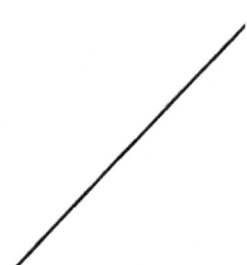

A simple line detector filter (left) and corresponding diagonal line feature (right). (Illustrations by the author.)

When we employ this filter on a given region of the input image, we compute multiplications between the filter and pixel values at that region. Now let's take an example of an image that we want to classify, and let's put our filter at the top of the cat's back.

Applying the line detector to an image of a cat; original image is on the left and visualisation of the filter on the image (near the top of the cat's back), is on the right. (Illustrations by the author.)

112

We multiply the values in the filter with the original pixel values of the image. If, in the input image, there is a shape that generally resembles the diagonal line that this filter is representing, then all of the multiplications summed together will result in a large value:

0	0	0	0	0	0	20
0	0	0	0	0	0	20
0	0	0	0	0	20	20
0	0	0	0	20	20	0
0	0	0	20	20	0	0
0	0	20	20	0	0	0
0	20	20	0	0	0	0

0	0	0	0	0	0	0
0	0	0	0	0	0	40
0	0	0	0	0	40	0
0	0	0	0	40	0	0
0	0	0	40	0	0	0
0	0	40	0	0	0	0
0	40	0	0	0	0	0

Visualisation of the receptive field on the cat (left), pixel representation of the receptive field (centre) and pixel representation of the filter (right). Convolution with our line detector filter on the back of the cat produces a large number: (20x40)+(20x40)+(20*40)+(20*40)+(20*40)+(20*40) = 4,800. (Illustrations by the author.)

Now let's see what happens when we move our filter:

0	0	20	0	0	20	20
0	20	20	20	20	20	0
20	20	20	20	20	0	0
0	0	0	0	0	0	0
0	0	0	0	0	0	0
0	0	0	0	0	0	0
0	0	0	0	0	0	0

0	0	0	0	0	0	0
0	0	0	0	0	0	40
0	0	0	0	0	40	0
0	0	0	0	40	0	0
0	0	0	40	0	0	0
0	0	40	0	0	0	0
0	40	0	0	0	0	0

Again, the visualisation of the receptive field on the cat is on the left, with pixel representation of the receptive field centre and the pixel representation of the filter on the right. This time, the multiplication and summation does not give a large number, in fact convolution with our line detector filter on the lower part of the cat produces zero!

The value is much lower – in fact, it's zero. This is because there wasn't anything in the image section that responded to the line detector filter. Remember, the output of the image convolution is an activation map (or feature map). So, in the simple case of a one filter convolution (and if that filter is a line detector), the activation map will show the areas in which there are most likely to be lines in the picture.

This is just for one filter; a simple filter that is going to detect lines that go from the bottom left to the top right. We can have other filters for lines in other directions and for various curves. The more filters, the greater the depth of the activation map, and the more information we have about the input. The above filter is a simplistic one to show how the convolution works – in real CNN applications they are more complicated. To summarise, the filters convolve around the input image and "activate" (or compute high values) when the specific feature it is looking for is in the input image.

Therefore, the convolutional layer is the core building block of a CNN. The layer's parameters consist of a set of learnable filters (or kernels). Each feature map shows the detection of some specific type of feature at some spatial position in the input. Using various filters creates a series of activation maps and these are stacked up to form what is known as the full output volume of the convolution layer.

To give you just a bit more information on how CNNs work, the hidden layers of a CNN typically consist of the convolutional layers we have just been discussing, as well as a RELU layer (to remove negative values and help with training), pooling layers, and fully connected layers. Pooling layers reduce the dimensions of the data by combining the outputs of neuron clusters at one layer into a single neuron in the next layer. Fully connected layers connect every neuron in one layer to every neuron in another layer – as in a traditional multi-layer neural network. The fully connected layers classify the images. I admit that this can all sound a little complicated when first explained, but the point is that you don't necessarily need to know about all the intricacies of CNN architectures in order to make good use of them. And as you use them, you inevitably learn more about their composition and modes of operation. It is true that in order to model very complex data you need complex models, but the great beauty of CNNs is that, once you know how to train them for given sets of data, the network itself generates the complex model automatically – without you having to fashion its complexity manually – as we used to have to do years ago, using formal mathematical modelling, statistics, or whatever tools were available to us. And as well as being laborious, the old methods were generally limited to modelling relatively simple or structured situations.

So, here's a summary of the situation regarding CNNs: convolutional neural networks automatically identify characteristics of a dataset that can be used as reliable indicators i.e. features. Historically, the conventional approach was for researchers to put vast efforts into 'hand-crafting' exhaustive sets of features for image classification. Since the advent of deep learning/CNNs, the conventional approach has been exceeded in accuracy for almost every data type. Impressive, eh? *Grazie padrini!*

The need to take one step at a time

"Take the first step in faith. You don't have to see the whole staircase, just take the first step."

— Martin Luther King Jr.

Having covered the basics of how AI and deep learning methods such as CNNs work, it is worth addressing the question of how we can usefully apply such technologies for significantly advancing science and technology in critical areas. The important points here are that *we need to take one step at a time* and *data is king*; or perhaps I should say data *are* king, since data is a plural (the singular is datum). For example, computers are very good, and have been for some time, at playing games. A famous example is provided by the series of chess matches that were played between the computer known as 'Deep Blue' and the chess grandmaster Garry Kimovich Kasparov. Such a six-game chess match was played in New York City in 1997 and won by Deep Blue. This 1997 match was the first defeat of a reigning world chess champion by a computer under tournament conditions. A mistake that is often made is to then assume that the computer concerned actually has *human intelligence* and *can think*, so that it would be able to replace a human expert in undertaking some complex reasoning tasks. By the way, I am not saying that computers will never be able to think like humans – if this were possible no doubt some great advances could be made, but we are not yet at such a stage. When discussing whether computers can think, I always tend to be reminded of the *Star Trek* episode, 'The Ultimate Computer'. In this rather good episode, talented computer scientist Dr Richard Daystrom presents his new computer - the 'M-5 Multitronic System'. This is an advanced artificially intelligent control system that is said to be able to control a starship; as Dr Daystrom put it: "The M5 *thinks*, Captain".

The Enterprise, with a skeleton crew, is ordered to test how the M5 performs in a series of war games. Kirk is, as you can imagine, not best pleased by the concept of being made redundant by a smart computer. If the M5 was able to think it must have had some serious (artificial) mental issues, since it starts destroying the other starships in the war games, thereby killing many people. Daystrom has a breakdown and it is left to Kirk to talk the M5 down and save the day (which is perhaps a somewhat too commonly employed means for solving issues presented in a number of *Star Trek* episodes).

What all this might indicate is that getting a computer to think in a truly useful and reliable way may well be quite a long way off – Star Trek was set over 200 years in the future and it seems that even at this stage in man's progress, genuine and reliable artificial intelligence had not been attained.

The M5 Multitronic Unit – from the *Star Trek* episode 'The Ultimate Computer'. (Illustration by the author.)

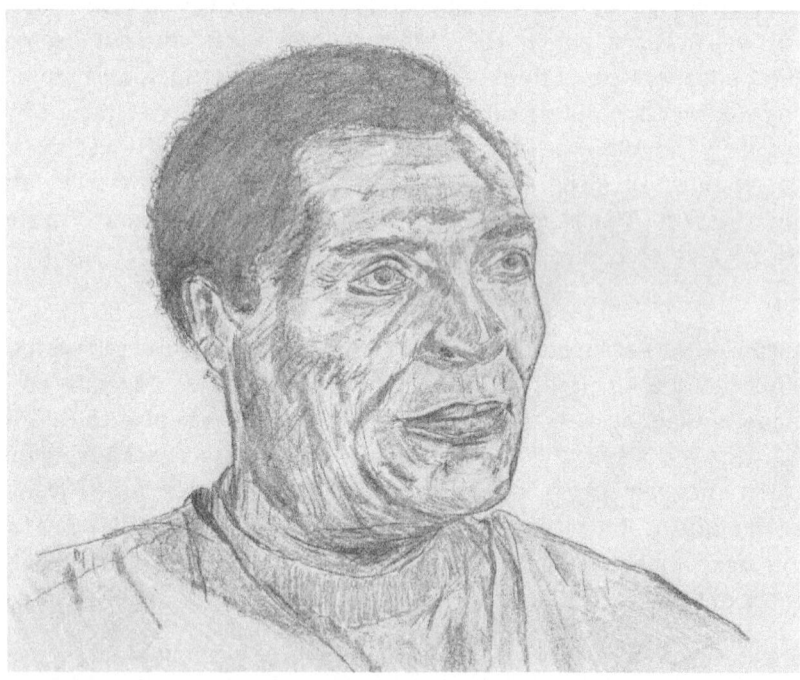

Dr Richard Daystrom – the electronics/computing genius who (happily) created many of the computer systems on the Enterprise but who went on (less happily) to create the ultimate computer - the M5. In the episode 'The Ultimate Computer', Daystrom is played (rather well) by William Horace Marshall. (Drawing by the author.)

The M5 seeks a new power supply – killing a crewman in the process. (Note details of Enterprise Engineering section in the background.) (Illustration by the author.)

Coming back to our century, all that deep learning and CNNs can do is to identify and recognise patterns; and in many cases, do this as well as or better than humans – but as discussed, this does not mean they have human intelligence. Acting upon this assumption can often lead to spectacular failures and a good example of this is IBM's Watson computer, which successfully competed on the US TV quiz Jeopardy! in February 2011. Watson was a supercomputer running software called 'Deep QA', developed by IBM Research. While the grand challenge driving the project was to win on Jeopardy!, the broader goal of Watson was to create a new generation of technology that could find answers in unstructured data more effectively than standard search technology.

There was much excitement about the commercial potential of Watson and in 2013, the MD Anderson Cancer Center launched a "moon-shot" project: diagnose and recommend treatment plans for certain forms of cancer using IBM's Watson cognitive system.

IBM's Watson computer. (Pen and ink drawing by the author.)

But in 2017, the project was put on hold after costs went beyond $62M without the system having been used on a single patient. Why did Watson succeed with the game but fail in the real-world application? There could be many detailed explanations for this, but most, if not all, are related to the observation that games operate with a limited set of clearly defined rules. In the case of some games, such as the chess mentioned above and the Jeopardy! quiz, the game can appear to be very complex, but this is only because of the highly extensive nature of the data that can be associated with the game (in the case of chess the enormous number of possible move combinations and in Jeopardy! the vast number of natural language phrases that need to be analysed to identify the various patterns/connections). In reality, the actual rules of how the chess pieces move or how the Jeopardy! phrases are generally related are relatively simple and straightforward. So, in the world of games, we are operating in a simplified universe, where data might be extensive or complex, but where they can be analysed in relation to a relatively simple set of rules or potential associations. In contrast to this, in the real world, where you and I live and where problems such as medical diagnoses need to be solved, complexity and non-standardisation, in virtually every aspect of data capture and procedures, are the norm. Computer systems, however powerful they are, are just not as good as humans at interpreting, understanding, and drawing significant conclusions from data in the forms in which they are usually employed by humans. This was illustrated when Watson processed leukaemia patient health records that exhibited missing and/or ambiguous data that were sometimes out of order chronologically.

It may well be that the relative failure of IBM Watson has more to do with shortcomings in the data it was presented with, and strict adherence to the limitations of standard practice in medical research, than a consequence of limitations in the computer's ability to process data and identify relationships/patterns. Or to put it another way, health care medical research methodologies can be somewhat more oriented towards a reverence to current practice rather than regarding data as king. This seems again to be associated with medical conservatism and resistance to new thinking – even when supported by data (why should I wash my hands, Vitamin C is only a dietary supplement, and aspirin a painkiller – they can't help fight cancer, and so on...). In the current health care environment, even if Watson had formed recommendations for patient treatment based on analysis of vast amounts of past patient data, they would not have been accepted if not linked to official medical guidelines and the accepted conclusions of clinicians from the existing medical literature. To be fair to the medical establishment, the problem with purely studying patient data is that there may be significant complications/irregularities within and between patient cohorts that may make it difficult to draw reliable conclusions. This is why so much emphasis is placed within medical research on consistency within patient cohorts and the use of randomised trials – so that complicating varying circumstances between patients can be, as far as possible, minimised. I have, myself, experienced the limitations that are placed on automated diagnoses as a result of non-standardised data. Some years ago, I undertook a review of the extent to which computer vision techniques have been applied to usefully detect skin cancer from analysis of images of patient moles. My finding was that many of the computer vision techniques showed promise for this very important application, but at that time a useful clinical role for the technology had not been demonstrated. The reason for this did not have to do with limitations in the computerised image analysis software, but in the variations in the data resulting from non-standard ways of capturing the images of the moles. Variation was present that arose from the use of different camera resolutions and lens set-ups, changes in lighting, distance from the skin and so on. These were observations that led to the development of the Skin Analyser that employs a standard camera and lighting configuration each time a mole is imaged. This provides repeatability in image capture that thereby enables change to be detected – which is an important indicator of possible skin cancer. In fact, I am convinced that combining the data from this device with deep learning can provide a reliable method for automating diagnosis of skin cancer – which for me is a very exciting possibility – but a subject that could itself form the basis of this whole book.

The Skin Analyser employs a standard camera and lighting configuration that provides repeatability in image capture, thereby enabling change to be detected – which is an important indicator of possible skin cancer. (Photograph by the author.)

Therefore, if there is a problem it does not really lie with Watson or IBM, but with limitations in the way medical data are currently captured. If AI is to realize its full potential and transform medicine, the computer systems need access to many more categories of factors than are currently represented in a typical clinical trial. This, of course, requires data capture and access on a vast scale, and so will need enormous investments in relevant technologies for capture and processing along with relevant infrastructure. However, the potential benefits of objective analysis of vast amounts of reliable and standardised patient data in an automated system offers great potential for new insights into disease causes and cures in a way that could constitute *truly personalized care*. In 2020, the UK National Health Service announced a £250 million investment into new ways of applying emerging AI techniques to healthcare – one hopes this will form a first step along this road.

Not that IBM Watson is a complete failure; some physicians are finding it useful as an instant second opinion that they can share with nervous patients, and say that it is useful, and quite good sales of it have been reported in Asia. It's just that, although Watson had demonstrated impressive natural language processing capabilities, after the $62M direct investment (and spending billions of dollars on company acquisitions that they expected to support the project), as well as over four long years of hard work, IBM did not create the super doctor they had aimed for. Is it possible to be even more precise as to why? Yes, it's because they didn't call it 'IBM Holmes'! Or, since they were in the USA, perhaps they could have called it 'IBM Sherlock'.

A sketch of Dr John H. Watson's service revolver. In 'The Adventure of the Speckled Band', Sherlock Holmes tells Watson that: "An Eley's No. 2 is an excellent argument with gentlemen who can twist steel pokers into knots". (An Eley No. 2 is a type of cartridge, rather than gun.) (Drawing by the author.)

Take a systems-based long-term approach and think big

"It is difficult to think of a major industry that AI will not transform. This includes healthcare, education, transportation, retail, communications, and agriculture. There are surprisingly clear paths for AI to make a big difference in all of these industries."

- Andrew Ng

What are the most promising future applications of AI? In 2018, Michael Wu endeavoured to answer this in his keynote session, "How AI Enables the Future of Business Intelligence," at the MDM Analytics Summit 2018 on Wednesday, 19th September in Denver. Here is part of what he said:

"AI is being used in a wide variety of ways by businesses across every sector. However, these are the four most prominent – and promising – applications of AI in business today:

1. Fully autonomous systems

Machines are learning to act and react on their own. This application is largely driven by the rise of self-driving cars, where the AI is constantly learning and ultimately enabling the machine to know how to react to all the potentially different environments and circumstances.

A similar application is relevant for distributors as well, particularly within fulfilment centres. For example, sensors within Internet of Things (IoT) devices can detect inventory levels and automatically place orders, automating the fulfilment process and enabling businesses to run more effectively.

2. Human-computer interface

AI is changing how humans and businesses interact with machines. Think of computer assistants like Alexa, Siri, and other chatbots. This form of perpetual AI mimics higher cognitive functions of humans and can be used in the form of "intelligent digital assistants" to help companies boost productivity.

3. Online personalization

AI can drive recommendation engines, helping companies like Amazon, Netflix, and Spotify learn from users' online behaviour to deliver highly personalized suggestions. Companies can leverage this application of AI to deliver personalized recommendations over time, improving the customer experience.

4. Automating business decisions

Organizations are using AI to improve their systems and gain a competitive advantage. The learning loops in this application of AI can give distributors data-driven insights that enable them to make better-informed decisions and identify opportunities to grow revenue.

By better understanding the different applications of AI, business leaders can determine which is right for their business. Only with this foundation of knowledge can they begin reaping the benefits of this technology."

Wu may be largely right in what he is saying; however, with the possible exception of self-driving cars which represent a significant and possibly life-changing technology (that is once it works reliably and safely on our over-crowded and complex road networks), the other applications mentioned represent AI providing somewhat increased levels of efficiency or productivity. But if I am ever to stand any chance of making a private trip to Mars, there need to be *revolutionary* technologies. It's not enough to just arrange a tweak of what we already have, but instead we need new types of systems that deliver novel and advanced capabilities in the form of automated solutions to complex and significant challenges. The four things that Wu refers to; specifically fully autonomous systems, human-computer interface, online personalization and automating business decisions could, for example, take the form of slight modifications to an online retailing system, such as www.amazon.com, that would be undertaken to improve the shopping experience for the customer and to enhance the seller's business operation. But what I am suggesting is needed is more of a revolution in technological solutions associated with the business operation. For the case of buying some items from Amazon, the tweak might be to have a better concept of the kinds of products the buyer is interested in and so more closely align online shop advertisements to those interests. Rather than just achieving this, the technological revolution would be something more like arranging for the items to be delivered to the customer automatically by AI-guided drones employing GPS and advanced vision capabilities.

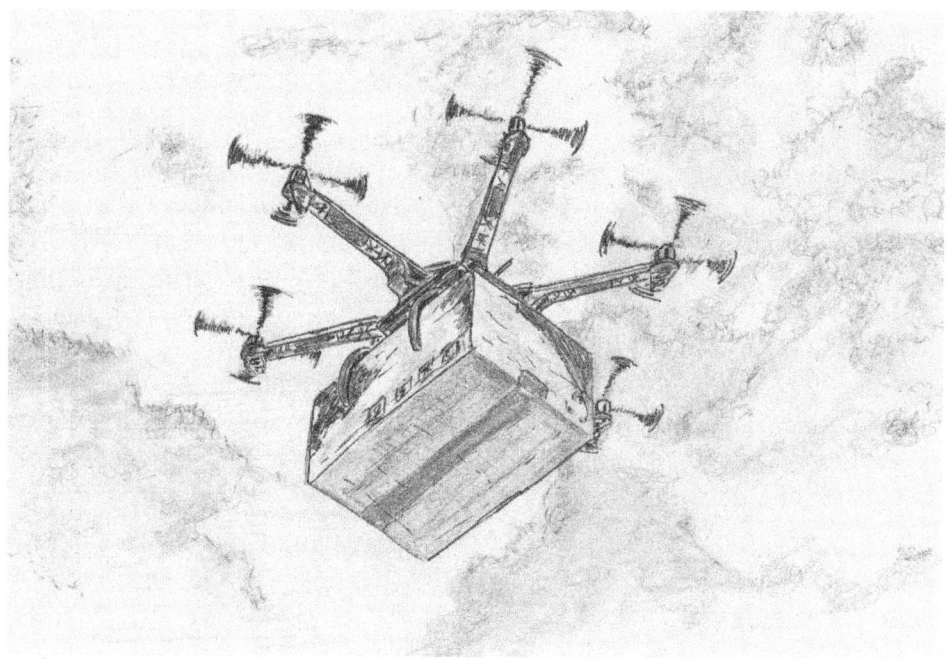

Automatic drones; the future of delivery? (Illustration by the author.)

By the way, for such a delivery the last mile and, in particular, the last few dozen yards would be the more critical part of the delivery. This is because for current manual delivery, often the last mile comprises up to half of the costs, and it is also when in close proximity to a person's home that GPS will prove less useful and there will be a need for advanced vision that employs AI for complex scene understanding and identifying exactly where the package should be delivered.

Therefore, for facilitating new high-performance and high-impact technologies that offer potential to improve our lives, we need to look beyond searches and analyses of databases, such as those relating to online customer interests and shopping behaviours. Instead, we need to employ autonomous systems that will typically be multi-sensorial, but which are certainly likely to employ vision systems powered by cutting edge AI techniques such as CNNs. This point is in fact worth dwelling upon since most research that is being undertaken in fields such as computer vision does tend to dwell more upon database analysis rather than the guidance of multisensory autonomous systems. If we were not feeling charitable, we might say that this is because processing databases is easier to do. Yes folks, inputting data that already exists for you in a formatted and standard fashion, is certainly going to be easier than developing your own system that can capture new data for you. Not that performing research on existing datasets is a complete waste of time; as mentioned above, it was, after all, studies on reliability of face recognition for well-known face datasets that originally led to the breakthrough in use of CNNs for pattern recognition.

But what taking a systems-based approach and thinking big really means is that the world is a very complex place and in order to generate new types of automated systems that can successfully operate in the real world, providing real benefits, the systems need to be able to interact with that world. Although the level of interaction might vary greatly depending upon the task to be undertaken, some ability to capture and interpret new data in a real-world interaction is definitely needed. The relative lack of emphasis of, say, university researchers, on real world autonomous systems, in comparison to the extensive studies on existing datasets, may help to explain why, despite the great promise of advanced capabilities arising from the marriage of modern high-performance cameras with AI, the actual impact i.e. number of autonomous vision-guided systems now usefully operating in the field, is so low.

Perhaps we should again refer to the canon for guidance. In 'The Adventure of the Greek Interpreter', Holmes says that his brother, Mycroft, is his superior in observation and deduction and then goes on to say: "If the art of the detective began and ended in reasoning from an armchair, my brother would be the greatest criminal agent that ever lived. But he has no ambition and no energy. He will not even go out of his way to verify his own solution and would rather be considered wrong than take the trouble to prove himself right. Again and again, I have taken a problem to him and have received an explanation which has afterwards proved to be the correct one. And yet he was absolutely incapable of working out the practical points which must be gone into before a case could be laid before a judge or jury." Holmes is saying that although his brother may be a brilliant reasoner, this is of little practical use due to his lack of application.

Mycroft Holmes, whom Holmes refers to as his younger brother who is his 'superior in observation and deduction'. (Drawing by the author.)

The same is true of AI-driven vision systems. Although we may generate some very powerful scene analysis algorithms, in practice these will be of limited utility if we don't get out in the field and use the system with new data from the particular situation that is of interest to us. And from experience I can confirm that there are many potentially very important situations where the marriage of high-performance imaging and state-of-the-art AI can provide solutions that may have the greatest significance in the long term.

It's not just commonly encountered problems that we can address, such as the location of weeds in grass so that we can eliminate them without spraying herbicide everywhere. No, there are a vast array of applications in a very wide range of sectors; to name just a few I have been involved with: animal identification and condition appraisal, monitoring of building site operations to assist with logistics and improve productivity, plant phenotyping, 3D face analysis at airports, 4D face analysis to identify medical conditions and to assess surgical outcomes, non-contact breathing monitoring, skin cancer detection, used book identification and condition appraisal, identification of security features on banknotes and wear classification, metal power characterisation, measurement of airfreight dimensions, non-contact wheel alignment, scratch detection on polished stone, assessment of aggregate morphologies, 3D face recognition for ticketless travel with gateless gate lines on the London Underground ... which brings us back to Holmes (did he not travel by steam on the Bakerloo Line?)

Early London Underground ticket. (Drawing by the author.)

So, yes, it would be great to be able to be transported to Mars, but to do so, we can't rely on 'reasoning from an armchair'.

Can computers be used to more effectively direct technological development?

"First, we thought the PC was a calculator. Then we found out how to turn numbers into letters with ASCII — and we thought it was a typewriter. Then we discovered graphics, and we thought it was a television. With the World Wide Web, we've realized it's a brochure."

— Douglas Adams

As discussed above, about 25 years ago, in a bid to limit CO_2 emissions, motorists were given incentives to buy diesel cars – in the form of reduced Vehicle Excise Duty. The results of this misguided policy were, of course, calamitous, with many cities worldwide finding themselves in breach of air quality legislative standards. Unfortunately, the politicians who had introduced the policy change had missed the fact that while a diesel engine may produce less CO_2 per mile than a petrol one, it also emits far more of other types of pollution. Some of the blame for this oversight could perhaps be attributed to the fact that most politicians tend to have humanities or law backgrounds rather than a grounding in science and so would be more prone to being unable to see the whole picture, as it were. The amazing thing is that this policy was not limited to one or two small regions, but covered vast areas on an international scale. Just about the whole of Europe seems to have been affected by this diesel mania, with the French being particularly enthusiastic advocates. This resulted in extremely high pollution rates in Paris, with the situation eventually becoming so bad that a rather draconian solution was sought in the form of dramatic increases in diesel fuel tax. Of course, the average French citizen did not take kindly to the price hike – seeing it as a typical manifestation of the superior attitude and lack of concern of the French political class for the average guy on the street. Cue massive riots and civil unrest in the form of the 'Yellow Vests' protests, and the burning out of God knows how many cars. One can appreciate the grievances of the protestors, but really, burning out all the cars – that seems a little too much – I know I would have been upset if my car had been consumed in one of their conflagrations. Anyway, in time-honoured French tradition, there were multitudinous violent demonstrations on the streets (but not quite a revolution thank goodness) and in the tradition of their overdoing things and subsequent defeat, the government/president conceded to the demonstrators' demands and reversed the diesel price increases (with all the lamentable long-term environmental consequences that we may expect to attend that).

So, one thing we can learn from all this is that just because something is believed by many, or even most people, that does not guarantee that it is correct. In fact, it can often mean that they are completely wrong and there are many examples of 'urban myths' or things that are for some reason popularly believed despite being erroneous. An example, albeit a prosaic one, is provided by the process of topping up your car's engine with oil – which is something that most of us do from time to time. There is an urban myth that if, in doing this, you mix mineral oil with semi-synthetic oils, sludging will occur. There is, though, precious little evidence of this; all that would occur in practice is that you would have created an oil mixture with an unknown specification (viscosity grade). Sludging is most commonly caused by not changing the oil at the recommended intervals. (There is another myth that once you have changed to a synthetic oil you can't change back – of course, in reality, you can do so at any time you wish.) Most semi-synthetic oils are actually manufactured by mixing mineral and synthetic oils! Poe made many astute observations and he effectively touches upon this (urban myths, not oil), in his short story The Purloined Letter, where his seminal genius private investigator Dupin says: *"'Il y a a parier,'"* replied Dupin, quoting from Chamfort, *"'que toute idee publique, toute convention recue, est une sottise, car elle a convenu au plus grand nombre.'"* Roughly translated, Dupin is saying that you can bet that any public idea, any conventionally received belief, is nonsense, because it appeals to the greatest number of people. (By the way, Dupin, along with his narrator was the inspiration and basis for Sherlock Holmes and Dr Watson – which was something that Sir Arthur Conan Doyle was very willing to acknowledge and did so in his story 'The Resident Patient'. Conan Doyle also famously noted at one point that Poe's detective stories represented "a model for all time".) The idea that the validity of a concept is more important than its popularity was also expressed in the famous quote by the great Galileo Galilei: "In questions of science, the authority of a thousand is not worth the humble reasoning of a single individual."

Away from such lofty sentiments, and getting back to the rather more everyday diesel car situation, this fashion for replacing petrol engines with diesels did not, mercifully, catch on in America as much as Europe, despite the fact that a number of European auto manufacturers did their best for it to do so. You may ask why diesel power is such a poor option for automobiles and the answer, of course, lies with not the volume of the pollution it generates, but its nature. Diesel engines produce nitrous oxides that are quite toxic as well as micro-particles that can cause cancer – to the extent that the World Health Organisation has designated diesel fumes as carcinogenic – which is not something they have done for petrol engine emissions.

The effects of the appalling decision to encourage motorists to invest in diesel vehicles were also exacerbated by the diesel emission scandal (or 'Dieselgate', discussed above), where VW was found to have installed, with the knowledge of senior management, software that rigged automobile tests and made vehicles appear less polluting than they actually were so that they could appear to be within emission limits and so be sold.

GALILEO GALILEI

Statue of Galileo in Florence. (Pen and ink drawing by the author.)

This is significant because it was not a mistake – it was a deliberate effort to mislead that resulted in all of us breathing in much more pollution than we should have for many years – the result is a vast number of deaths occurring that could and should have been avoidable. There is a case for viewing this as manslaughter – and it is not surprising that an arrest warrant has been issued in the USA for the CEO of VW. (This gentleman, Martin Winterkorn, was pictured above. He lives in Germany, which does not currently extradite its citizens to countries outside of the EU, so he is safe from arrest – as long as he doesn't decide to visit America.) But what has all this to do with employing computers, and perhaps deep learning/CNNs, to more effectively direct technological development? Well, auto companies have been manufacturing petrol and diesel engines for many years and vast amounts of data are available on their respective gaseous emissions. At the same time, the health effects of inhaling different types of gases is something of interest to public health investigators over the long term; for example, the relative toxicity of NO_2 has been well-known for many years. These data could have been used to train a neural network to evaluate the relative risk to health of petrol and diesel as automobile fuels, thereby highlighting the danger of a dramatic switch to diesel. Or, failing that, at least more statistical analyses could have been done.

The example of identifying dangers associated with diesel emissions is, of course, a very simple one and may not have required extensive training of a deep neural network to generate a useful result. What it does show is that, again, data are king, and our decisions need to be based on real data rather than assumptions or beliefs, no matter how widely held they may be. Automatic acceptance of mistakenly held views might explain why machines in general, and perhaps automobiles in particular, do not seem to have progressed as much as one would have expected when considering the long time they have been in existence and the prodigious resourcing that has been invested in their development. Auto manufacturers tend to assume that auto customers want something traditional – or somewhat similar to what their father bought and which they were drove around in as a child – despite the fact that in their father's day global warming was a little-appreciated threat. So, the problem may be due in part to the general conservative nature of the sector, but limitations in the thinking related to the technological developments involved must also play a role. One of the most significant of these developments relates to the need for effective and efficient design. The traditional approach to engineering design is to employ a trial and error method whereby something is designed - possibly after employing some modelling such as FEA (Finite Element Analysis) and if it works well it is adopted, otherwise changes are made and it is re-manufactured. This tends to lead to a generally operational outcome, but is very wasteful in terms of materials, labour, and time, and there is no guarantee an optimal solution will be generated. Wouldn't it be much better to make more use of the extensive engineering-related data that already exist in order to gain direction for technological development (e.g. direct R&D activity for cars away from diesels and towards petrol or, even better, electric power), and then to assist with optimisation of the design of the various engineering devices/systems involved? The problem with doing this in the past has been that, although data exist, effective utilisation has been difficult due to the under-developed data-processing methods that companies generally employ - e.g. databases that are effectively look-up tables or very simple (usually straight-line) models. In engineering, complexity and non-linearity is the norm. Output characteristics of a given manufacturing operation are usually dependent upon multiple input parameters, and we cannot assume a linear relationship between inputs and outputs. So how can we make use of the existing voluminous amounts of data? Deep learning, and CNNs in particular, are powerful techniques for recognising patterns and relationships in vast amounts of data - even when there are significant variations within the data due to variations in environmental parameters. The actual optimisation of the design of the engineering devices/systems can be achieved by introducing minimal constraints (in the form of what you wish the device or system to be capable of) and then relying on the CNN to identify suitable solutions based upon patterns the network finds in the available training data. For example, suppose you wish to manufacture an engineering component that will fasten two other components together in the presence of forces that would tend to separate them. The constraints would be the relative orientation and position of the two components to be fastened, the forces to be exerted on them and, if possible, the maximum permissible weight and/or cost of the fastening component. The CNN could employ vast amounts of existing data to determine the optimal morphology and size of the fastening component, along with the material composition and manufacturing method that would provide the needed mechanical properties and strength. In fact, it could make use of the extensive amounts of FEA data that have been generated over the years – or perhaps even generate its own FEA data for a given problem. Here the CNN would be taking the place of the human who traditionally uses FEA systems to try to optimise designs – which may not be a bad thing, since using such systems is, in my experience, not the most exciting activity in the world as well as being very time-consuming. This interesting idea is further discussed, in slightly more detail, in just a mo.

CNNs are a rare demonstration of a true breakthrough in AI, and the above scenario is just one example of how applying AI to automate design could result in improvements in productivity/product quality. While we are here, it is worth noting that there have been numerous attempts in the past to incorporate AI into design. I myself completed a PhD in the mid-1990s that was concerned with development of a knowledge-based system for assisting with design of parts to be manufactured by power metallurgy (or PM, which is a specific engineering process that involves forming final parts from powdered metals). A knowledge-based system (or KBS, also known as an expert system) is an attempt to represent the expertise of subject experts in a computer, to assist others who may be less expert, in designing parts

131

to be manufactured. The knowledge-based system employs rules to interrogate a proposed design to see if it is suitable for manufacture by PM. The system also includes a materials selector to ensure that steels with the needed mechanical properties can be selected by the user and there is also an interface to a finite element (FEA) system that could be employed to fine-tune the design for the process. The problem with all of this is that none of it really comprises a breakthrough in AI – everything this KBS did could have been done by a relational database perhaps also interfaced to an FEA package (relevant software includes Oracle or SQL from IBM). My God, I worked hard on that PhD – I wrote 10 papers on it and there was much talk of knowledge-based systems being like a 'tiger in a cage' – but, unfortunately, the tiger never got out of the cage! In the late 1980s and 90s there was also much enthusiasm for neural networks (NNs) – and I also dabbled in this, having developed NNs for tasks such as irregular metal powder characterisation and calibration of cameras in computer vision. The problem with all these systems and approaches has to do with something called *knowledge engineering*, which is the process by which the *domain knowledge*, or expertise in a particular area such as design for PM, is captured and represented within the computer. To be more specific, knowledge engineering can be very laborious and the way it is undertaken has an enormous influence over whether the KBS will be of any use in practice. Typically, a KBS will either not go into enough detail to be practically useful, or if it does the requirements of doing so may necessitate the area addressed being so limited as to make the KBS of little use in general. The problem is that knowledge engineering (for example, identifying factors or features that are particularly important for solving particular problems i.e. 'hand crafting' features of interest), is laborious and different people may tend to do it in different ways – thereby limiting standardisation and applicability. The great advantage of CNNs is that the hand crafting is eliminated – identification of features of interest is achieved automatically within the CNN, based on the available data – so that the subjectivity and possible introduction of errors associated with traditional identification of useful features is taken out of the equation. The result is something that really does approach artificial intelligence in an almost uncanny way. Whereas we used to talk about AI in design in the 1990s, now we can actually implement it!

Interestingly, CNNs allow us to do things that many people in the 1990s thought could be done with neural networks. For example, consider a system able to identify pencils in sets of images. Many people used to think that this could be done by training NNs with all sorts of images of pencils – whereas in reality it could not – the images had to be manually processed so that all pencils were presented to the camera in similar ways, with similar lighting conditions and so on – otherwise there would be no guarantee a pencil could be correctly identified. But in contrast to this, CNNs can use all sorts of training data, and if there is enough, they will be able to reliably identify a pencil in a given image. Coming back to the fastening component, by training with extensive databases of previously designed components, a CNN could suggest a design for a given requirement and then go into lower levels of recommending how the component could actually be manufactured. Earlier, finite element analysis was mentioned. This is a numerical modelling technique that can be used to simulate the strain a component, with a given geometry and material type, would experience when subjected to a specified load. Those who studied physics or engineering at school or college will remember that strain = change in length ÷ original length and is how much something distorts (or stretches) when experiencing typical working forces. FEA is, in fact, a very involved subject – particularly when plastic deformation is involved – this is where a component stretches but then does not go back to its original size when the load is removed. Apart from involving very complex maths, the setups required, and computations involved, are extensive and very time-consuming. The subject is indeed so involved that many bright individuals specialise in it and can spend their entire lives on it. Imagine that – spending your entire life on FEA simulation of a pressure applied to a metal pipe coupling to see what chance there is of cracks appearing during use. Very boring? Perhaps, but if the metal coupling is for something critical such as the primary cooling circuit for a nuclear reactor, then no doubt it's needed and somebody has to do it. Thinking about it though, maybe a better solution is to employ a power source that could not be subject to catastrophic environmental effects in the event of a system failure. Bill Gates claimed to have actually done this for nuclear power in the case of his 'slow wave' reactor – but it was unlucky for him that as he was trying to launch this new technology the Fukushima Daiichi nuclear disaster occurred, which turned many people (including his potential investors) off nuclear power of any sort for the foreseeable future. Later on, I will return to the subject of nuclear power.

But could CNNs be used in the design of components much more complex than simple fasteners? Perhaps CNNs could help automate FEA for generating vast amounts of data for various types of engineering components. The emerging data could then be used to train another CNN for advising on design of similar components. The result would be expected to be an AI system able to reliably quantify strain during use for components without all the time-consuming computations needed for conventional FEA every time a slightly modified component is to be designed (CNNs can be consulted very quickly). In the case of completely new designs for components, perhaps after simply being presented with the constraints of a problem, a CNN could be employed to generate innovative design solutions for existing problems, as well as providing information for directing the FEA analysis. The CNN may also be able to employ the FEA system in a more systematic (i.e. again, less trial and error) way – which should improve the chances of reaching an optimal solution. All the simulation data thus generated could be stored and used in future CNN advisory systems for related designs – thereby providing objective and quantitative assistance with the fine tuning – the final stage of the component design process. In this way, we could replace much of the current 'black art' or conventional practices, with component designs driven by real data and employing optimal 3D morphologies and industrial processes. Such optimisation would assist with avoiding 'over engineering' and improve performance as well as minimising costs and, of course, this would apply to just about all fields of engineering in addition to mechanical engineering/component manufacture.

The Fukushima Daiichi nuclear disaster ended Bill Gates' 'slow wave' reactor dream. (Illustration by the author.)

To summarise, deep learning networks such as CNNs represent a potentially powerful approach for informing strategies for adopting preferred technologies, as well as eliminating the traditional 'black art' or guess work that is still widely employed in engineering. By providing data-driven optimal solutions that will work the first time, they surely comprise an initial step along the Martian road. Or, to put it another way, all these far-out ideas about deep learning directing engineering are blowing my mind! And if it looks like CNNs can help direct engineering design, is there any chance they can do the same thing for science research?

Can computers be used to significantly increase our scientific understanding?

"Machine learning allows us to build software solutions that exceed human understanding and shows us how AI can innervate every industry."

-Steve Jurvetson

Rutherford once famously said that there are two types of science: physics and stamp collecting. It's easy to appreciate where he was coming from with this – physics provides a fundamental, quantitative, and systematic understanding of how the Universe is constructed and functions. It can be imagined that if we have a sufficiently in-depth understanding of physics, this will lead to understandings of chemistry and biology (consider, for example, the physical model of the atom as electrons orbiting a nucleus, helping with appreciation of electron interactions controlling chemical reactions, with such reactions leading to understandings of the biochemistry of living organisms). It is not for nothing that physics is known as the mother of the sciences. However, despite its importance, progress in physics research seems to have been somewhat limited in recent decades. It must be worth considering to what extent computers, and deep learning in particular, may offer potential for accelerating developments in this area.

When considering the factors that might be holding back physics discoveries and understanding, it is hard to avoid the conclusion that the problem may be that directions of enquiry may be being influenced by emotionally-related human considerations, such as what type of enquiry, for one reason or another, may be in fashion at any particular time. Humans each have individual senses and different ways of thinking that modify the way we perceive and interpret the world. These differences may be, to some extent, due to our genetic make-up (although there seems to have been a general over estimation of how much we are controlled by our genes) and certainly conditioning and environment, particularly in the early years of life, will have an effect. We are also each profoundly influenced by the culture and language of the country we happen to have been born in. Since we have so many subtle differences, it should come as no surprise that there are pronounced variations in the way humans understand physical reality. While this may be an advantage for a writer of novels who could do with some diverse characters to bring their fiction to life, for physics it is something of a nuisance. Science needs to be objective and standard in its approach – it does not benefit from local colour, or metaphorical allusions that are so common in many languages. As mention above, in science a spade is a spade – it's not a spade some of the time and, say, an 'agricultural implement' the rest of the time. Computers do, of course, comprise a powerful means of assisting with standardisation of data capture, storage, analysis, and presentation. The French did a great job of setting up the metric system for units and measurements – credit where it's due (although it seems very ungrateful of the population to chop off Lavoisier's head at the revolution, just after he had sorted out the metric system for them). Later, with involvement from James Clerk Maxwell, William Thomson (later Lord Kelvin) and others working under the auspices of the British Association for the Advancement of Science, metric units were formed into the International System of Units (SI), which has been adopted by most of the globe; apart from, apparently, the USA. I love the way that our American cousins are quaintly refusing to adopt metric units; but, let's face it, decimal systems make sense since, last time I looked, I had 10 fingers (by the way, it may be a pity that we don't have 16 fingers, since Hexadecimal has many advantages; but that's another story...).

Imperial Uncle Sam versus the world metric system. (Illustration by the author.)

Metric units are great for storing the actual data about the universe, so if you are a serious scientist you will be keen to embrace metrication. What I suggest we need now is another standard system that relates to not just the actual data, but the metadata as well. Metadata is information on data – it tells you something about

136

some data you have been presented with. If there were a standard way of presenting metadata, then it would be much easier for computers to process it and draw useful conclusions from it. Currently a major problem in computer systems that are designed to employ AI to solve difficult tasks is the large variation that is present, not in the actual data itself, but in the way it is recorded and presented. CNNs are in fact better able to process data that contains variations in presentation than most other computer analysis approaches.

Consider the agricultural example that I have been using of a system designed to detect weeds in grass. There may be variations in images due to the angle of the camera relative to the sun (e.g. causing various shadows or overexposures), as well as apparent changes due to perspective and camera angle, time of day, weather, and vibration. A surprising amount of this can be accommodated by the CNN while still generating accurate performance in weed detection. Metadata, in this case, might comprise information on which images actually contain weeds. Gathering such information can be laborious and time-consuming (believe me, closely studying thousands of images of grass to see whether each contains any weed takes a long time and is not the most interesting job on earth). CNNs can even deliver when there is a complete absence of metadata – in the case of weeds in grass this would involve no annotations about the possible presence of weeds on any of the images. The way CNNs can accommodate this is to employ a technique known as unstructured learning, which is something that has, up to now, been considered rather difficult to achieve. Here the CNN will analyse large numbers of images and, by itself and without direct human indication, recognise that a number of images contain a relatively similar and consistent pattern – specifically that of a weed. However, many tasks, particularly in complex and challenging fields such as physics research, are considerably more complex than just determining if a weed is present in a section of grass - nature will never give up her secrets willingly (I think Sir Francis Bacon could have elaborated here).

Consequently, we can be pretty sure that to provide ourselves with a good chance of making progress in physics research, we need to standardise our metadata as much as possible. To the question of 'once we have done this, what further approaches do we need to employ?', I answer simply: 'deep learning!' As discussed, this is a powerful approach that can uncover subtle correspondences/patterns/correlations, and in vast amounts of data to boot! What I am suggesting is a data-driven approach to the directing of physics research; one that will bypass all of the fashionable/biased/prejudiced or in short emotional motivations (which may of course be subconscious) that will, to a greater or lesser extent, influence the thinking of even those scientists who try to be completely open minded and dispassionate. One way of making progress using these approaches may be to apply them to historical research and influential physics experiments of the past (e.g. Rutherford's discovery of the nucleus, Thompson's discovery of the electron, Michelson and Morley's disproof of the presence of the aether, and so on). Data relating to each experiment would need to be collated and configured so that it obeyed a system for standardisation of metadata, as discussed above. Then extensive deep learning would be undertaken for each of the experiments.

The intriguing question is: would this approach be capable of using input data from past physics experiments in order to generate metadata for future experiments that could take the research forward? If so, this would certainly be an exciting development – one can imagine inputting, for example, data on known particles or interactions, with the CNN then outputting information on unknown particle/interactions or metadata related to experiments that might enable us to check the existence of such particles/interactions. But first things first; at the moment, our data are all over the place rather and our metadata are mixed (rather than our metaphors). So, it's all about data; and perhaps everything in this chapter can be (or *was*, or *is*) summarised by that quote from Holmes mentioned earlier: "It is a capital mistake to theorize before one has data. Insensibly one begins to twist facts to suit theories, instead of theories to suit facts." And to this we can add: "Data! Data! Data! ... I can't make bricks without clay!"

(Drawing by the author.)

138

The nuts and bolts of a rocket to Mars

"Mars is there, waiting to be reached."

- Buzz Aldrin

The previous chapters covered various approaches that might have some potential for improving our knowledge of the physical sciences and engineering capabilities, since that is what is needed for us to be able to create an affordable transportation system to Mars, right? Wrong! We have technologies available to us today that are perfectly capable of providing regular transportation to Mars and beyond at relatively affordable costs and with limited environmental impacts. We can use rockets to go to Mars if we choose, the problem being that most of the time mankind has a tendency to use them for somewhat less constructive purposes, such as threatening others with nuclear obliteration.

When employing the term rocket, you might be thinking of a device such as the Saturn V rocket that took man to the moon – that is to say a chemically-based, expensive device that was not re-useable (in the case of its successor, the Space Shuttle it was intended to be reusable, but this was still very expensive to launch as well as being somewhat unreliable). But when I talk about a 'rocket to Mars' I am not necessarily thinking of this kind of craft. To escape from any massive body, all we need to do is to accelerate to its escape velocity – which is dictated by the mass of the body. Since the mass of the Moon is much less than that of the Earth, launching a rocket to Mars from the Moon would be much easier than from the Earth (one would also not need to worry about complicating factors caused by air resistance).

But whichever body we launch from there is a technology that might well provide significant benefits, specifically the *mass driver* or *accelerator*. A mass driver consists of a very long and mainly horizontally aligned launch track or tunnel for space launch, curved upwards at the end. The concept was proposed by Arthur C. Clarke in 1950. Clarke, by the way, was in fact quite a futurist, who many years ago predicted now common technologies such as communication satellites, mobile computerised telecommunication, and the internet. The mass driver could launch vehicles directly to space by accelerating them to very high velocities. This would be facilitated by having the vehicles floating just above the track by using maglev repulsion – rather like some current German trains. The track would probably need incorporation of superconducting magnets to accelerate the vehicle to the necessary very high speeds. The track would be constructed so that it terminated at a relatively high altitude and at an angle that would enable a high-speed vehicle to fly into a low-earth orbit. The power required would probably be provided by superconductive energy storage units distributed along the track. Vehicles could then employ a relatively small on-board rocket motor to change orbit. The main challenge when launching humans into orbit using such technology is that it does require quite high accelerations and most people would not be able to tolerate a sustained acceleration of more than about 2g (i.e. twice that caused by gravity on the surface of the Earth). Therefore, manned vehicles would need relatively long tracks ... but, how long? That's a good question. Well, to get into orbit a craft needs to travel at around 7.9 km/s and Newtonian physics tells us that $v^2 = u^2 + 2as$, where v = final velocity = 7900m/s, u = initial velocity = 0, a = acceleration and 1g is around 10 m/s^2 and s = distance. Therefore $s = v^2/2a$. Putting the values in gives us a track length of about 1560 km! This is indeed rather long; but it is worth bearing in mind that if we just wish to accelerate equipment into space a much higher g could be employed — use of 40g would result in a track length of just 78 km which would seem quite attainable.

Fictional concept of part of a mass accelerator for launching objects into orbit. (Drawing by the author.)

Although building such a length of mass driver track would still be quite an expensive undertaking, it is important to note that this is only a one-off cost; once built the track could be used to accelerate objects up into orbit frequently and at low cost. As mentioned, it would be much cheaper and easier to launch a rocket to Mars from the Moon, or in fact from Earth orbit, rather than actual *terra firma*. But the chief difficulty is the high price of launching equipment from Earth to these locations using presently available chemical rockets. Currently, prices are around $10,000 per kg – the amazing fact is that a mass driver could offer potential to reduce this by a factor of 100, to only around $100 per kg! But what about the previously mentioned problem of needing a very long track for launching humans? Well, build a longer track! Railways longer than 2000 km exist and have existed for many years and many were originally built with the limited technologies available in the nineteenth century. A 1560 km long mass driver would be the ultimate solution to low cost transport of humans to Mars; but if in the nearer term a method was required that was not quite as ultimately low cost but perhaps easier or quicker to implement, then a shorter mass driver could be used for launching needed equipment and following this humans could travel up to orbit, or the moon, by riding a good old-fashioned chemical rocket (NASA had few serious problems in reliably achieving repeated manned flights to the Moon even when all they had was 1960's technology).

To summarise all this, we can expect to be able to employ technologies that are not currently inconceivable, or unaffordable, to launch men and, particularly, equipment into Earth orbit and on to the Moon and Mars. Is this worth doing? Ray Bradbury thought so.

"We should go to the Moon and prepare a base to fire a rocket off to Mars and then go to Mars and colonize Mars. Then when we do that, we will live forever."

- Ray Bradbury

Yes, it's as much worth doing as man leaving the warmth of his campfire to walk and look over the nearby hills – exploration is our business. Or as Kirk used to say, "risk is our business":

"They used to say if man could fly, he'd have wings … but he did fly. He discovered he had to. Do you wish that the first Apollo mission hadn't reached the Moon, or that we hadn't gone on to Mars or the nearest star? That's like saying you wish that you still operated with scalpels and sewed your patients up with catgut like your great-great-great-great-grandfather used to. I'm in command. I could order this. But I'm not … because … Dr McCoy is right in pointing out the enormous danger potential in any contact with life and intelligence as fantastically advanced as this. But I must point out that the possibilities, the potential for knowledge and advancement is equally great. Risk … risk is our business! That's what this starship is all about … that's why we're aboard her!" (You can imagine all the Shatnerisms of being dramatic and speaking/moving in little sharp bursts.)

William Shatner as Captain Kirk in the *Star Trek* episode 'Return to Tomorrow': "Do you wish that the first Apollo mission hadn't reached the moon, or that we hadn't gone on to Mars or the nearest star?" (Drawing by the author.)

Sorry, I got a bit carried away there. But what if we, like Kirk, do decide to explore as far as we can. Mars is relatively cold and inhospitable, but modern astronomical observations tell us that there are multitudes of planets – or exo-planets – in our Galaxy that are in the habitable zone of their star. This is very intriguing; can we travel to them and explore? The problem here is that the distances involved are truly vast and so to cross them we will need craft capable of very high velocities. This is where some of the considerations of the last two chapters will become relevant. It is fine and dandy to use a mass driver to launch men and equipment efficiently from the surface of the Earth or Moon, but what happens then? How do we accelerate up to the very high speeds needed to achieve inter-stellar travel in reasonable timescales? Currently, all we essentially have is the good old chemical rocket – which is an invention dating from thousands of years ago and one that has several serious limitations. One of the most serious is the need to carry large amounts of fuel on board in order to accelerate to high speeds, which currently makes launch difficult if not impossible. This is where new understandings of physics could lead to new concepts for propulsion mechanisms, and novel capabilities in engineering design and manufacture will enable fabrication of these new generations of rocket motors. My hope, as described, is that this can be facilitated in the not too distant future, perhaps through judicious application of the new deep learning methodologies outlined earlier. As well as building a rocket capable of high speeds, we also have the little issue of the laws of physics to worry about. For example, in *Star Trek* it was very easy for Kirk to issue an order to accelerate to warp seven and Scotty would promptly make sure his engines obliged the captain. But warp seven meant a speed well in excess of light and to quickly accelerate the Enterprise up to such a speed, even if it were possible, would result in such g forces that, horrible to contemplate, the Enterprise crew of 430 would be immediately squashed to a pulp!

The starship USS Enterprise from the TV series *Star Trek*. (Illustration by the author.)

But let us return in thought for a moment from the prospects of galactic exploration to our good old Earth; what's the latest report on prospects for planet 3? Are there any clouds emerging on the horizon and how serious or insurmountable might any potential threats actually be?

Part 2.

Potential and definite threats and possible responses

"We stand today on the edge of a new frontier - the frontier of the 1960's - a frontier of unknown opportunities and perils - a frontier of unfulfilled hopes and threats."

- John F. Kennedy

I have included this image from Venus at the start of this section, since perhaps the most serious threat that humanity faces is global warming. If a vicious circle were initiated for global warming, accelerated by release of vast amounts of carbon dioxide, methane, and other greenhouse gasses from the oceans, then man's outlook would indeed be bleak. To give an idea of possible consequences, we can consider the planet Venus – which has an extremely dense atmosphere, sulphuric acid rain, and a surface temperature that is about twice as hot as the oven in your kitchen. (Illustration by the author from images sent by Russia's Venera 13 spacecraft on 1st March, 1982. The craft just had time to capture a few images, before being roasted by the extreme heat.)

Part 1 addressed what progress has been made in science and technology and outlined some approaches that may help the rate of progress and particularly their impact on our societies. So, these discussions relate to how things can operate when we are all sailing along at a reasonable clip, as it were. Or, in other words, when no emergency situations are arising. But what happens when threats materialise? There is a theory about world events that uses a biological metaphor – by referring to 'black swans'. I read a book that put this theory forward and I seem to remember the author going around the houses for what seemed like about 500 pages, but to cut a long story short the idea is that unexpected events occur that can be very disruptive. By the way, I am a great believer in cutting a long story short – particularly when it comes to scientific or technological theories or descriptions. Science does not have time for artistic renderings or flowery prose. And succinct and clear descriptions are also a good idea in many other fields, if you ask me. Many writers may have had some good ideas but falter somewhat in their use, or over-use, of language. Consider, for example, the psychologist Jung, who had some interesting theories on development of the individual but seems to have experienced some difficulty in expressing them in an accessible way. He also had ideas on parapsychology such as 'synchronicity', that many people wish to immediately dismiss but which, for me, are pretty intriguing. Synchronicity refers to the simultaneous occurrence of events which appear significantly related by meaning, but which have no discernible causal connection (you know, like BBC 'celebrity' DJs/presenters being paid huge salaries), whereas parapsychology is the study of mental phenomena such as hypnosis or telepathy, which are excluded from or inexplicable by orthodox scientific psychology. I mean, who among us has not been lying in bed at night and telepathically received a sensation of icy fingers on their spine? (Not me, thank God; but some have!) Meanwhile, Jung's one-time mate and fellow psychologist, Freud, may have been a reasonable writer but also seems to have been keen on dreaming up some very wacky ideas that could perhaps be described, technically, as *baloney*. I mean, Oedipus Complex, Interpretation of Dreams and, can you believe it, Penis Envy? Give us a break! The chief problem is that these theories seem to have been taken seriously by legions of Freudian psychologists, with the result of them writing vast tomes on Freudian-psychological interpretations of the characters appearing in the classic stories written by famous authors. Yes, in Poe's short story 'The Black Cat', the cat is, apparently, a Freudian mother figure for the narrator … curiously, I had been thinking it was a cat. But to be fair to Freud and company, they didn't have much to build upon; before them, all there really was, was the (pseudo)science of phrenology. This is a process that involves observing and/or feeling the skull to allegedly determine an individual's psychological attributes. (This may explain why, when I was a child and had done something that I shouldn't have, my mother used to say: "You need your head felt!" She was interpreting my behaviour as warranting a psychological examination by a phrenologist.)

Jung, with his specs, (who believed in Synchronicity, which seems a bit mystical), Freud with his cigar, (who seemed to think that everything is based on sex, which seems a bit crazy) and Nietzsche with his walrus-handlebar moustache, (who ended up actually going crazy). Here's my quick appraisal of how they appear: Jung looks like your nice uncle who wants to tell you a story, I wouldn't want to meet Freud on a dark night, and it looks like Nietzsche has already started to go bonkers! But very nice mustacho Friedrich! (Drawings by the author.)

But really, expecting that feeling the bumps on one's head will facilitate a psychological profiling seems, at least to me, to be a bit naïve. Anyway, when it comes to wishing to cut a long story short, or to be succinct, there were some contemporaries of Jung and Freud who really did have this as a goal. Take the philosopher Nietzsche for example; he said: "It is my ambition to say in ten sentences what others say in a whole book." Unfortunately though, he seems to have gone nuts before he had a chance to do so and came out with some bombastic rantings such as *The Anti-Christ*. And who can read his torturous book *Thus Spoke Zarathustra* without wondering what the guy was on? Good grief. I mean, here is a typical Nietzsche quote: "Whoever fights monsters should see to it that in the process he does not become a monster. And if you gaze long enough into an abyss, the abyss will gaze back into you." High, clearly, (although, perhaps there is something in that quote...).

But apologies for the digression. Returning to the concept of black swans, I am sure there is something in it, since apparently random events do occur which, really, only an all-out genius could have predicted – an example being 9/11. But in my view, it's not just all about regular swans and black swans – there are also a good few grey swans kicking about. In other words, there are potential crises that we may have an inkling of and might be able to take some pre-emptive action to alleviate possible negative effects of, before the phenomenon concerned were to become a full-blown crisis. You could say we are just about aware of these potential threats – we perceive them as dots on the horizon. It doesn't seem unreasonable that we should take action just in case they come our way. In this part of the book, several such potential threats are considered – in no particular order – just the order in which I wished to discuss them. They are: Brexit, contact with extra-terrestrials (ET), interstellar objects colliding with the earth, and viruses. I think it will become clear that if we were to adopt a more proactive and less reactive approach in addressing these potential threats, the negative effects that they could have on society would be greatly reduced. The final threat I will address, climate change (or global warming as it is often known), is somewhat different, since rather than just being a potential threat, it is generally acknowledged that it is a serious, real and present phenomena that may be expected to have rather profound long-term effects on society. Therefore, I wish to address our possible responses to it in rather more detail.

Brexit

"Brexit was not a historical accident, after all. It taught us where the EU's real problems lie. And if we do not solve them, we will not prevent the anti-European currents in many EU countries, but rather encourage them."

I have included Brexit in part 2 of this book for two reasons: it has been consistently presented by some as a threat, and it provides a good example of the kinds of factors that cause distractions and wasted effort, thereby diminishing the chances of us being able to get to Mars and beyond. My response to these two considerations is that it is likely to be more constructive to view it as an opportunity rather than a threat, and that it is really a relatively simple matter that has been blown up into a major issue for political reasons. This is something that happens quite regularly, with another example being the 'Millennium Bug', but here the motivation was profit rather than being political in nature. You may remember that there was fear that at midnight on 31st December 1999 computers across the world would go into meltdown due to not being able to handle the digits '2000'. Of course, no such thing happened, and it is generally considered now that the fear was being stoked up by some software companies who wished to sell 'patches' to cover this non-existent software bug. In the case of Brexit, the motivations for creating fear and stalling the process are principally political – the EU wishes to make the UK's leaving of the EU as difficult as possible so as to deter other countries from leaving in an attempt to avoid its own disintegration. In reality, the situation is quite simple; the UK voted in June 2016 to leave the EU and this decision was confirmed in three subsequent national votes (one European election and two general elections).

That is really all that it is necessary to say – the votes meant that the UK had to leave, and once it has left it is in the strong interests of everybody for the EU and UK to continue to trade as before. It would perhaps be best to do the latter through use of a trade deal but if this cannot be agreed upon before the deadline, trade must continue through the use of WTO rules. So, it is simple; the UK needs to leave the EU and the UK and EU need to continue to trade ... next? This should not be interpreted as a political comment – I am not saying that leaving the EU is a good thing or something that should happen according to my opinion – it is just an objective observation that a democratic process necessitates it. Nor does it mean that we should not have excellent political relationships and, in fact, great friendships with our neighbours i.e. the nations of the great continent known as Europe.

A tremendous amount has been said about Brexit; unfortunately, most of it is effectively partisan twaddle. There was, however, one person who had a profound understanding of Britain's place in the world and in particular its relationship with Europe and America; his name was Sir Winston Churchill. Perhaps I can do no better than quote the interesting, but often misrepresented speech on Europe that he gave at the University of Zurich just after World War II (on the 19th September 1946):

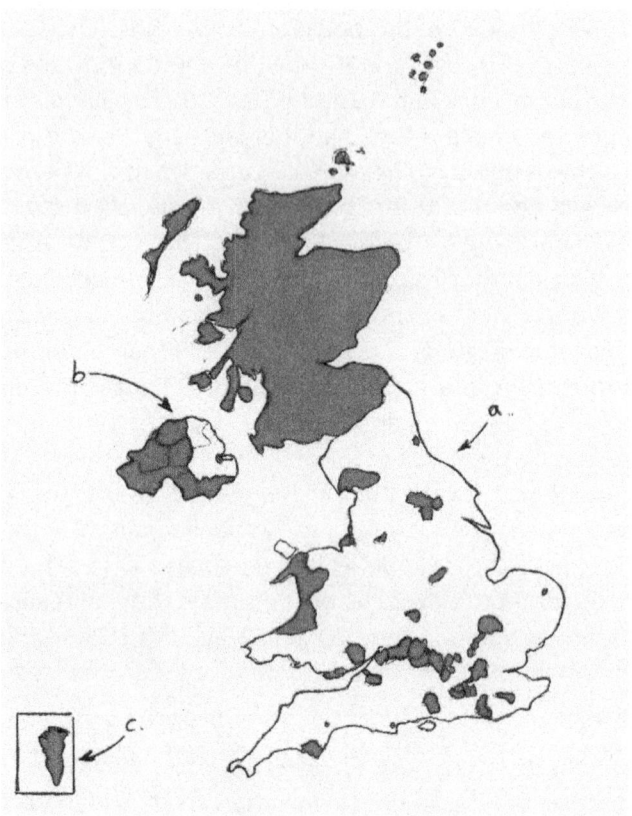

How the UK voted to leave the EU in the June 2016 referendum. Shading indicates remain; a – Britain, b – Northern Ireland and c – Gibraltar. (Illustration by the author.)

"I wish to speak about the tragedy of Europe, this noble continent, the home of all the great parent races of the Western world, the foundation of Christian faith and ethics, the origin of most of the culture, arts, philosophy and science both of ancient and modern times. If Europe were once united in the sharing of its common inheritance there would be no limit to the happiness, prosperity and glory which its 300 million or 400 million people would enjoy. Yet it is from Europe that has sprung that series of frightful nationalistic quarrels, originated by the Teutonic nations in their rise to power, which we have seen in this 20th century and in our own lifetime wreck the peace and mar the prospects of all mankind. What is this plight to which Europe has been reduced? Some of the smaller states have indeed made a good recovery, but over wide areas are a vast, quivering mass of tormented, hungry, careworn and bewildered human beings, who wait in the ruins of their cities and homes and scan the dark horizons for the approach of some new form of tyranny or terror. Among the victors there is a Babel of voices, among the vanquished the sullen silence of despair. That is all that Europeans, grouped in so many ancient states and nations, and that is all that the Germanic races have got by tearing each other to pieces and spreading havoc far and wide. Indeed, but for the fact that the great republic across the Atlantic realised that the ruin or enslavement of Europe would involve her own fate as well, and stretched out hands of succour and guidance, the Dark Ages would have returned in all their cruelty and squalor. They may still return. Yet all the while there is a remedy which, if it were generally and spontaneously adopted by the great majority of people in many lands, would as by a miracle transform the whole scene and would in a few years make all Europe, or the greater part of it, as free and happy as Switzerland is today. What is this sovereign remedy? It is to recreate the European fabric, or as much of it as we can, and to provide it with a structure under which it can dwell in peace, safety and freedom. We must build a kind of United States of Europe. In this way only will hundreds of millions of toilers be able to regain the simple joys and hopes which make life worth living. The process is simple. All that is needed is the resolve of hundreds of millions of men and women to do right instead of wrong and to gain as their reward blessing instead of cursing. Much work has been done upon this task by the exertions of the Pan-European Union, which owes so much to the famous French patriot and statesman Aristide Briand. There is also that immense body which was brought into being amidst high hopes after the First World War - the League of Nations. The League did not fail because of its principles or conceptions. It failed because those principles were deserted by those states which brought it into being, because the governments of those states feared to face the facts and act while time remained. This disaster must not be repeated. There is, therefore, much knowledge and material with which to build and also bitter, dearly bought experience to spur. There is no reason why a regional organisation of Europe should in any way conflict with the world organisation of the United Nations. On the contrary, I believe that the larger synthesis can only survive if it is founded upon broad natural groupings. There is already a natural grouping in the Western Hemisphere. We British have our own Commonwealth of Nations. These do not weaken, on the contrary they strengthen, the world organisation. They are in fact its main support. And why should there not be a European group which could give a sense of enlarged patriotism and common citizenship to the distracted peoples of this mighty continent? And why should it not take its rightful place with other great groupings and help to shape the honourable destiny of man? In order that this may be accomplished there must be an act of faith in which the millions of families speaking many languages must consciously take part. We all know that the two World Wars through which we have passed arose out of the vain passion of Germany to play a dominating part in the world. In this last struggle crimes and massacres have been committed for which there is no parallel since the Mongol invasion of the 13th century, no equal at any time in human history. The guilty must be punished. Germany must be deprived of the power to rearm and make another aggressive war. But when all this has been done, as it will be done, as it is being done, there must be an end to retribution. There must be what Mr Gladstone many years ago called a "blessed act of oblivion". We must all turn our backs upon the horrors of the past and look to the future. We cannot afford to drag forward across the years to come hatreds and revenges which have sprung from the injuries of the past. If Europe is to be saved from infinite misery, and indeed from final doom, there must be this act of faith in the European family, this act of oblivion against all crimes and follies of the past. Can the peoples of Europe rise to the heights of the soul and of the instinct and spirit of man? If they could, the wrongs and injuries which have been inflicted would have been washed away on all sides by the miseries which have been endured. Is there any need for further floods of agony? Is the only lesson of history to be that mankind is unteachable? Let there be justice, mercy and freedom. The peoples have only to will it and all will achieve their heart's desire. I am now going to say something that will astonish you. The first step in the re-creation of the European family must be a partnership between France and Germany. In this way only can France recover the moral and cultural leadership of Europe. There can be no revival of Europe without a spiritually great France and a spiritually great Germany. The structure of the United States of Europe will be such as to make the material strength of a single State less important. Small nations will count as much as large ones and gain their honour by a contribution to the common cause. The ancient States and principalities of Germany, freely joined for mutual convenience in a federal system, might take their individual places among the United States of Europe. But I must give you warning, time may be short. At present there is a breathing space. The cannons have ceased firing. The fighting has stopped. But the dangers have not stopped. If we are to form a United States of Europe, or whatever name it may take, we must begin now. In these present days we dwell strangely and precariously under the shield, and I even say protection, of the atomic bomb. The atomic bomb is still only in the hands of a nation which, we know, will never use it except in the cause of right and freedom, but it may well be that in a few years this awful agency of destruction will be widespread and that the catastrophe following from its use by several warring nations will not only bring to an end all that we call civilisation but may possibly disintegrate the globe itself. I now sum up the propositions which are before you. Our constant aim must be to build and fortify the United Nations Organisation. Under and within that world concept we must recreate the European family in a regional structure called, it may be, the United States of Europe, and the first practical step will be to form a Council of Europe. If at first all the States of Europe are not willing or able to join a union, we must nevertheless proceed to assemble and combine those who will and who can. The salvation of the common people of every race and every land from war and servitude must be established on solid foundations and must be created by the readiness of all men and women to die rather than to submit to tyranny. In this urgent work France and Germany must take the lead together. Great Britain, the British Commonwealth of Nations, mighty America - and, I trust, Soviet Russia, for then indeed all would be well - must be the friends and sponsors of the new Europe and must champion its right to live. Therefore, I say to you 'Let Europe arise!'"

Sir Winston Leonard Spencer Churchill, KG, OM, CH, TD, DL, FRS, RA (1874 – 1965) was British Prime Minister of the United Kingdom from 1940 to 1945, and led the country from its darkest hour through to victory in the Second World War. His many awards include the Nobel Prize for Literature in 1953, and in 2002, in a BBC poll attracting more than a million voters, Winston Churchill was voted the greatest Briton of all time. Considering all the letters after Churchill's name, there can be little doubt that Sherlock Holmes would have said of him (as he did regarding the 6th Duke of Holdernesse in 'The Priory School'): "-half the alphabet! ...Well, well, this man is certainly one of the greatest subjects of the Crown!" (Drawing by the author.)

Contact with extra-terrestrials (ET)

"I'm sure the universe is full of intelligent life. It's just been too intelligent to come here."

— Arthur C. Clarke

In moving on from Brexit to ET, you may think that I have gone from the sublime to the ridiculous, but I would assert that the reverse is true – I have actually gone from the ridiculous to the sublime. (I am not saying that Brexit itself is ridiculous, rather the furore that has emerged around it is). Many people believe the idea of extra-terrestrials, or ET, to be the stuff of fantasy or science fiction. It is, however, much more likely to be a matter of scientific fact rather than a fantasy. In just our own galaxy, the Milky Way, there are estimated to be 11 billion Earth-sized planets orbiting in the habitable zones of Sun-like stars (based on 2013 Kepler space mission data). And it might blow your mind to know that astronomers say there are at least a trillion galaxies in the observable Universe – which is only a small fraction of the whole Universe!

"The universe is a pretty big place. If it's just us, seems like an awful waste of space."

— Carl Sagan, Contact

The laws of statistics say, therefore, that you can be nigh on certain that life exists beyond the earth – in fact statistics would indicate that life exists on billions of 'exo-planets', or trillions, or perhaps more. However, that does not necessarily mean there are trillions of intelligent ET lifeforms in existence who have technologies similar to ours. Coming back to the Milky Way, 11 billion potential habitable planets does not imply 11 billion planets where humanoids are driving around in automobiles and watching TV. There may be life lurking in primeval protein 'soups' on the surface of many of these planets, but it may not yet have progressed beyond that stage (after all it took 4.5 billion years to evolve on Earth). Or it may be that the life never crawled out of the sea, or evolved the thumbs needed to manipulate the tools and instruments that are used to build technologies. Or perhaps huge reptiles evolved, similar to the ones that ruled the Earth in its distant past. In the case of the Earth, there is much geological evidence that an asteroid around 10 km across hit Earth 65 million years ago. The impact, near the Gulf of Mexico, created a huge explosion and a crater about 180 km wide. Debris from the explosion was thrown into the atmosphere, dramatically altering the climate, and leading to the extinction of roughly 3/4 of the species that existed at that time, including the dinosaurs. This gave the smaller mammals, and ultimately us, the chance to rule the roost. But this seems like a very fluky thing; do we owe our existence to this seemingly very unlikely impact causing the extinction of the dinosaurs and thereby giving the mammals a chance to thrive and to eventually evolve into humans? If similar situations arose on exoplanets we would expect such impacts to be very rare and therefore, perhaps, the rise of the mammals on such planets to be correspondingly rare – unless the dinosaurs eventually led to an evolution of intelligent reptiles... (which, by the way, was something James T. Kirk knew something about; following his famous contest with the Gorn on Cestus III, A.K.A. Vasquez Rock).

The Gorn captain with Cestus III, A.K.A. Vasquez Rock, in the background; from the *Star Trek* episode 'Arena'. (Pen and ink drawing by the author.)

There are many unknowns (or insufficient data as Mr Spock would say); however, for the sake of argument, let us assume that 1 million of these 10 billion potentially inhabited planets in the Milky Way have evolved intelligent life and have developed technologies that are comparable to, or superior to, ours. Then why have we not heard from them? Well the fact is that the Milky Way is an enormous structure – in fact it is around 100 thousand light years across. So even if there were 1 million intelligent life forms located randomly within it, it is unlikely that any would be located particularly close to us. Suppose there happened to be one positioned at a distance of 50 light years from us – that's about 450 trillion km – quite a long way away I would say and they would need a strong transmitter before we would stand much of a chance of receiving a signal from them. If they were sending out very intense signals that we might be able to detect, they would need to make them highly directional, so that rather than broadcasting in every direction they would scan their transmission across the heavens, with the time they would happen to be sending them in our direction being very short. We would also need to be looking exactly in their direction at the instant they were transmitting – hence their signal would be very easy for us to miss. (Also, if we sent them a message, we would have to wait 100 long years to get an answer – making it a bit tricky to have a quick chat with them.) So, you see, the fact that we are not hearing anything from ET does not mean that he, or she, or it, does not exist – rather, probability indicates that the existence of ET is pretty much certain. The thing we don't know is how far away ET is and in which direction our nearest neighbour is to be found.

Due to the extreme distance involved, if an ET were transmitting a signal to us it would need to be tremendously powerful and highly directional – and we would need to be looking for it at the exact right time – so the fact that such signals have not been verifiably detected does not indicate ETs do not exist. (Illustration by the author.)

This chapter is entitled contact with extra-terrestrials (ET) and the type of contact we have considered so far is that of communication by transmitted signals. But what about physical contact; what are the chances of an ET paying us a visit? We have noted how distant an ET exoplanet is likely to be located, so it follows that, considering the rudimentary nature of our spacecraft technology, the technology (and therefore the culture) of any ET capable of visiting Earth would be far in advance of ours. This may be why the noted physicist Professor Stephen Hawking considered the possibility of a visit from an ET lifeform to be a considerable threat:

"If aliens ever visit us, I think the outcome would be much as when Christopher Columbus first landed in America, which didn't turn out very well for the Native Americans."

- Stephen Hawking

On the other hand, Carl Sagan - physicist and all-round good egg that he was - was rather keen on the idea of alien contact. He even wrote *Contact*, which is a hard science fiction novel. The book, which appeared in 1985 and made the top 10 in the New York Times bestseller list, is concerned with contact between humanity and a more technologically advanced ET life form. In 1997, the book was turned into an enjoyable film starring Jodie Foster.

But Hawking was concerned that, in Earth's history, when more advanced cultures come into contact with less advanced ones, the latter tend to suffer. He gave the example of when European explorers colonised the Americas, where the natives were pretty much devastated. And it is not just America; this pattern has been repeated over the ages over much of the globe. This consideration is what led Gene Rodenberry to create the *Prime Directive* for his fictional *Starfleet*. Gene was a futurist and a bit of a genius. He was also an optimist and envisaged a *United Federation of Planets* where beings on planets joined together in a cooperative union that was protected by Starfleet, with the latter comprising a fleet of starships (of which the USS Enterprise was one) and a network of star bases. His Starfleet is sworn to uphold the Prime Directive, which states: "The Prime Directive prohibits Starfleet personnel and spacecraft from interfering in the normal development of any society, and mandates that any Starfleet vessel or crew member is expendable to prevent violation of this rule". And, "As the right of each sentient species to live in accordance with its normal cultural evolution is considered sacred, no Starfleet personnel may interfere with the normal and healthy development of alien life and culture. Such interference includes introducing superior knowledge, strength, or technology to a world whose society is incapable of handling such advantages wisely. Starfleet personnel may not violate this Prime Directive, even to save their lives and/or their ship, unless they are acting to right an earlier violation or an accidental contamination of said culture. This directive takes precedence over any and all other considerations and carries with it the highest moral obligation." All this is pretty prescient if you ask me; I mean he is imagining a rule that will apply in the 23rd century and is telling us about it in 1966! And one thing I would like to know is this: if Roddenberry told us all about the Prime Directive in 1966 then why did Richard Nixon ignore it and dramatically escalate the Vietnam War in the following eight years and why did George W. Bush and Dick Cheney organise and prosecute the Iraq war in 2003, both of which are now generally considered to have been calamitous. Don't they have television in the White House?

Personally, I like the *Star Trek* vision of how alien contact is made. According to the 1996 film *Star Trek: First Contact* this was achieved by Zefram Cochrane, who was apparently born in 2030, and in 2063 tinkered together humanity's first warp-capable vessel, the Phoenix, in Bozeman, Montana, out of an old Titan II nuclear missile. Apparently, on April 5, 2063, Cochrane made Earth's first warp flight, playing the suitable anthem of Steppenwolf's 'Magic Carpet Ride' during blast-off. Legend has it that the Phoenix's warp flight was detected by a Vulcan survey ship, the *T'Plana Hath*, which then made peaceful first contact with humans, including Cochrane, at the Phoenix's launch site. Well done, I say! The character of Zefram Cochrane actually appeared twice in *Star Trek*; once in the original TV series in 1967 and then in the 1996 film (played by different actors each time).

Zefram Cochrane, the *Star Trek* inventor of warp drive; played by Glenn Corbett in the 1967 TV episode 'Metamorphosis' (top) and James Cromwell in the 1996 film *First Contact* (bottom). (Drawings by the author.)

Seriously though, humans coming into contact with ETs is quite a possibility and it could represent an existential threat to mankind. Consequently, we should put some effort into considering the possibility and the preferred response to it. It is worth noting that we can expect the ET I have been referencing to have just about nothing in common with Spielberg's sentimental creation in the film of the same name. Nor, considering their expected vast technological superiority, will any 'shoot them up' response provide any useful outcomes – in fact, it might be rather like a pea shooter versus a tank. Probably the best thing we can do is recite the Prime Directive to them and then start looking into recommended ways of dealing with 'culture shock'.

Near Earth Objects colliding with the Earth

"Asteroids have us in our sight. The dinosaurs didn't have a space program, so they're not here to talk about this problem. We are, and we have the power to do something about it. I don't want to be the embarrassment of the galaxy, to have had the power to deflect an asteroid, and then not, and end up going extinct."

- Neil deGrasse Tyson

On 30 June 1908, an explosion ripped through the air above a remote forest in Siberia, near the Podkamennaya Tunguska river. The fireball is believed to have been 50-100m wide. It depleted 2,000 sq. km of the taiga forest in the area, flattening about 80 million trees. Many of those trees are still lying flat now with the power of the explosion being around 200 times that of the Hiroshima atomic bomb and with seismic vibrations being observed as far away as the UK. That's a pretty big bang, quite enough to completely flatten a city if it had happened to occur in a populated area; apparently in 1908 only around 5 hours separated Helsinki from obliteration. But I don't think most people know much about the 'Tunguska Event'. Even now there is some uncertainty as to exactly what caused it, although it is generally believed to have been the result of the collision of an asteroid or comet. While impacts on this scale are rare, thousands of tiny pieces of space rock, or meteorites, hit the ground each year. However, the majority of these events are unpredictable and go unnoticed, as they land in vast swathes of uninhabited forest or in the open waters of the ocean.

Meteors are pieces of rock that enter the atmosphere, with 90% of them burning up, which can be seen as streaks of light (i.e. shooting stars - if you go out on a night when the stars are visible and look for long enough, you will be likely to see one – I saw one last night as a matter of fact) when the rock is the size of a grain of sand, or flashes of light for a somewhat larger rock fragment. I observed one of these myself one night while looking out of a roof window – the flash was quite conspicuous – it made an impression in the darkness of the night and I posted the event on Twitter. Other slightly larger fragments have caused automobile damage – including the Grimsby meteorite that landed in Ontario, Canada in 2009, breaking the windshield of an SUV, as well as the meteorites that crashed into the back end of a Chevrolet Malibu in Peekskill, New York, in 1992. No one was injured during these events. Unfortunately, this cannot be said about the Chelyabinsk meteorite, which comprised an asteroid the size of a six-story building that entered Earth's atmosphere in February 2013 over Russia. It broke apart 24 km above the ground and generated a shock wave equivalent to a 500-kiloton TNT explosion, injuring 1,600 people. These events have convinced many people that rocks falling from space are in fact a real and considerable threat to humanity. One approach for addressing the threat is to keep a look out for Near-Earth objects (NEOs), which are defined as asteroids or comets of sizes ranging from metres to tens of kilometres, that orbit the Sun and whose orbits can bring them into the vicinity of Earth. Of the more than 600,000 known asteroids in our Solar System, over 20,000 are NEOs. That represents quite a lot of space debris that is whizzing around our solar system which could, at some point, come our way.

Tens of thousands of Near Earth Objects (NEOs) are constantly tracked by NASA scientists to ensure that they don't collide with our planet. (Illustration by the author.)

Although NASA doesn't believe that any of the NEOs it is currently tracking are on a collision course with our planet, in the future NEOs could potentially hit Earth and, depending on their size, produce considerable damage. While the chance of a large object hitting us is very small, it would produce a great deal of destruction. NEOs thus merit active detection and tracking efforts. Consequently, the European Space Agency has set up something called 'NEO Segment', which aims to: 'map the current and future position of NEOs relative to Earth, estimate the likelihood of Earth impacts, assess the consequences of any possible impact and develop NEO deflection methods'. (They are getting their data from the Minor Planet Center in the USA, which is keeping a close eye on the trajectories of asteroids and comets in our solar system).

What really interests me is the idea of developing NEO deflection methods – since there is limited value in knowing a big rock is coming towards you unless you can do something about it (other than trying to rush away from its expected impact point). This is also, ironically, the aspect of all this which is currently under-developed. It is true that the US Jet Propulsion Laboratory has undertaken some theoretical work, entitled 'NASA/JPL NEO Deflection App', which studies how NEOs could be deflected from an Earth-bound trajectory; but at the moment there does seem to be rather a shortage of detail on practical ways of meeting this threat. So, we need a device that can defend us from approaching asteroids.

It seems that Gene Roddenberry (with a bit of help from Margaret Armen and Arthur H. Singer), also had a contribution in this area. In the *Star Trek* episode, 'The Paradise Syndrome', Kirk, Spock, and McCoy come across an obelisk with strange markings on it. It is an asteroid deflector built by 'The Preservers' - an ancient race that resettled various endangered humanoid populations on other planets in order to ensure their survival.

In this episode Kirk loses his memory and gets romantically involved with a native (called Miramanee) on a planet threatened by an approaching asteroid. This is how the episode ends: As the asteroid nears the planet, the sky darkens, thunder roars, and strong winds blow, while the elders tell Kirk he must go into the temple to stop the storm. As Kirk pounds fruitlessly on the side of the obelisk, the tribe turns against him, stoning him and Miramanee. Spock and McCoy materialize, frightening the villagers away. Spock uses a mind meld to retrieve Kirk's memories, while McCoy tends to Miramanee's wounds. Kirk is able to open the trap door and Spock activates the deflector with minutes to spare. McCoy tells Kirk that Miramanee will not survive. Good stuff! Asteroid deflector technology, native culture, romantic storyline, and Greek tragedy; what else could you ask for?

The obelisk with strange markings on it, which is an asteroid deflector built by 'The Preservers' in the *Star Trek* episode 'The Paradise Syndrome'. (Pen and ink drawing by the author.)

One way to build an asteroid deflector might be to apply a force to the rock by creating an explosion nearby from, say, an H bomb, thereby pushing it off course. We would have to do this as far away from us as possible, so that collision avoidance could result from a small change in the angle of the asteroid's trajectory (which, for massive asteroids might be all that we could potentially achieve). Perhaps launching and transporting the H bomb to the needed location would be a good application for the mass accelerator discussed earlier. In any case, it seems that in utilising the H bomb in this way we would have finally found a possible positive application for a device that up to now was thought to be unusable except in the case of Armageddon.

Mr Spock, as played by Leonard Nimoy. Spock was said to be half Vulcan and half Human, but called himself Vulcan; which meant that, although he felt emotions, displaying them in his behaviour or speech was considered poor taste (this is rather like being British, if you ask me). (Drawing by the author.)

In order to determine the urgency with which an asteroid defence system should be installed, it is worth looking at the frequency with which impacts occur. Monitoring of Earth's atmosphere through infrasound and satellite observation over the last 60 years indicates that asteroid impacts with energies comparable to those of nuclear weapons routinely occur, although Tunguska-sized events, on the order of tens of megatons of TNT, are much rarer. Impacts on the order of tens of kilotons are estimated to occur annually, with Tunguska-sized events occurring about once every 100 to 300 years. The conclusion of all this is, I fear, that it is only a matter of time before we find a substantial asteroid on a trajectory towards a populated area – which convinces me that following the example of The Preservers is not a bad idea.

Viruses

"A healthy body is not easily infected by external bacteria and viruses, a healthy mind too is not easily infected by external insults and undesirable events."

— Awdhesh Singh

In 'The Adventure of the Dying Detective', Holmes seems to be ill, but instead of suffering effects from his intravenous use of cocaine, he appears to be critically ill due to a somewhat exotic (if that's the right word) disease.

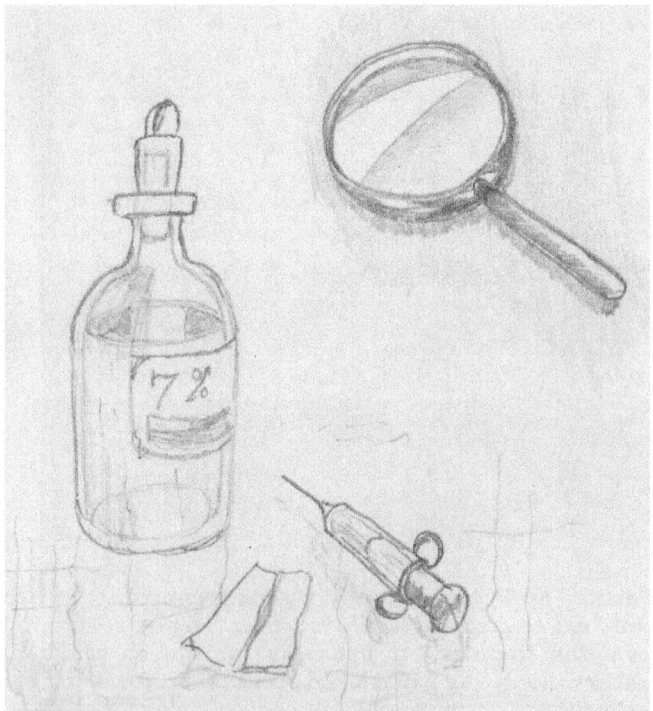

Some of Holmes' accoutrements, including his '7% solution' of cocaine. (Drawing by the author.)

Holmes says: "There are many problems of disease, many strange pathological possibilities, in the East, Watson." Considering the disease effects that are occurring as I write this, specifically the COVID-19 worldwide pandemic, which originated in China, Holmes seems to have been on the ball, again. I am not a medical expert, nor do I work in healthcare or in the essential services. I do, however, have the utmost respect for those who do fit these criteria. Imagine risking your life to help others – this is what these people do, and in doing so I can imagine they feel 'a great Hand' in theirs.

"A man loses his fortune; he gains earnestness. His eyesight goes; it leads him to a spirituality... We think we are pushing our own way bravely, but there is a great Hand in ours all the time".

- Sir Arthur Conan Doyle

Hindsight is a great thing, and it is easy to look back at just about any set of events and make pronouncements about what should have been done to mitigate the effects of threats that pressed down upon us. Yet what this part of this book is about is perceiving potential threats as early as possible and then avoiding a serious manifestation of the threat.

In Western medicine, there has always been more emphasis on curing disease rather than preventing it, but prevention has the obvious benefit of enabling avoidance of suffering or death as well as all of the expense associated with treatment. In the case of infection, we have Fleming to thank for the brilliant and revolutionary consequences of having antibiotics available. I know that some GPs have a tendency to over-prescribe antibiotics and there are problems of resistant bacteria emerging as a result, and/or patients' immune systems can be somewhat weakened; but anybody who has any doubts about the overall benefits of antibiotics should spend some time studying what was going on in septic wards before they were available.

To summarise, antibiotics have greatly reduced the threat posed to humans from infections. Unfortunately, however, progress against viruses has not been so great and they still pose a significant threat to mankind. To minimise this threat, I strongly feel that we need to adopt a more intelligent approach to addressing it. Regrettably, this did not initially happen in Western countries when Coronavirus descended upon us.

To give a very brief summary of the history of the pandemic, it originated in Hubei Province in China, in a city known as Wuhan, in late 2019. China did not inform the rest of the world early on as to what was happening. Instead, they persecuted persons who tried to raise the alarm (including a young doctor who later died of the virus). While they did eventually stop travel from Hubei to the rest of China, they did not prevent travel from Wuhan to the rest of the world and some in the West believe this was because they did not wish to see COVID-19 have less of an economic impact in other countries than it was having in China.

Most amazing, however, was the fact that Western authorities did not prevent people from infected areas from entering their countries! The intelligent solution would have been to prevent foreigners from the infected regions from entering the country and for nationals returning home to undergo two weeks of quarantine. This would have prevented the virus from getting a foothold and would probably have made a total lockdown unnecessary.

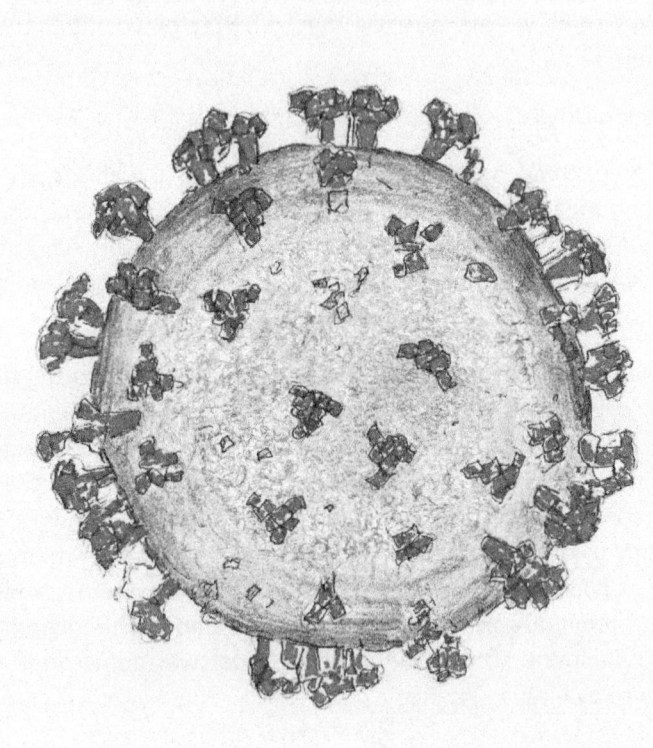

Coronavirus, which first originated in Wuhan, Hubei, China in late 2019, causing the global COVID-19 pandemic. (Illustration by the author.)

In contrast to this, multitudes of infected people were allowed in and, once the seriousness of the resulting situation was realised, a series of lockdowns were implemented that will have economic repercussions that are likely to persist for many years. This seems like a triumph of PC attitudes over common sense, where people say 'we can't stop people entering our country' despite the fact that doing this as early as possible would prevent disease and death on a prodigious scale and stopping entry would be necessary at some stage in any case. (In fact, travel bans/quarantines from high risk countries were eventually implemented several

166

months after the disastrous COVID-19 peak in the UK – which brings to mind images of bolted horses and stable doors.) I, for one, don't find the explanations that the politicians give for not doing this to be at all convincing. The intelligent solution also involves testing for the virus on a grand scale so that the progress and spread of the virus is known, in combination with the use of smartphones to track the movements that have been made by infected individuals and warn those who might have been in contact with them. Smartphones comprise an advanced technology that provides vast amounts of data on the location and behaviour of people, which up to now has been put to very little genuinely beneficial use. Fighting COVID-19 is an example of an application where they could have been employed to save many lives but getting this off the ground proved very slow. Mercifully, a more intelligent approach does now seem to have been adopted and a smartphone app has been launched to detect and alert people as to the movement of those who have been exposed to the virus. The frustrating thing about the pandemic is that other viruses have become epidemics in recent years and other countries such as South Korea have learnt from the experience with the result of a very minimal death toll this time around – the same could have been true of the West.

One more point must be made in relation to the origin of coronavirus in China. Some have wondered exactly where the virus emerged from, and also wished to study its behaviour in the early days of its progress, in order to help them fight the current and any future outbreaks. National governments and international organisations have, therefore, asked China to open its doors to an independent, international investigation into the origins of the novel coronavirus that has caused the current COVID-19 pandemic, as well as into the nation's early response to the outbreak. However, the Chinese government has said it does not wish to cooperate, claiming that the request for an independent investigation is 'politically motivated', and 'would hamper China's efforts to combat the virus'. China's lack of cooperation, its silence, and signs that China is stifling research into the origins of the disease by its own scientists, have fuelled theories that the virus accidently leaked from a lab there. Whether or not this is the case, China's attitude, and unwillingness to take responsibility or apologise for the outbreak, speak of a power-structure that is very different from the West – more secretive, undemocratic. It is behaving like what it perhaps always was: an authoritarian mercantile dictatorship; and if that continues it is likely that the West will have to be more realistic about its relationship with China and re-appraise the extent to which it threatens Western security and prosperity. Having said this, I would like to make clear that the above comments on China refer to the Chinese Communist Party, rather than the Chinese people themselves. I have numerous friends and close associates who are Chinese; and I have also supervised a number of PhD students, originally from China, who did excellent work. I would say that I find the Chinese I have worked with to be intelligent, hardworking, and with a very good attitude.

But what of the 'intelligent approach' to dealing with the virus? Well, this is something we will need to perfect and apply to coronavirus and other viruses on an on-going basis, since there is no certainty that immunity or vaccines will protect us in the future and we can by no means expect that coronavirus will be the last pandemic-threatening virus that we will have to deal with.

As I write this, the UK, and in fact the world, is still in the grip of the coronavirus pandemic. The response of the UK and indeed most Western countries has been to impose a strict lockdown. While there can be little doubt that the restrictions imposed are saving lives and are thus necessary, at the same time the impositions of such restricting measures on humans, who are, after all, social animals, has created much anxiety as well as various forms of inconvenience and, in fact, real suffering. As usual, it is the poorest and most disadvantaged in society who tend to suffer most; but there is little that can be done about the restrictions until the peaks of the pandemic have passed. All that we can do is sit tight, endure, and be reassured that the disease will pass, and brighter, better times lie ahead.

In the meantime, we may take heart and gain some comfort by thinking about other times in history when the people of Britain have been sorely tested. To anyone who is perplexed by the lockdown situation or who needs inspiration, I say this: consider the British situation in the autumn of 1940. A Nazi war machine, highly powerful, efficient, and ruthless had overrun nearly all of Europe and had ambitions to take over the world. The only country making a stand against Nazi tyranny and a new Dark Age was the UK; and much rested on the country's shoulders – the future of the freedom-loving world – for years to come – or perhaps even decades or centuries. And Britain stood ALONE (except for excellent troops from various parts of the British Empire/Commonwealth that were staunch to the end – and like the mother country they consistently punched above their weight). In 1940, most of the world thought that Britain was finished, but with characteristic courage and determination she beat the odds; and with a dogged perseverance and tenacity was eventually successful and emerged victorious. While the coronavirus is, of course, tragic for those who have suffered or died, and their families, the threat to our country in 1940 was immeasurably greater; and now the UK also has great and powerful allies and friends who are all pulling together with us to overcome this emergency. So, my advice is to have a cup of tea, read 'The Last Enemy' and watch 'Darkest Hour'. Churchill may have witnessed our finest hour, but the best is yet to come – if we stay calm and carry on the future will be a great one.

STOP PRESS! Saw a newsflash just after writing this: "The first effective coronavirus vaccine can prevent more than 90% of people from getting Covid-19, a preliminary analysis shows. The developers - Pfizer and BioNTech - described it as a "great day for science and humanity". Their vaccine has been tested on 43,500 people in six countries and no safety concerns have been raised." Latest data shows that the BioNTech/Pfizer vaccine is effective in 95% of cases and there are also other vaccines on the way – such as the Oxford/AstraZeneca one – for which there are good indications and high hopes. So, it's early days for the vaccines, but the news is definitely good. Hooray! (Another example of how science and technology can save our lives...)

Global warming

I live in Sedgemoor on the Somerset Levels and I must say I love it – an area of special scientific interest – which has the advantage that, mercifully, it is almost impossible to get planning permission to build new houses. One thing I have noticed though, is that there is often a tremendous wind blowing - the wind is so seemingly powerful and consistent that I feel it could provide for most, if not all, of the UK's energy needs. I am also convinced that the wind blows more strongly and frequently than it did when I was a small boy. This is, of course, just a subjective observation – I could be wrong. Another thing that has happened in Somerset in recent years is unusually severe flooding.

Severe flooding near Glastonbury on the Somerset Levels, in 2014. (Illustration by author.)

During three solid months, from December 2013 to February 2014, *the rains came*, as my mother used to say. As a consequence of this, the Somerset Levels hit the national headlines as the area suffered from extensive flooding. At one point in the winter floods, 65 km^2 of land on the Levels were underwater. The floods were the most severe ever known in this area. What do the apparent increases in wind and rain have in common? You guessed it – they could be phenomena caused by global warming.

I must be nuts to try to do climate change and global warming justice in a mere one chapter of a book – if I spent a whole book discussing it, I would still only be giving something of an introduction. Also, I have by no means made any kind of particular study of it, while many others devote their entire lives to its analysis. But it's such an important topic that I have got to give it some consideration; so here goes.

Global warming is believed to be caused by the 'greenhouse effect'. The latter is welcome in your greenhouse – where you like some heat in order to help your plants grow. But, in relation to the Earth's atmosphere, it is powering what may be the most serious threat mankind has ever faced. Why does it lead to increased wind and rain? Well, in a nutshell, the sunlight passes through the atmosphere and warms the earth. Although the hot soil gives off radiation, since it is a lot cooler than the surface of the sun its wavelength is much longer – so much so that this radiation cannot pass back out through the atmosphere but is trapped – thereby increasing the average temperature of the atmosphere. An increase in temperature means weather systems have more energy – something moving around that has more energy tends to move faster – hence the increased wind. A higher temperature also naturally means more water will be evaporated from the world's oceans, in the form of vapour that cools – forming clouds. What goes up must come down – in this case in the form of increased amounts of rain.

Although it is hard to be certain that global warming caused specific phenomena such as the 2014 Somerset flooding, more extreme events of this nature, and their more frequent occurrence, is consistent with what scientists expect to result from increases in global temperatures.

There is much discussion – or perhaps I should say character assassination – in the media in relation to 'climate deniers'. Such people purport to deny that global warming is occurring; and it seems that some criticism of them may well be justified since, we may as well face it, global warming is a real phenomenon – it *is* occurring.

According to National Geographic (and NASA, the UK Met Office, Al Gore, and just about everyone else) there is conclusive evidence that the Earth is warming up. Thermometer measurements taken over the past century and a half show Earth's average temperature has risen by over 1 degree Celsius (and considerably more in parts of the Arctic).

As I have already mentioned, Sherlock Holmes said "I have no data yet. It is a capital mistake to theorise before one has data. Insensibly, one begins to twist facts to suit theories, instead of theories to suit facts." No doubt he was right; but we have not made the capital mistake, since we have the data – as shown in the above figure. The theory is that the climate is changing and (as the great detective would have said) 'it is beyond debate'. The main things we might wish to now consider are: is global warming caused by man, how much of a threat might it constitute for mankind, and if there is a significant threat, what can we do about it? By the way, scientists prefer to discuss climate change rather than global warming – but, let's face it, we are all talking about the same thing – basically, things warming up.

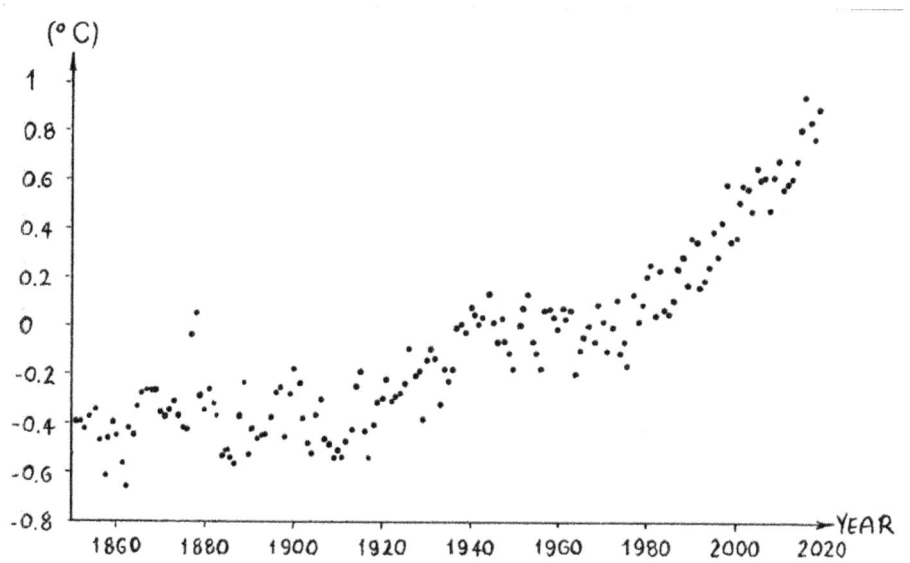

Graph showing the increase in measured global average temperatures since 1850, with zero set at 1951-1980 average. The data combine land data from Berkeley Earth and ocean data from the UK Hadley Centre. (Graph by the author.)

Let's deal first with the question of how much of a threat climate change poses. Scientists are pretty sure that global temperatures will continue to rise for many years, largely due to greenhouse gases that have already been generated by human activities. Examples of such activities include running cars – the exhaust produces carbon dioxide, which is a greenhouse gas (in other words it increases the tendency of the atmosphere to let heat in but not out – like the glass of a greenhouse), and even such prosaic activities as making a compost heap – the latter gives off methane, which is actually a very potent greenhouse gas. There is a body called the Intergovernmental Panel on Climate Change (IPCC), which includes thousands of scientists from all over the world. They forecast that global temperatures will rise by 1.5 to 5.5 degrees Celsius over the next century. Other likely damaging effects

171

that they predict, many of which we are already observing, include: heat waves and more droughts, stronger and more damaging hurricanes, the Artic becoming ice-free in the summer, and a possible rise in sea level by 2100 of up to 2 metres (due to melting polar ice and the expansion of seawater as it warms). All this is not particularly pleasant – but we can survive it. However, things become much more serious if a 'vicious circle' is set up. As you know, the latter occurs when factors are at play that intensify and aggravate each other, leading inexorably to a worsening of the situation. In this case, rising CO_2 levels cause a greenhouse effect that raises temperatures. This causes more wildfires, reducing the number of trees, further increasing CO_2 by reducing CO_2 absorption capacity. Ice caps start to melt, which reduces sunlight reflection (less snow), resulting in more heat absorption. Sea levels rise, causing flooding that destroys more plants and trees, further diminishing the CO_2 absorption capacity. Oceans acidify, lowering their CO_2 absorption capacity as well, and so on and so on... But all this would pale into insignificance in comparison to the potential effects of the release of greenhouse gases from huge carbon reservoirs that are believed to lie under the oceans. These contain vast expanses of carbon dioxide and methane distributed across the seafloor. They form as volcanic activity releases heat and gases congeal into liquid and solid hydrates, which form into large expanses of carbon-based gunge. Such undersea carbon reservoirs are usually relatively stable, but recent studies indicate that these natural reservoirs are vulnerable to the effects of a warming ocean and their destabilisation might result in a rapid release of 'geologic carbon'. If man-made global warming were to warm the oceans sufficiently to thus release vast amounts of carbon dioxide, methane, and other greenhouse gasses, then humanity would really be up against it. Analogies involving 'shit creek' and a paddle come to mind, since this would represent the ultimate vicious circle for global warming. To give an idea of possible consequences, we can consider the planet Venus – which, it seems, likely experienced something akin to this at some stage in its long history.

The surface of Venus looks rather like Mars but has major differences – such as the surface temperature being 462 degrees Celsius! (Illustration by the author.)

The result is a planet with an extremely dense atmosphere, sulphuric acid rain, and a surface temperature that is about twice as hot as the oven in your kitchen. I don't want to be a doom merchant, but anyone landing on the surface of this planet would be simultaneously poisoned, crushed, and burnt to a cinder. Humans in such an environment wouldn't stand a snowball's chance in hell of surviving – which is a good analogy since the surface of Venus is very close to what we must imagine hell to be like. God preserve us and save us from such an appalling future cataclysm. But as I write this, I see on the news the surprising discovery that scientists have detected a gas in the atmosphere which is associated with life - phosphine. It's reported that on Earth this gas is produced by microbes living in the guts of animals like penguins, or in oxygen-poor environments such as swamps. So, despite all the above facts about Venus, people are now wondering whether there might be living organisms floating in the clouds of the planet. Life is certainly robust and tenacious … almost anything is possible; who knows, there might be some form of life in the atmosphere of Venus, but the chances of finding it on the planet surface are, for the reasons given above, vanishingly small.

Since the future effects of global warming appear to range from unpleasant to catastrophic, it is natural that we should consider what we might be able to do about it – or at least how we could mitigate the threat as much as possible. Patrick Geddes, the planner and conservationist, introduced the term "Think globally, act locally," in 1915 but it is just as valid today. So, what can we, as individuals, try to do locally to play our part in tackling global warming? Well, we certainly can do a few things that may, in a modest way, help to limit emission of greenhouse gasses. Examples include: changing our energy provider to one who makes more use of renewables, eat less meat (meat production involves more release of the greenhouse gas CO_2 than vegetables), waste less food, take the train instead of flying and simply consume less in general. No doubt implementing such lifestyle changes would be helpful, but I can't help thinking that this is largely tinkering around the edges with the problem rather than addressing it with the seriousness which the situation demands (particularly when considering the possible disasters outlined above that might transpire if we pretend there is not a problem and carry on as normal). In short, government action is needed, beyond the limited responses, campaigns, or initiatives we have seen so far. In other words, we need less lip service and more legislation. Here are some things which governments could do, and will need to do if we are to stand any chance of tackling global warming: enormous investment in renewable energy (there is no point in introducing subsidies on solar power and then removing them after a short period – all this does is create uncertainty and erode confidence), huge incentives for people to buy and run electric cars (when in California in 2019 I seemed to see Tesla cars everywhere, but they appear to be something of a rarity in Europe and Japan – hybrids just won't cut it, I'm afraid), along with very significant investment in schemes to improve home insulation. An example of a major scheme that the UK

Government could have funded that would have had an enormous impact in reducing CO_2 emissions is the Severn Barrage. This one facility could utilize clean and everlasting tidal power in the Bristol Channel to produce around 6-10% of the UK's electricity requirements – enough to effectively replace the contribution from the current generation of aging nuclear reactors that are due to be retired by 2025. A Severn Barrage could also provide the additional significant benefit of flood protection. Building it is, in my view, a no brainer, but the powers that be don't seem to be particularly interested. Instead, the Government decided to go ahead with building the Hinckley Point C nuclear reactor, with the heavy involvement of China. For political and social reasons that are outlined in other parts of this book, it seems to be a mistake to involve the People's Republic of China intimately in a capital project closely concerned with Britain's infrastructure and essential energy supply (to say nothing of security and the huge problem of dealing with nuclear waste as well as safety concerns). Consequently, I believe it is only a matter of time before this ill-advised project is cancelled. The associated losses will be very large, but I suspect we need to take it on the chin and learn from it. The sooner the situation is resolved the better and, ultimately, less expensive it will be. It is possible that I may be wrong about Hinckley Point C – in fact, I hope I am since that would save us all a lot of money – but unfortunately that's how I see the situation. Again, I would like to make clear that the above comments on China refer to the Chinese Communist Party, rather than the Chinese people themselves.

Finally, there is one simple thing the Government could do that would cost relatively little and would reduce CO_2 emissions significantly; I am referring to the simple expedient of not putting the clocks back in the autumn. People are generally more active in the evening than in the early mornings, and data indicate that having the clocks forward an hour results in a reduction in electricity consumption due to reduced need for artificial light in the evenings. To be more specific, Cambridge University research shows that an extra hour of daily sunlight in winter could save £485 million each year, as people would use less electricity and heating. This is equivalent to eliminating the carbon emissions of 70,000 people. This overall reduction in CO_2 emissions is estimated to represent around 450,000 tonnes across the UK each year – significant indeed. And it's not just about carbon emissions; keeping British Summer Time all year would be expected to give a boost to leisure activities and tourism, reduce crime, save a great deal of money and, most importantly, save many lives. We could, of course, go beyond just not putting the clocks back and look at putting them forward all year. If we changed to Single/Double British Summertime (SDST), (adjusting the clocks to GMT+1 in the winter, with GMT+2 in the summer), Brake have estimated this would prevent 80 deaths and more than 200 serious injuries on UK roads every year. The initial, one-off cost of making and publicising the change is estimated at about £5 million, which would be more than offset by the benefits of the change, the latter amounting to

£138 million per year. Analysis has projected a net benefit of £2.5 billion over 20 years, from reduced casualties.

Having got all that off my chest, let me turn to less grandiose subjects. There are many simple measures governments could take to limit greenhouse gas emissions by encouraging a greener economy. I am sure we could all think of many examples, which may seem modest but when multiplied over large populations could be very significant. Consider, for example, packaging. Many companies still overdo packaging for various reasons – one of the main ones being to, allegedly, make products appear more appealing. An example I noticed the other day relates to shampoo – where a relatively small amount of the product is sold in a plastic bottle that has been engineered to look as big as possible – to make the customer (perhaps subconsciously) believe they are getting better value.

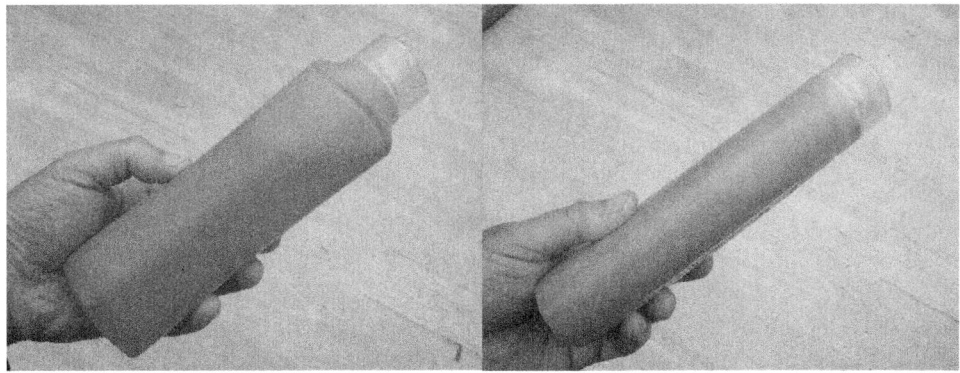

The shampoo bottle looks large from the front (left), but from the side it can be seen to be quite shallow in depth (right) – such a shape requires more use of plastic than a more cylindrical bottle – leading to greater greenhouse gas emission. (Photographs by the author.)

As you can see in the images, the bottle is relatively high and wide (and so quite thin), but in fact it only holds 350ml of shampoo. The problem here is that employing such a shaped bottle requires much more use of plastic than would be the case if the bottle were more perfectly cylindrical; and, of course, the manufacture and (hopefully) recycling of more plastic means more emission of CO_2. In order to check my idea, I bought a standard Sainsbury's 500 ml plastic bottle of still water (which has a relatively cylindrical morphology), poured out the water and weighed both the water bottle and the shampoo bottle. The water bottle (including the cap) weighed 17 g, while the weight of the shampoo bottle was 32 g. This confirms what I had thought – even though the shampoo bottle only contains 70% of the volume of liquid that the water bottle holds, it uses very nearly twice as much polymer. This could seem like a trivial example, but when considering that the bottle might be manufactured in quantities of millions, or tens of millions, or more, then it can be appreciated that the cumulative effect for emission may be substantial in the long term. To quantify this somewhat, according to my calculations, the shampoo bottle contains 20 g of unnecessary polymer. If 10 million bottles are manufactured, then the amount of unnecessary polymer that has been used (with all the consequences for the environment and global warming), is 200 metric tonnes – not insignificant, I think you will agree. And this is just one example I happened to notice. Domestic goods manufacturers and food processors employ a multitude of similarly unnecessary non-biodegradable packaging, all across their wide product ranges. To be honest, I doubt if they will do anything by themselves to reverse this – it will be up to the Government to introduce legislation to control and minimise the amounts of unnecessary packaging – particularly for items/materials that are non-degradable – such as most plastics used in packaging.

And, beyond packaging, I'm sure we can think of many more examples of commercial practices that seem to be flying in the face of limiting greenhouse gasses. The first that comes to my mind really does involve flying – I am thinking of duty free. Duty free; good grief - what in the hell is the point in that? At my local airport there is a big duty-free section that you have to walk through to get to the departure lounge. A meandering pathway takes you through a vast array of luxury goods. As a consequence, the lounge and, it seems, facilities such as seating and toilets seem to be rather limited in their provision. But if I'm in the market for a bottle of French perfume, a big bottle of whisky or some kind of obscure trinket, then I'm really in business! There is just one thing – if I wanted to go shopping it's very likely I would have gone to a shopping centre or supermarket; if I have gone to an airport then it is not impossible that my motivation was in fact to get onto an aircraft. Nevertheless, my understanding is that current practice is still to have passengers buy multiple duty-free bottles of spirits on their outward journeys and then carry them on the aircraft to fly all across Europe to Greece (or wherever) and back (so they can take them home for future drinks), with all of the associated waste of fuel and unnecessary greenhouse gas emission. At the very least, they could have a system whereby the bottles are stored in a safe place at the airport so that they are not carried on an unnecessary trek through the skies. While I'm having a whinge, let me mention a couple of other things that are unrelated, other than seeming a bit nutty to me:

1. Printer cartridges with built in page counters. Laser printers and similar devices have cartridges you insert that contain the ink (they often also contain expensive precision components such as a light-sensitive roller). Once the ink runs out, the ecological thing to do would be to simply pour more in, but some cartridges are designed to prevent you doing this by incorporating counting 'chips' that stop the printer working when a pre-programmed number of pages have been printed out – thereby requiring you to buy a new entire cartridge. Imagine all the CO_2 emission associated with all the manufacturing involved – and all unnecessary since all you

wanted to do was add more ink to do some printing (usually the light-sensitive roller is fine – capable of printing out thousands more pages – throwing it away in such a condition seems like a waste to me). Some manufacturers even go so far as to sell the printer with a cartridge that is half (or less) full of ink, so that they can sell you the expensive replacement as soon as possible – and to hell with the environment. Nutty I think you will agree.

2. Supermarkets (or anyone else for that matter) selling imported bottled water. I don't buy bottled water (other than the 500 ml mentioned above). Reasons for this include the fact that transporting heavy water over long distances takes a lot of energy and so produces much CO_2 and, unlike tap water, it isn't regulated. I am not convinced the quality is as good or consistent as tap water (or at least tap water in the UK). My quality concerns stem, in part, from a scandal that arose some years ago in relation to contamination of bottles of Perrier bottled water, as well as recent research in the USA which found that bottled water from a number of well-known suppliers contained a considerable quantity of plastic particles. Another reason why I am against bottled water is that it is the enemy of the reliable supply of nice fresh clean water to the taps of our houses. The more we purchase, and therefore effectively support, bottled water, the less interest and ultimately investment we may expect to see in piped water supply. You might think this an incredible idea, but I believe that, at least to some extent, it has already occurred in some places. For example, a good friend of mine, who is Indian, has advised me that if I ever visit India, I am not to drink the tap water (nor in fact any bottled water that may be offered me, unless I carefully examine the bottle and satisfy myself that the plastic seal on the cap has not been broken). Thinking about water supply, my grandfather had an old-fashioned water pump in his yard, and I was told that, if you can believe it, many years ago when this pump was their only water supply, he tried to resist the (ultimately successful) attempts that my grandmother made to have piped-in water installed (although why he resisted it is less clear – perhaps he was just a very big traditionalist). I remember that when I was a very young child, I used to like to push the pump's lever and watch the water gush out of its nozzle. By the way, he had a very good well; during very hot summers when neighbour's wells dried up, his would always remain operational, so sometimes they would come around to collect water from him - or at least, that is what I was told when I was little. (Yes, at one time, even I was little!) Then, much later, while I was living in Pennsylvania, I remember noticing a machine outside a supermarket in Penn State, where you inserted a quarter and you could fill a one-gallon plastic container. (By the way, I very much like Penn State, or "Happy Valley" as the residents call it, and really enjoyed my time there. In fact, I have a sentimental affinity for the U.S.A. in general. There may be two reasons for this: I am an Englishman, and I met my wife there.) This reminded me of my grandfather's pump – the only difference was he didn't charge a quarter. This inevitably seemed a little retrograde i.e. going back to a situation where we don't drink water that is piped into our houses. I know

there can sometimes be an issue with water being rather heavily chlorinated and/or having some contamination due to old lead piping, but in this day and age sorting this out is surely not beyond possibility, and putting more resources into this, rather than having to go somewhere to collect good quality drinking water, must, surely, be the way forward. While I am thinking of my grandfather, I will just say one or two more things about him. I remember he had long fingers and thumbs and he always seemed to be taking clocks and instruments apart to investigate and repair them. I can see him now, rolling things out onto his table using his long thumbs – God knows what he was doing – probably another clock or radio repair. He was an engineer with a capital E, and to give you some idea of how good he was and how much he was liked by his colleagues; when he left Vickers Small Tools Limited in Croydon, in 1917, in order to get married, his friends bought him a grand wedding present – consisting of a chiming marble clock and a large pair of metal Marley horse figurines after Guillaume Coustou. Now; I have seen some examples of similar figurines on the internet – sometimes for sale on eBay, but these are always less elaborate than my grandfather's. In his case, each figurine consisted of two rearing horses and their groom restraining them, all on a wooden base. So, for many years my grandfather had four horses and two grooms on his mantelpiece. I remember that there was hardly room on his mantelshelf for them all; but this did not stop him from keeping them there for, can you believe it, over sixty years! That tells you how much pride he had in his work and what being an engineer meant to him. But I seem to have meandered away from the subject of bottled water. Before leaving it completely, I would like to say one more thing. When you go into a supermarket, you see this big range of bottles of water, many coming from different countries and each, apparently, with its own distinctive flavour – or aroma. Good Lord, it reminds me of the classic 'Water Pub' sketch by *The Two Ronnies*; and if you haven't yet seen this excellent offering from those two absolute legends of British TV then I implore you to do so as soon as possible.

The Two Ronnies' 'Water Pub' sketch: "What kind of water would you like sir?"
(Pen and ink drawing by the author.)

The Water Pub reminds me of a time in a restaurant in a DoubleTree hotel in Salt Lake City. A guy approached our table, whom I had taken to be the wine steward, but it turned out he was, it seems, the *water* steward. When he showed us a selection of bottles of water and asked us which we would prefer, I began to wonder what the tab for the meal would end up looking like. Luckily, it was being covered by our (very accommodating and generous) industrial client. We were very appreciative.

So, after all those digressions, what is our situation regarding global warming? Well, we can say for sure that the average temperature on Earth is rising and has been doing so for over a hundred years.

It's hard to be equally certain about what is causing this – but the available evidence strongly points towards the increasing greenhouse effect caused by human industrial activity increasing the proportion of greenhouse gases in the atmosphere. Can the trend be stopped, or even reversed? We cannot be certain about this – scientific opinion is somewhat divided, with some such as Robert B. Laughlin being convinced that it will continue no matter what measures humanity may attempt to implement to tackle it. Considering the potentially existential threat to humanity, as outlined above, it certainly seems sensible to put in place as many of such measures as we can, as soon as we can. I am not a climate scientist, but my expectation is that if we did this with utmost zest, we would be able to significantly reduce the rate of temperature increase. Will this be sufficient to avoid the vicious circle dystopian future described above? Nobody can say with certainty. Again, I think there is a good chance it will. But the wildcard with greatest significance may well be the question of release of vast quantities of gas from the under-sea carbon reservoirs mentioned above. Geologists believe that this happened a number of times in the distant past, with results that included the ending of various ice ages. But they are less certain about what actually caused the carbon release. Pulling us out of an ice age seems like a positive result for the carbon release but, of course, currently we are not in one (despite the fact that some maintain one is overdue). No, if rapid and accelerating global warming occurred now it would definitely not be good for humanity. We would expect the Earth to become uninhabitable for humans certainly within a few centuries and possibly within a matter of decades. If the latter occurred it seems likely there would be little we could do to save humanity.

I remain the eternal optimist and believe that such dramatic planetary heating will not occur in any kind of foreseeable future, and if it did it would take on the order of centuries to develop. But supposing we were to find ourselves in a situation where we knew the Earth would become uninhabitable within, say 200 years? Would we be physically able to save humanity? And if that were possible, could we find the wisdom to place aside all religious and cultural differences that would be needed to enable everyone to all pull together to achieve the enormous effort that would almost certainly be involved? For what we would need to do would be to literally reach for the stars, and to give us any chance of doing that we would require a method for travelling through space quickly – very quickly, in fact – to allow us to reach neighbouring stars and planets within reasonable timescales, in our quest for a new home for humanity. Consequently, the prospects for us being able to do this are discussed at length later in this book. But before we can develop a real warp drive (as they called it in *Star Trek*), we need to make some significant progress in our scientific understanding and technological capabilities. No doubt Walt Disney was right in saying, with his Carousel of Progress, that "There's a Great Big Beautiful Tomorrow". In case anyone is unaware, Walt Disney's Carousel of Progress is an engaging rotating theatre audio-animatronic stage show attraction that is located in Tomorrowland at the Magic Kingdom theme park at the Walt Disney World Resort in Bay Lake, near Orlando. I can't resist the nostalgic 1950's take on progress and the future and strongly recommend visiting it if you are ever in the area.

A scene from Walt Disney's audio-animatronic stage show Carousel of Progress. (Pen and ink drawing by the author.)

But what, from a 2020 perspective, might we realistically expect the future to hold in terms of science and technology?

180

Part 3.

What the future holds

Developments in science and technology
"The future belongs to those who believe in the beauty of their dreams."

— Eleanor Roosevelt

This section of the book considers what the future might hold, but before doing this I will give a brief review of past technological developments. Few photographs capture the juxtaposition of such developments as well as the one above. It was taken during Concorde's final flight; and in the background the Clifton Suspension Bridge (which was mentioned towards the start of this book), is visible. So, the image combines two world-famous Bristol icons and forms a suitable epilogue to the career of this astonishing aircraft. (The photograph is used with the permission of South West News Service.)

The past

"You realize that our mistrust of the future makes it hard to give up the past."

— Chuck Palahniuk

I wonder whether, like me, you have noticed that most books, most of the time, are discussing things that have already happened. Even texts that purport to be about the future seem to be largely focused on events of the past. Why is this? We all understand that we have to have some appreciation of the past to help us see where we might go in the future, but I believe there is more to it than this. There are, I think, quite a few factors that tend to lead authors towards historical discussions. The first and most obvious is the fact that since past events have occurred and have usually already been discussed in some detail by others, we know a great deal about them and so can say much about them without fear of being in error. Most people also enjoy reading about the past – we all, to some extent, like to be told things we already know, and sometimes an historian can approach a subject from a slightly new angle and perhaps we can gain some new insights on familiar themes. However, in-depth study of the past does have one obvious disadvantage – *we cannot have an influence on the past*. Yes, historical events, on their face and by their very nature are not things we can do anything about – if it's part of history, *ipso facto* it cannot be changed. In stark contrast, the future is all in front of us and, by our decisions, we can have a very profound influence on how it plays out - at least for us as individuals; that is, assuming you are not a person who believes completely in fate, who some would term a predestinarianist or determinist (or possibly simply a fatalist). So, given that the future is critical for our wellbeing and is something that we can have some effect on, why do not more books discuss it? Well, predicting the future is bloody difficult; and I'm not just talking about palm-readers – anybody can understand that giving specific details on future developments is nigh on impossible, but even predicting general trends in the future is certainly a non-trivial task. Even people who are acknowledged experts in their field find predicting future developments very difficult. Curiously, there even seems to be some evidence that the more of an expert a person is, the harder they find it to reliably predict the future – *even for matters that are within the scope of their own expertise*. That may seem amazing, but I feel it is true. There is much anecdotal evidence to support this claim, in fact far too much to go through in detail here. So, I will just provide a few examples from the past of experts who have famously and spectacularly gone wrong in their predictions of the future. In 1935, the esteemed journal *Nature* reviewed a book about rockets passing through space, saying that "...the whole procedure sketched in the present volume presents difficulties of so fundamental a nature that we are forced to dismiss the notion as essentially impracticable." In 1941, the distinguished Canadian astronomer Professor J. W. Campbell wrote a paper in *Philosophical Magazine* where he stated his belief that "...it would appear that the statement that rocket flight to the Moon does not seem so remote as television did one hundred years ago is over optimistic." Then in 1956, the new Astronomer Royal, Dr Richard van der Riet Woolley, remonstrated with the press, saying "Space travel is utter bilge" - just a year before the appearance of the world's first artificial satellite, Sputnik I. And in the same year as Sputnik went up into orbit, Lee de Forest, an inventor who worked on wireless telegraphy, broadcast radio, and synchronized-sound films, boldly proclaimed that sending a man to the moon and returning him to Earth alive was: "a voyage [that] will never occur regardless of all future scientific advances." He made his remarks just 12 years before NASA proved him wrong. It must have been considerations of these and similar events that led the science fiction author and futurist Sir Arthur C. Clarke to formulate his First Law, which states that: "When a distinguished but elderly scientist states that something is possible, he is almost certainly right. When he states that something is impossible, he is very probably wrong."

Futurist and science fiction author Sir Arthur C. Clarke, who published a scientific paper in 1945 that predicted global communication satellites. (Drawing by the author.)

183

This law, by the way, makes me think that, eventually, travel at speeds greater than that of light might be attained – since many distinguished/elderly scientists appear to believe it to be impossible. More on this later. (Arthur Clarke also formulated two other interesting laws: 2, the only way to discover the limits of the possible is to venture a little way past them into the impossible. 3, any sufficiently advanced technology is indistinguishable from magic.)

Having given all this as a preamble, you may be asking what chance I stand of being able to predict future developments in science and technology; and I am also wondering the same thing. To be honest, one stands little chance of being able to predict specific developments in the near future, and such predictions for the far future are virtually impossible – so any attempts I make at the latter can be taken more as thought provocation than accurate estimates. What I can do is identify expected general trends in terms of the kinds of tasks/facilities the technology will be expected to accomplish/provide. Notwithstanding my comments above about history, I will start by reviewing some technological developments/inventions of the recent past – since these may provide some pointers to the future.

A miraculous quarter of a century

Consider all the amazing scientific and technological developments that occurred between 1939 and 1969. A comprehensive list would take up too much space, so I will just list some of the more significant developments (in alphabetical order): affordable (reliable and safe) automobiles, antibiotics, artificial satellites, atomic power, beating smallpox, computers, discovery of DNA, electronics (particularly transistors), gas turbines, helicopters, high-speed trains, integrated circuits, the internet, jet aircraft, mapping of the human genome, oral contraceptives, organ transplant, probes exploring the planets and beyond, RADAR, robotics and automation, space travel by humans (including putting a man on the Moon and returning him safely to Earth), television, video recording ... and the list goes on. Incidentally, during this period many dramatic social changes/events also occurred, including: the cultural revolution in the 1960s that led to changes in behaviour, dress, and attitudes and an explosion in popular music, decolonisation, decriminalisation of abortion and homosexuality, feminism, the Green Revolution in agriculture, mass aviation, Woodstock and Youth Culture. There is a strong argument to be made for this miraculous quarter of a century being the time when the modern world was somehow invented; before it everything that happened seems old fashioned and remote – almost Victorian – after, it all appears modern. 1969; the dawn of the modern era: with events that summer that include the lunar landings, the first flight of Concorde, and Woodstock (Scooby Doo also debuted in that year, which is something that I have always considered important and also, somehow modern). So, these three short decades seemed to have resulted in absolutely momentous developments and change in many areas that must, surely, greatly outstrip anything that has been seen since. Why did this occur at that time? Of course, many people will suggest that it has to do with the war and there is no doubt some truth in this. For example, the race to manufacture faster and faster aircraft spurred Britain and Germany on to produce jet-powered aircraft, and without the invention of Hitler's V2 vengeance weapon, what would have been America's chances of actually designing and building that Saturn V rocket that was needed to get Armstrong and Aldrin to the Moon before the end of the 1960s? But this is only part of the picture, since rapid technological development did not cease in 1945; in fact, if anything it seemed to accelerate, resulting in the emergence of marvels of new technology such as colour television and the Concorde – a unique commercially operating jet airliner that cruised at twice the speed of sound!

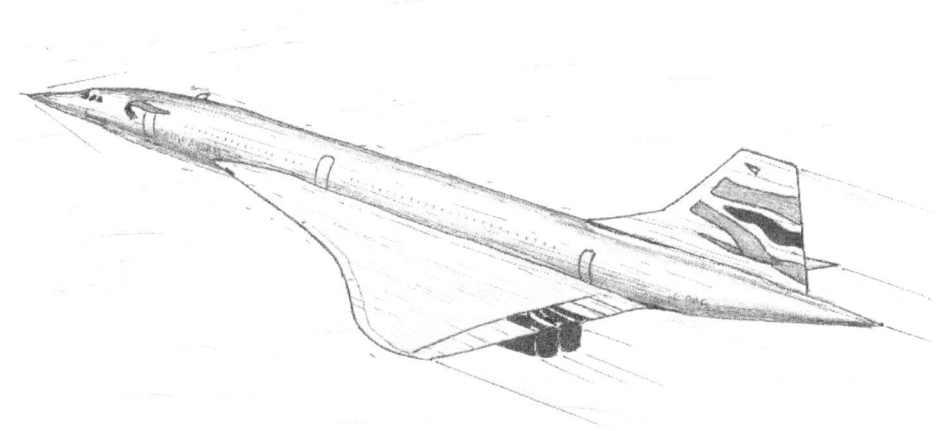

The Concorde had its maiden flight over half a century ago but remains the world's only commercial supersonic aeroplane. This beautiful aircraft is capable of sustained cruising at Mach 2. (Illustration by the author.)

The situation since 1969

What is the difference between the situation in those heady days and the world as we experience it today? One obvious thing that did not really exist back then was political correctness and all the other related issues that were discussed in some depth in Part 1, and no doubt all these considerations have contributed somewhat to the situation. However, even considering all these effects, I do not feel they fully explain the apparent difference in technological achievements from 1939-1969 and, say, 1989-2019; so, what does? Many of the advances prior to 1969 emerged either from tax-funded universities or from other publicly funded organisations. An early example is the pioneering work of Charles Babbage, the father of all computing, which was directly funded by the British government; while later the first programmable electronic computer was built in the University of Manchester. Even the internet emerged through a publicly funded organisation - the world's first web server was used by Berners-Lee at CERN.

Sir Timothy John Berners-Lee and the computer with which he created the world's first web site, in 1991. (Drawings by the author.)

What all these endeavours, and nearly all the inventions mentioned above, required, was a good deal of courage on the part of the inventors concerned. However, courage is perhaps not a characteristic one would tend to naturally associate with today's publicly funded institutions. In fact, after 30 years of working in academia I can confirm that universities are, without a doubt, risk averse. By the time we have undertaken all the multitudinous risk assessments, ethical applications, and cost analyses and predictions, there is little time or energy left to actually develop any new technology. And it is not just universities that are like this – most other publicly funded bodies are saddled with enormous amounts of admin that are, apparently, intended to reduce risk (either physical safety or economic risk analysis). I know from personal experience that the NHS, for example, is completely overloaded with admin in this area; and I must wonder if someone were to have invented, say, the CT scanner yesterday; whether there would be any chance of it gaining approval for its medical use in our lifetimes, despite the huge potential such a device offers for improved diagnoses that can often help to save lives. So, perhaps the limitations that seem to have been placed on technological developments in recent decades can be principally attributed to something as simple as *risk aversion*.

Not that there are no innovations currently occurring; developments of recent years that people have undoubtedly found useful include, for example, the internet, low-cost flights to a very wide range of destinations worldwide, very significant increases in available computing power – particularly in the form of the ubiquitous personal computer, and truly impressive mobile technology that facilitates widespread use of smartphones and other devices (but I wish the battery in mine would last seven days instead of seven short hours). So, yes, we have seen some impressive technological advances; and it is worth doing a quick appraisal of what technologies have just been invented and those we might expect to be realised in the near future, to provide us with a steppingstone to imagining what the future may hold.

The present and near future

Table 1 below identifies some technologies that are now in existence.

Sector	Invention
Electronic communication	The internet
Telecommunication	Smartphones
Transportation	Electric cars
Aerospace	Orbiting space station
Artificial intelligence (AI) and machine vision	Automatic face recognition (with performance similar to human capabilities)
Engineering	Simple robots able to undertake 1 specific task (e.g. vacuuming)
Engineering	'Tele-operators' enabling surgery to be undertaken remotely
Artificial Intelligence (AI) and Machine vision	Automatic scene interpretation, as needed for undertaking real-world tasks automatically (e.g. selective removal of weeds from grass)

Table 1. Technologies that are now in existence

In Table 2, I have gone on to list technologies we might expect to be realised in the near future (when I say, 'near future', I am thinking of the next few decades).

187

Sector	Invention
Artificial Intelligence (AI) and machine vision	AI, sufficient to enable robots to sense and interpret their environments to allow them to act appropriately
Engineering	Robots, able to undertake more than one task, and agile and safe enough to interact effectively with humans
Transportation	Self-driving electric cars that can re-charge automatically
Aerospace	Human travel to Mars and beyond
Artificial intelligence (AI) and machine vision	Human-computer interaction capabilities enabling, for example, complete automation of a personalised shopping experience
Engineering, with artificial intelligence (AI) and machine vision	Robotic systems, capable of undertaking advanced diagnostics and selected surgical tasks in semi-automatic/automatic modes
Engineering, with artificial intelligence (AI) and machine vision	Automation of laborious tasks in various sectors (e.g. mining, farming, manufacturing, and so on)

Table 2. Technologies we might expect to be realised in the near future

I was considering going into some detail in relation to the technological breakthroughs that have occurred and are occurring that are enabling the tasks outlined in the above tables to be undertaken automatically. However, as interesting as these methodologies may be (at least to me), they are being described in the technical papers and articles that are now emerging in AI and latest technology-related publications. Many of the breakthroughs in the tables can, in fact, be summarised in the following way. The world is a complex place; the second law of thermodynamics applies – which states that the total entropy of an isolated system can never decrease over time. In other words, there is a tendency for entropy, i.e. randomness, to increase over time (and this gives an official explanation for why my desk looks like such an untidy mess so much of the time). All this randomness introduces a great deal of variation in just about all situations that we might wish to automate. For example, if you buy a robot vacuum cleaner that purports to be able to automatically clean your floor, it's of little use if it can't deal with variations that occur such as, for example, chairs being in various random locations. For the device to be really useful it needs to be able to deal with such variation – the robot vacuumer is clearly of little value if you have to put more effort into ordering the environment of your rooms than you would have to expend by simply vacuuming manually as usual (unless of course you bought it to impress your friends). All this is, however, being overcome by the big breakthrough which is now occurring – specifically the development and useful application of deep learning. This technology is providing a facility for interpreting environments rather as humans would – by using vision to recognise features in a given scene and then employing the resulting information to direct robotic operations. For example, it could be used to direct the robotic vacuumer to avoid obstacles such as tables and chairs that may have been moved to new locations since the last vacuuming.

Emerging vacuuming robots use sensors to detect and avoid objects in their environments and to create floor plans to make vacuuming more efficient.

In fact, the vacuuming robots now emerging do employ sensors such as cameras, gyroscopes, and laser rangefinders to detect and avoid objects in their environments and to create floor plans that make vacuuming more efficient. Having said that, reading the users' reviews, it seems there are many ongoing performance issues that need to be resolved, as well as practical factors that limit their current usefulness. These include their tendency to be rather small (therefore taking a long time to vacuum a floor and needing frequent dust container emptying) as well as being relatively expensive. Therefore, so far, the economic case for them has not been proved, meaning that currently they are more like expensive toys than

189

practical household devices. Of course, as the technology matures, we can expect this to change.

But possible future applications go way beyond robotic vacuuming. Up to now robotic systems have been confined to very structured environments, but the power of deep learning can allow them to function in all sorts of real-world complex situations that had previously been considered too challenging. Consider, for example, outdoor robotic applications – such as in farming. Outdoor situations are quite challenging for automatic machines, due to factors such as dramatic changes in light and alterations in the apparent appearance of various objects, as well as variations due to the seasons and changes in the weather. But all of this does not present such a challenge when employing deep learning – techniques such as convolutional neural networks can recognise features of interest in images even when there is a remarkable amount of variation present – they are surprisingly robust. We have got to a situation now where CNNs can recognise things of interest in scenes about as well as most humans (e.g. detecting the presence of a weed such as dock in grass when there is less than 5% of dock present). This is a great enabling technology and we are now on the cusp of a revolution in the potential for undertaking difficult and/or dangerous tasks automatically. You could say that deep learning is the game changer that will enable robots to successfully perform some of the kinds of tasks that people years ago thought they could, and may have seen them do in the movies, but who became disillusioned at the time when they realised that robots were not actually capable of them. I previously mentioned a tiger in a cage that was a bit of a disappointment, but the combination of AI with machine vision and robotics will represent some tiger - one that could break out of the cage and achieve a hell of a lot for humanity - if we allow it to do so.

So, AI breakthroughs are proving to be the key to technological revolution in the near future and the possibility of robotic solutions to many of the difficult, dangerous, or dirty jobs that men still have to undertake in the modern age is an encouraging and exciting prospect. But what of the more distant future? Of course, this is much harder to predict, but it is intriguing, since the possibilities that may open up might well blow your mind. For example, will there ever be a time when 'Beam me up Scotty' will refer to scientific fact rather than science fiction fantasy?

The far future

Transport

"The reality about transportation is that it's future-oriented. If we're planning for what we have, we're behind the curve."

Man's ability to live, thrive, and survive has always been to some extent dependent upon his ability to move himself, and his supplies, around in a reasonably effective and reliable way. Up to about 5000 BC the only way to move relatively heavy items was to pass them over wooden rollers – in the way that it is supposed the ancient Britons moved the twenty-odd-ton stones that were needed to construct Stonehenge. Then, the invention of bronze chisels enabled wood to be formed with sufficient accuracy for reliable axle-wheel assemblies to be constructed – providing something of a revolution in the speed with which heavy goods could be transported (the wheel is often described as the greatest invention of all time but this accolade could be more accurately attributed to the axle).

The next dramatic increase in speed of transport did not occur until the nineteenth century, with the invention of the steam locomotive and railways. The twentieth century then saw the greatest increase in speed of travel that mankind has ever experienced, (which might never be exceeded) – specifically a 200-fold increase from a 100 mph train to a moon rocket travelling at over 20,000 mph. Will we see any further substantial increases in the future? The answer to this is surely yes, but whether they will occur in our lifetimes, or that of our children, is a different matter. When travelling on the surface of the Earth, one problem that high speed travel has to contend with is that of air resistance, which creates a drag force, the size of which is proportional to the square of the speed and to the cross-sectional area of the moving object. Consequently, travel at very high speeds means a very high drag, necessitating a great power or expenditure of energy (this explains why most cars can accelerate to 100 mph quite easily, but a very powerful engine is required to exceed speeds of, say 200 mph). One way around this in the future would be to build long airtight tubes which would have all of the air pumped out. Inclusion in the walls of the tube of devices similar to the mass accelerators described earlier, would then enable very high-speeds to be attained – perhaps of the order of tens of thousands of mph for transporting goods. The maximum speeds for humans would depend upon the g forces that passengers could endure in the periods when they would be accelerating up to, and down from, the high speed. Of course, building the tubes over long distances, and installing/operating the mass accelerators, may well turn out to be very laborious and expensive (but then, when jet engines were first invented most people thought they would be too expensive to run for human transport purposes – which, of course, proved to be very far from the truth). Although constructing a junction for these tubes (analogous to a junction on a railway line), would appear to be a task of prodigious complexity, it may be that no junctions would be required – particularly if these high speed transports were primarily employed for very popular routes for which high volumes of traffic would be expected. One can, for example, imagine such a tube being constructed between Southampton in England and New York. In fact, two tubes would be required – one for travel in each direction, and they could be suspended a relatively short distance below the ocean's surface – say 200 feet. This would allow them to be missed by any ships passing overhead while being sufficiently close to the surface to allow reasonably easy maintenance as well as avoiding all the demanding and expensive physical strength that would be required if the tubes were experiencing higher pressures at greater depths. The route would be fixed without requiring junctions, since once coming up onto land they would enter termini that could employ railway hubs (or perhaps other tube hubs in the USA), for onward travel to the traveller's exact destination. I must say I like the idea – I should seek a patent for it (but this has probably already been filed).

These types of transportation systems do not require great scientific breakthroughs – they could be developed using modest developments of the technologies available to us today. It may be that they would be expensive to build, but once operational they could offer transport speeds that up to now have only been dreamed of, as well as affordable operating costs and on-going substantial environmental benefits. But what about high-speed travel in the air? It is, of course, easy to imagine aircraft that could travel at significantly higher speeds than current airliners. In fact, for many years we had one regularly operating between London and New York – the previously mentioned Concorde, which could comfortably cruise at Mach 2. Since it travelled faster than the rotation of the Earth, it famously enabled passengers to disembark in New York *before* they set off from London (at least according to the local times). I know I have already included images of this stunning aeroplane, but I had to do so again because it is so beautiful.

The Concorde, which enabled passengers to disembark in New York before they set off from London. (The photograph is used with the permission of South West News Service.)

Yes, Concorde was certainly a great engineering achievement – perhaps the most beautiful commercial airliner ever built – but efficient it was not. Its Rolls Royce Olympus engines may have been the epitome of reliability, but they could not be described as frugal. Concorde, alas, is no longer flying, and in recent years there has been a move away from speed towards saving money, so that nearly all of today's airliners employ *turbofan* engines which (for reasons we will not go into here) are much more efficient than *turbojets* such as the Olympus, with the disadvantage being that they operate best for aircraft that are traveling at a maximum speed of around 0.8 Mach. It would, however, surely be possible to design aircraft that could travel at speeds well in excess of that of sound while still performing with reasonable efficiency – perhaps by flying very high in the atmosphere while employing the 'Ram Jet' principle. Such supersonic ram jets, or scramjets, have been the subject of theoretical and practical studies where their potential to travel at up to Mach 6 has been explored; but up to now little has emerged in terms of developments that indicate capabilities for commercial air travel. Perhaps the technology is considered too expensive or risky, or maybe the major carriers feel that the average customer can be kept happy with extended/premium services to cover the extra time that is needed to make a journey at a lower speed. No doubt their business cases and projections show that a far greater profit can be made by providing increased service instead of increased speed.

Another travel environment to be considered is the vacuum of space. The main problem encountered with space travel is that in order to get thrust to move forwards, we need to push backwards on something; or to put it another way, we have to obey Newton's third law, which states: 'every action has an equal and opposite reaction'. In space, it's clear that there is precious little to push against (just the occasional hydrogen atom) – which is why the only types of drive that have been employed, in practice, in space are rockets – here the thing we push back against is the gas escaping from the back of the rocket.

There are other types of drives that have been experimented with, such as ion drive, where a gas is ionised and then accelerated in an electric field before exiting at the back of the drive, providing thrust. Plasma drive is similar but involves a plasma which is accelerated via an electric current. Another type of drive that could theoretically accelerate (very small) spacecraft to high speeds is laser drive, where a high-power laser (usually on the ground) is used to aim a laser beam at a craft, to which momentum is transferred, thereby accelerating it (the effect being enhanced through use of a laser-pushed 'lightsail'). Although these methods are perfectly reasonable from the physics point of view, the magnitude of the forces that they have been shown to be capable of providing, at least up to now, are far too small to accelerate spacecraft containing humans up to usefully high speeds in reasonable time periods (of course, that is not to say they will not undergo further development in the future and become practical methods of propulsion).

There are, by the way, one or two other species of spacecraft thrusters that seem implausible but have generated a good deal of interest in certain sections of the media. One such device is the *EMDrive*, or *radio frequency resonant cavity thruster*. It is claimed that it generates thrust by reflecting microwaves internally in the device. Unfortunately, in doing this it would be in violation of the law of conservation of momentum and Newton's third law. Also, it seems that there has not been independent verifiable evidence from tests that it can generate thrust forces any greater than those attributable to experimental error. However, if at any time such forces are demonstrated in the verified tests, I will be all ears...

So, what does this leave us with? Yes, the good old rocket engine. Old is certainly the operative adjective – the Chinese were launching crude rockets over 1000 years ago.

The first rockets were propulsion systems for arrows that are believed to date from the 10th century Song dynasty, in China. (Illustration by the author.)

Rocket engines, although cumbersome and occasionally unreliable, are perfectly capable of providing thrust for rockets aimed at exploring our solar system – as all the robotic probes launched in recent decades have illustrated. The problem arises when much higher speeds are required to enable interstellar travel within liveable time periods (i.e. perhaps years rather than millennia). To state it simply, if a rocket is to contain enough fuel for the motor to burn long enough for it to reach very high speeds, it would be too heavy to actually launch! But I did say I was going to address the developments of the far future and, as mentioned, the rocket is an invention that is a thousand years old. So, let's dispense with it and let our imaginations roam more freely. If we were to ignore the constraints of current technologies for the time being, what might we imagine transport mechanisms of the far future would be able to do and how could they work? And why did I just ask myself a question that is just about impossible to answer?

When thinking of the farther future, for me *Star Trek* often comes to mind. What an original show and one that, for once, envisioned the future as an exciting place where you would want to live, full of all sorts of fantastic possibilities; rather than some kind of grim, fashionable, dystopian nightmare. One of these fantastic possibilities is, of course, the transporter mechanism; but is it really a possibility? In my view, it is one of the least believable 'gadgets' that appear in the show, perhaps partially because one finds it difficult not to think of it as slightly too convenient – a simple business of stopping the camera briefly so that the actors can walk off set, then start it again so that they seem to disappear. Use an optical printer to combine this with a glittery effect (film of someone shining a light through a cascade of glitter) and, hey presto, the guys have beamed out! Suppose they have beamed down to a planet – the next scene can show them in a glittery re-appearance on the planet surface (AKA Desilu Studio 3 on the Paramount Lot, Culver City, LA). Having said that, my God, I love those old *Star Trek* special effects; of an era perhaps, a bit cheesy no doubt, but great! But in any case, the simple expedient of stopping the camera for an apparent 'beam down' is so much more convenient and cheaper than all of the optical effects that would be needed to show Kirk and the boys getting into, say, a shuttlecraft and gliding all the way down to the planet surface.

But what does the transporter actually, or should I say allegedly, involve? Dr (Bones) McCoy, used to say in a depreciative tone of voice, that he did not wish to have his 'atoms spread across the galaxy' or something similar. But the only thing that is moving in the case of the transporter is information. The process essentially involves three stages, the first being to break the human body down one atom at a time. (By the way, I should have expected this, but have just found that Sherlock Holmes had this idea ahead of us, or rather, his creator did. 'The Disintegration Machine' is a science fiction short story written by Sir Arthur Conan Doyle and published in *The Strand* magazine in January 1929. The story describes a machine capable of disintegrating objects and reforming them as they were. Conan Doyle chose his wealthy eccentric adventurer Professor Challenger as the hero of this tale, rather than Holmes.) The next two stages involve transmitting the associated information and then re-assembling the body an atom at a time in a different location. Such *matter transmission* is not instantaneous, it takes a certain amount of time – for example, the transmission would be done using electromagnetic waves that travel at the speed of light. Transmitting a single atom would not take long, but when we consider that there are of the order of 10^{27} atoms in a human body, calculations show that transmitting a single whole body would be expected to take millions of years! It is interesting to note that Gene Roddenberry and his writers were well informed as to the scientific aspects of *Star Trek*; it may be that between the making of the original Series and *Star Trek: The Next Generation* (STNG) they became aware of the long time we would expect a transporter to take to transmit a whole human. Consequently, in STNG the transporter mechanism is described as a system that transmits a very large number of channels of information in parallel (in fact millions or more). If enough of such parallel channels were employed, then it could be imagined that the time needed for transmission of a man could become more manageable in magnitude. However, the main difficulty I have with the transporter does not have to do with speed of transmission; rather it is that, although one can imagine transmitting the material that makes up a man, I can't envisage that one could transmit the *essence* of the man himself. By this I mean that the man is more than just a set of atoms; rather, he is a complex combination of energy states and special configurations that would be extremely difficult to accurately read and replicate. Without this the copy would not have the memory, personality, thoughts, or in fact *identity* of the original man.

I mentioned accuracy and this is an important point; in order to transmit and replicate a given atom of the body, the device would need to accurately record its original state. The Heisenberg Uncertainty Principle states that there is a fundamental limitation to the accuracy with which this can be done. It is important to note that this limitation arises from fundamental quantum physics rather than being due to limits in the resolution/quality of our instrumentation – there is a limit, even in theory, to the accuracy with which the measurements of the atom could be taken (interestingly, Einstein did not believe this; he famously said "God does not play dice with the Universe" and thought that the fundamental error in possible measurement specified by the Heisenberg Uncertainty Principle was due to our incomplete understanding of the physics factors involved – but most modern physicists consider that Einstein was wrong about this). So, if there are fundamental limits to how accurately we can record and so re-create a human, what implications would this have on the quality of the copy?

And this discussion does not even address more metaphysical aspects – for example, what you might call the *soul* of a person. And, as others have pointed out, there is also the alarming possibility of the transporter being used to create multiple versions of the same person. In fact, I seem to remember this happened to Jim Kirk on more than one occasion – usually featuring a good Kirk and a bad Kirk which, in the episode 'The Enemy Within', were actually supposed to have emerged from the transporter at slightly different times during a storm. You might consider this a slightly weak plot, but at least this episode provided some good opportunities to display a good selection of Shatnerisms in the acting – or should I say over-acting (good stuff I say; over-acting may not be to everyone's taste, but I feel it is suited to a sci-fi TV series such as *Star Trek* and that it keeps the entertainment level up). Anyway, all things considered, perhaps Bones was right.

The *Star Trek* transporter in operation. (Illustration by author.)

Maybe, after all, a matter transmitter or transporter mechanism is a little too fantastic for "suspension of disbelief" (as Coleridge termed it in 1817).

What other advanced modes of transport might we expect to see appearing in the far future? One that is quite popular is the idea of controlling gravity. This is something that has always been featured in *Star Trek*; in fact the artificial gravity on the Enterprise is itself a good example of suspension of disbelief on the part of the TV audience. How, after all, would this be implemented and why, no matter how wrecked or damage a spacecraft is, does the artificial gravity system appear to be fully functional? Talking about suspension of disbelief reminds me of *Space*

1999; a not inconsiderable sci-fi TV series that was obviously inspired by *Star Trek*, and which featured a large budget and optical effects by Gerry Anderson (creator of, amongst other things, *Thunderbirds*) that were more impressive than most of the acting.

The 'Eagle' - a space shuttle craft used between the Earth and the Moon in Gerry Anderson's *Space 1999* TV series. (Illustration by the author.)

The series was set on a Moon base in 1999, but unfortunately featured the slightly ridiculous plot line that an explosion in a dumpsite for nuclear waste created an explosion sufficient to blast the Moon out of its orbit and off into interstellar space. Apparently, the main actor, Martin Landau, was annoyed by the viewers refusing to suspend disbelief sufficiently to accept this outlandish plot concept. In other ways, *Space 1999* was not that bad a TV series, but the performances of the lead actors, Martin Landau and Barbara Bain, are likely to forever remind us about how bad things can get for a TV series when the main characters are just not interesting and don't have engaging interactions or a decent rapport (or even arguments ... or anything!)

Coming back down to Earth, or getting our feet on the ground (if you will forgive the puns), how might we use control of gravity to provide a means of transport? One way was imagined by H. G. Wells in his engaging novel *The First Men in the*

Moon. This was originally serialised in *The Strand* magazine (as nearly everything I mention, bar *Star Trek*, seems to have been), from December 1900 to August 1901. The book tells the story of a journey to the Moon undertaken by the two protagonists: a businessman narrator, Mr Bedford; and an eccentric scientist, Mr Cavor. These characters discover that the Moon is inhabited by a sophisticated extra-terrestrial civilisation of insect-like creatures that they call 'Selenites'. Good grief! I know that Wells was quite a knowledgeable scientist and can only imagine that he somehow managed to synthesise lysergic acid diethylamide in 1900 (38 years before Swiss chemist Albert Hofmann was credited with doing so), since I can think of no other explanation for how an author could come up with stuff like that. Whether or not he was into drugs, I do think that Wells was a great author who produced some exceptionally *novel* novels.

We are told that a novel should be unique but most authors of fiction, even nowadays, seem to frequently produce wordy love stories – modern day versions of Jane Austen's tales. In contrast, consider *The Time Machine* – completely unique when it emerged and full of new concepts and far out ideas. The same can be said of his other books like *War of the Worlds* and also, of course, *The First Men in the Moon*. In the latter, Bedford befriends Cavor when he learns he is developing a new material, cavorite, which can mask the force of gravity. Bedford sees in the commercial production of cavorite a possible source of "wealth enough to work any sort of social revolution we fancied; we might own and order the whole world" (which is a bit of megalomania that reminds one of the titular character in another of his great works: *The Invisible Man*). Cavor comes up with the idea of a spherical spaceship made of "steel, lined with glass", and with sliding "windows or blinds" made of cavorite by which it can be steered, and persuades a reluctant Bedford to undertake a voyage to the Moon. Strong move, no doubt.

There is only one slight problem: such a thing is impossible – or as near to impossible as we can get. The reason for this is that a material such as cavorite would break a fundamental law of physics – the law of conservation of energy. This law states that energy cannot be created or destroyed - it can only be transferred from one type to another. For example, when you start a journey in your car, chemical energy (the petrol in the tank) is converted into heat energy in the engine and the kinetic energy of your car moving along the road. After the journey, some of the chemical energy has been transformed into other forms, (the fuel gauge has gone down a bit), but the overall amount of energy is exactly the same. This law has never been observed to have been broken and is believed to apply throughout the Universe.

This is not to say that gravity control is impossible – just that it would require application of a good deal of energy for it not to break the law of conservation of energy. If a portable/lightweight power source were invented that could be used to power an 'antigravity' machine, then it could indeed comprise a convenient means of transport - allowing one to hover in any location and to move freely in any direction. Such a facility would certainly comprise a transport revolution. It must, however, be borne in mind that, of all the forces in nature, gravitation is the least understood in modern science. In physics, fundamental forces are realised through particle exchange, or 'mediation'. For example, electromagnetism is mediated by the photon, the strong interaction by gluons, and the weak interaction by the W and Z bosons (apparently). Physicists are reasonably sure of this since the behaviour of these forces are in close agreement with modern models of particle physics. In contrast, in the case of gravity, it is hypothesized that forces between masses are mediated by an as yet undiscovered elementary particle, dubbed the 'graviton'; the behaviour of which is somewhat less understood. According to Wikipedia: "There is no complete quantum field theory of gravitons due to an outstanding mathematical problem with renormalization in general relativity." And I won't beg to differ.

So, as you can imagine, I would not be surprised if it takes a while before we get complete control over the force of gravity. If you ask me, this is a shame, since if I could turn gravity down a bit I am sure it would help with my current back pain. The best way to do this would probably be to make some adjustment to G, the Gravitational Constant (am sure this happened in one of the episodes of STNG). The other solution to my back pain would be for me to lose weight. Being able to adjust G might seem unrealistic, but it is probably more likely than me being able to stick to a diet.

Robotics

"It's very dangerous to put astronauts on a moon base where there's radiation, solar flares and micro meteorites. It'd be much better to put robots on the moon and have them mentally connected to astronauts on the Earth."

- Michio Kaku

There was some discussion above of robotics – particularly in terms of capabilities that could arise from combining robotics with AI. The kinds of developments we might expect to see in the next few decades could offer great opportunities for implementing labour-saving systems – and this is certainly commendable and should provide many societal benefits. However, most of the systems that are likely to emerge in the near future are essentially comprised of 'smart automation'. In other words, they would consist of automation generally similar to what has existed in the recent past, but with the significant difference of being able to accommodate the substantial variations that we see in practice in the world around us.

Looking beyond this to the farther future, what developments might we expect to see? The main one would be that the task-specific automation will give way to the general-purpose *robot* – and this is an exciting development indeed.

The promise of Hollywood

"Hollywood is not only a geographical place on the map of the world, but an idea and frame of mind. There is something that happens in a Hollywood studio that evokes brilliance, serendipity, and nostalgia all at once."

- Tommy Dangcil

As a prelude to considering what robots might look like in the far future, let's first discuss how robots have been depicted in visual media. To begin, at the beginning (as Dylan Thomas expressed it), perhaps we should mention Fritz Lang's 1927 film *Metropolis*. I have spoken to quite a few people who are critical of this film and H. G. Wells described it as silly; it does, however, contain many special effects that are impressive for the time and ground-breaking. Chief among these is the *Maschinenmensch* (German for "machine-person"), which is played by actress Brigitte Helm in a rather striking robot costume. The latter, which was created by sculptor Walter Schulze-Mittendorff from a whole-body plaster cast of Helm, certainly does look very metallic, and I would say it has the appearance of being both highly futuristic and aesthetic.

But does the film say much about what robots could actually do? Perhaps not. When watching it, I noticed that the workers were employed doing very simple and repetitive tasks, while at the same time the robot was obviously the product of a very advanced technology. So, perhaps this speaks of a civilisation that has vast and astonishing gaps in its technological development – either that or Fritz Lang didn't know much about technology.

Perhaps I should not have begun at the beginning, since the first film featuring a robot that really engaged me was *The Day the Earth Stood Still*. (I mean, of course, the 1951 picture with Michael Rennie and Patricia Neal, not the 2008 re-make; why would anyone want to re-make something that is already just about perfect?) What a great film; and as for 'Gort' - what a robot! What with Gort's disintegrator ray and Klaatu's warning that Gort is so powerful that it could "easily destroy the Earth and possesses limitless potential", the whole robot depiction is impressive and terrific (in more than one sense of the word). All I can say is: "Klaatu barada nikto!"

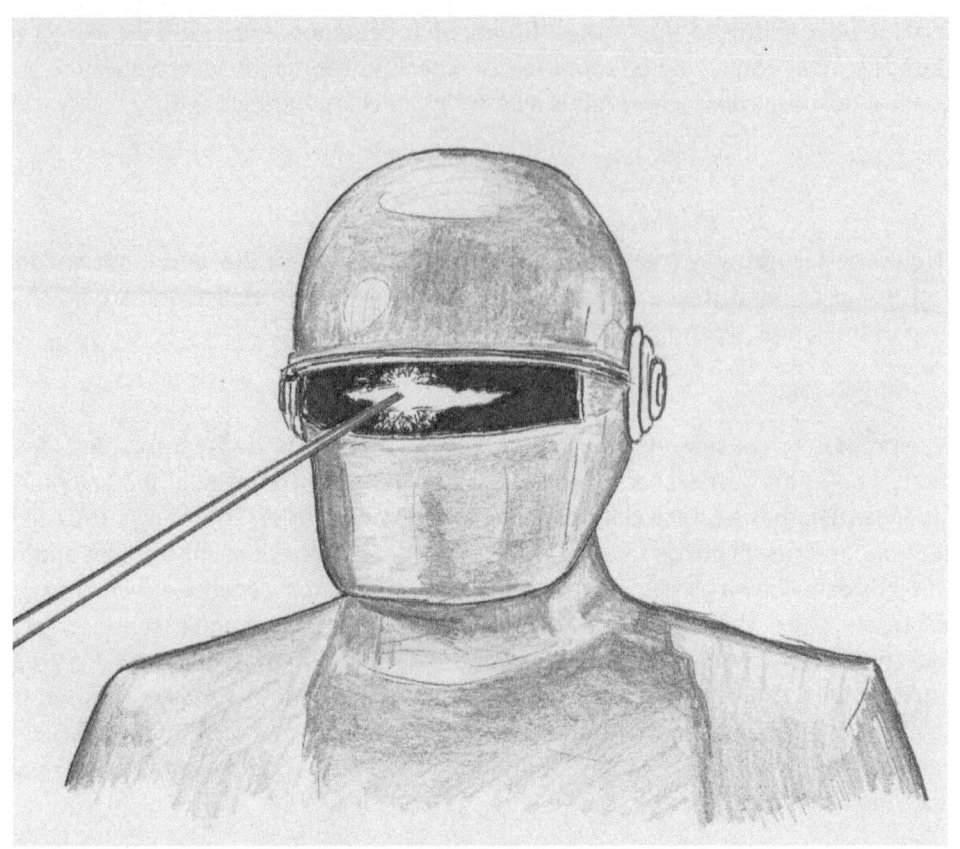

The robot Gort from the film *The Day the Earth Stood Still*, fires its laser weapon. (Drawing by the author.)

Another robot that impressed me even more than Gort was, of course, Robby. Is *Forbidden Planet* the best science fiction film ever made? If not, then it is certainly, as far as I am concerned, one of the best. The plot of this film is based on Shakespeare's *The Tempest* and the Prospero figure is a philologist called Dr Morbius. At one point, Morbius mentions that Robby's strength is sufficient to "quite easily topple this house off its foundation". Morbius also mentions that he 'tinkered' Robbie together during a couple of weeks – how did Morbius, a philologist, manage that? He subsequently explains how he got a 'brain boost' in the lab of a previous advanced civilisation (later in the film Doc Ostrow tries the brain boost himself but, unfortunately, only has time to say "You ought to see my new mind, up there in lights…" before expiring). Robby was, in fact, constructed by MGM's art and prop departments and they certainly achieved an impressive result – the first robot in cinema that did not look like an actor in a tin can or some kind of suit. In fact, Robby was one of the most expensive single film props ever created up to that time - representing 7% of the film's total budget.

A scene from the film *Forbidden Planet* where the spacecraft United Planets Cruiser C-57D is landing on the planet Altair IV. (Illustration by the author).

Another scene from the film *Forbidden Planet*: Robby the Robot Lt. 'Doc' Ostrow (left) and Commander Adams (right). (Pen and ink drawing by the author.)

Robby the Robot ultimately became something of a science fiction legend and even a well-loved figure in popular culture – appearing in around 30 films and various TV shows. The latter included a Season 5 episode of Rod Serling's *Twilight Zone* - which was also filmed at MGM Studios – and made extensive use of props and costumes originally created for *Forbidden Planet* - perhaps most memorable of which were Robby himself (or itself) and the film's saucer spaceship (United Planets Cruiser C-57D). In 2017, at the age of 61, Robbie was sold by Bonhams in New York for $5,375,000 – one of the most expensive movie props ever sold. MGM's Robby the Robot may well have been influenced by Isaac Asimov's seminal robot stories – in particular the short story, 'Robbie', which was first published in 1940 as part of his robot anthology *I, Robot*. It turns out that Isaac Asimov had a significant influence on Hollywood science fiction. He took an interest in *Star Trek* from its earliest days and used to say that it was his favourite TV show. Then, later, in the STNG episode, 'Datalore', we are told that the android Data is the result of Doctor Noonian Soong's desire "to make Asimov's dream of a positronic brain come true". Data was, in fact, a very capable android who formed one of the main hero characters of STNG – subsequently becoming a firm favourite with the multitudinous fans of the show.

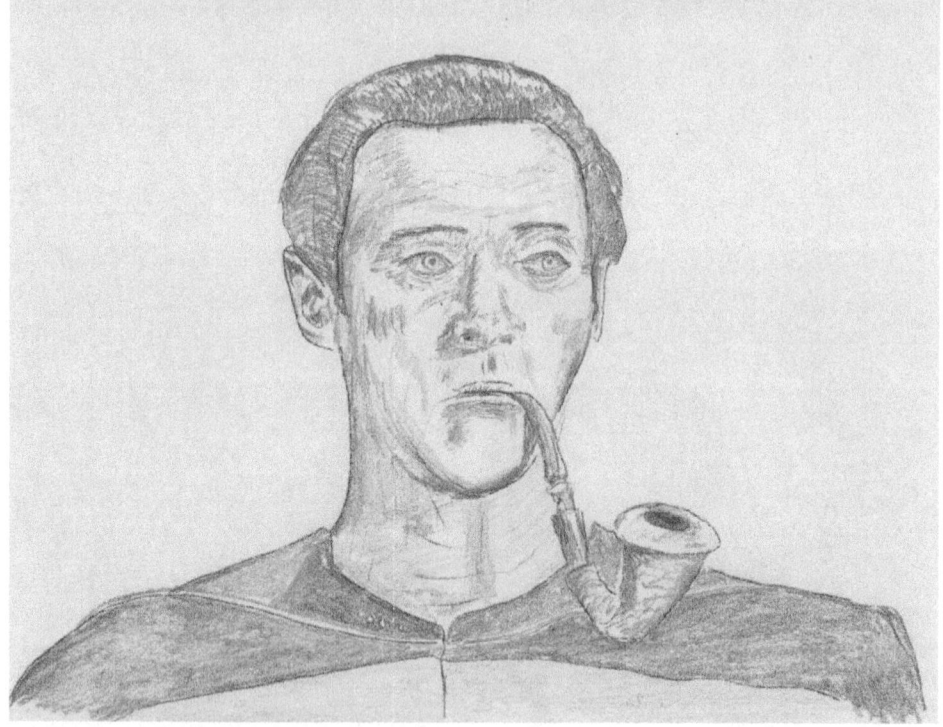

The android Data, from *Star Trek: The Next Generation*; which has no emotions but, as you can see, did have an interest in Sherlock Holmes and was given, on occasion, to masquerading as the great detective. This illustration combines three of the major themes of this book: robotics, *Star Trek* and Sherlock Holmes. (Drawing by author.)

A robot that features in a more recent film is 'TARS' - one of four former U.S. Marine Corps tactical robots (along with PLEX, CASE, and KIPP) that feature in the science fiction film *Interstellar*. I must say I enjoyed the sequences in this film that featured TARS; in fact, I thought the whole film was great – loads of interesting physics content, including time dilation, direction by Christopher Nolan and acting from the likes of Matthew McConaughey and Michael Caine – what more could you ask for? One thing I would say though, is that the grandeur of Robby is derived from a real presence – whereas TARS appeared somewhat more dependent upon cinematographic special effects. For me, the former will always create much more of an impression.

Why, you may be asking, have we gone into such detail regarding robot depictions in science fiction films? The reason is that these and other films and TV shows have presented robots in very impressive and believable roles. It turns out that the 'magic' of moviemaking has set our expectations very high. When we see what current robots can actually do, it can be somewhat disappointing. Aside from some specialised tasks such as vacuuming or lawn cutting, most domestic robots only really excel at arm-waving, while industrial robots are best suited to pick-and-place operations or moving through fixed and repetitive trajectories. In the late 1980s, there was something of a boom in industrial robotics – I was in fact part of it working at Cranfield University with a number of robot/automation companies. Unfortunately, as mentioned earlier, it didn't last - the boom largely turned to bust, due to the frequent employment of expensive robots to undertake simple tasks that could be achieved at a much lower cost using simpler equipment. To summarise, robots were looking like a solution in search of an application. The chief problem then was that re-programming industrial robots was so expensive that they were often scrapped at the end of their first use. In other words, software limitations meant that their flexibility was not being exploited – they were being employed as hard automation – and in that role they looked expensive. However, it may be that the AI breakthroughs discussed in this book, such as CNNs, will enable this software hurdle to be overcome.

So much for past events; what about the future and, intriguingly, the far future? Will robots be able to undertake anything like the kinds of impressive and wide-ranging tasks they commonly accomplish in the movies? What will they look like – do films give us any realistic indications? Is there any chance that the dominance of mankind could be threatened by robots – are they our servants or usurpers? Having said this, I can't help thinking of the *Twilight Zone* episode, 'To Serve Man'. Here, after tall somewhat weird-looking aliens known as Kanamits land on Earth, the humans have trouble deciding whether they are a threat. When a Kanamit book entitled *To Serve Man* is discovered, everyone thinks all is well and the Kanamits genuinely intend to bring humanity the benefits they have been promising. But, after someone manages to translate some of the book, you can imagine their consternation when they discover that it is in reality a cookbook! Due to this final dramatic twist, this is one of the most famous episodes of the series. By the way, since *Twilight Zone* was made by MGM you will not be surprised to learn that the spacecraft that the Kanamits travel in is the same one that appears in *Forbidden Planet* – specifically the United Planets Cruiser C-57D (it also appears in many other *Twilight Zone* episodes).

Robot intelligence

"I have always been convinced that the only way to get artificial intelligence to work is to do the computation in a way similar to the human brain. That is the goal I have been pursuing. We are making progress, though we still have lots to learn about how the brain actually works."

- Geoffrey Hinton

There is no reason why robots of the future should not comprise multi-purpose mechanisms. As mentioned above, the chief problem with robots up to now has been the prohibitively high cost of re-programming them for an altered task. This leads companies such as auto manufacturers, to simply buy a new set of robots (and all the needed ancillary equipment), every time the tasks for the robots is changed somewhat. As you can imagine, this is not a particularly economic solution and it was factors such as this that led to the bursting of the robotics investment bubble that occurred around 1990 (which I have already alluded to a couple of times), with all its attendant disappointments. In contrast to this rather unprepossessing past, the future for robot re-programming is bright since we can expect it to be largely automated. All that is needed for this is implementation of effective machine learning algorithms and the availability of vast amounts of data relevant to the task. Drawing on historical data from online databases might help the latter, but perhaps more importantly, the new robot could learn *on the job*, just as humans have done for centuries. This could be called, if you will, robot apprenticeships, or work-based learning (WBL) for robots (WBL is something that has come into fashion in recent years in tertiary education). The great advantage of this approach is that it would not be long before the knowledge/expertise of a new robot being trained and so generating new data, exceeded the knowledge of the older robot guiding it through the training. After a while, its knowledge will also exceed that of any human that has undertaken the same task. This is an illustration of how, in the not too far distant future, robot knowledge can be expected to exceed that of humans. This is not to say that such a robot would have greater intelligence than humans, or in fact intelligence at all as we understand it. Another way of stating this is that it is not clear whether robots will be capable of independent original thought – we can't say for certain that robots will be coming up with new and innovative ideas – it's just too early in the history of real AI. (I

camera) and the latter will require high computation capabilities in the robot's brain. This requirement is not to be underestimated. Consider, for example, what a small angle of view humans can see at high resolution (which is known as the vision span). Although the visual field of the human eye spans approximately 120 degrees of arc, most of this is peripheral (i.e. low-resolution) vision. The human eye does, however, have much greater resolution in the macula, where there is a higher density of cone cells, but the field of view that is observed with sufficient resolution to read text typically only spans about 6 degrees of arc. So, despite all the image processing power of the human brain (which is, after all, the most complex thing known in the Universe), evolution has arranged it so that the amount of data it reviews at high resolution is really very limited. Presumably a greater amount of data would be asking too much of the brain and it would be overwhelmed.

So yes, the robots of the future will require high resolution vision, but the actual amount of data captured might be limited by the amount of processing of continuous data that the robot brain could undertake in real time. Consequently, it does not seem unlikely that robotics will follow the human example and only capture a small number of degrees of arc at very high resolution. One way of doing this would be to have actuators re-orientating cameras towards objects of interest – as human eyes move to survey a scene. However, robotic technology might provide an advantage here in that a camera could be capable of capturing a wide field of view at high resolution but only a relatively small region of interest would be analysed at any given time. (This can, in fact, already be done to some extent in modern industrial cameras – particularly those based on CMOS technology.) The advantage for the robot here comes in the form of no moving parts being needed and also an ability to move the region of interest much more quickly than a human or animal can rotate their eyeballs.

While we are on the subject of potential advantages for the robot, it is worth mentioning that robot vision could be capable of detecting 'light' with a far greater range of wavelengths than humans can manage. While our eyes are only sensitive to a relatively narrow band of the EM spectrum, from red up to violet light, there is no reason why robot vision could not extend into ultraviolet and above, as well as into the longer wavelengths of infra-red (IR). Here, some interesting possibilities arise; for example, a robot detecting ultra-violet (UV) radiation could raise an alarm for any humans in its vicinity, since UV is harmful to humans and can even cause blindness. Likewise, detecting well into the IR would effectively provide the robot with a 'thermal camera' and such a device can be used to monitor the temperature of humans. If an elevated temperature were detected it could be providing an indication that the person has a fever – thereby flagging early that the person might have a virus and need to be tested and, if positive, their movements should be tracked. (All of which is, of course, very relevant to the current COVID-19 pandemic.) Going into even longer wavelengths, we enter the range of 'terahertz radiation', which occupies a middle ground between microwaves and infrared light. The emission and detection of terahertz radiation is something of an emerging technology, but it offers the capability to penetrate fabrics and plastics. The potential applications of this can be readily imagined. In surveillance, for example, terahertz security screening could be used for covert detection of concealed weapons on a person (and, interestingly, many materials of interest have unique spectral 'fingerprints' in the terahertz range).

To be honest, all this reminds me of Geordie LaForge – the engineer in STNG who was blind since birth but who employed a visor to see. Geordie LaForge was one of the main STNG characters being, of course, popular with the fans, but I can't help wondering whether the actor who played him, LeVar Burton, might have been slightly annoyed with the series writers for the way in which Geordie always seemed to have little success with women, while Will Riker was apparently getting intimate with females (alien and otherwise) just about every other week! I guess the Will Riker character was written to be a little similar to that of Captain Kirk in the original series – in that he often found that the solution to a serious and dramatic situation that he found himself in could be attained by kissing the nearest attractive woman. Anyway, although Geordie's visor allowed him to 'see much more than other people', he said he would have preferred to just have normal human vision. (The visor was replaced by ocular prosthetic implants in the last three films of the STNG franchise.)

What of the other senses? In the case of hearing, there is no reason to suppose that future robots will not have great sensitivity and a facility for detecting a wide range of sound frequencies (humans are limited to 20 to 20,000Hz). As for the other well-known senses – touch (tactile), smell, and taste, these will all be needed and, like hearing, they will benefit from advanced capabilities that will be offered from future sensor technologies – capabilities that would be expected to greatly exceed those of humans. By the way, the sense of balance is provided in humans by structures in the middle ear – in the case of robots this could be facilitated through use of gyros (perhaps explaining why gyroscopes are shown spinning around at the top of Robby's 'head'). It should be mentioned that robots are also likely to employ additional sensing technologies that are not available to humans – examples include object detection using RADAR and GPS position recording.

Therefore, even from this brief discussion, we can conclude that it is unlikely that future robots will be lacking in sensory technology. However, due to the discrete and compact technologies we can expect to be available in the future, this does not necessarily dictate the way in which they will appear. Instead, this may be more dependent upon sociological and practical considerations.

Geordie LaForge – the engineer in *Star Trek: The Next Generation*, who was blind since birth but who employed a visor to see. (Drawing by author.)

The appearance of robots in the far future
"Here I come
Cryogenic heart, skin a polished silver
One thing I am glad of
For this I thank my builder
I can never rust"

- Louis Shalako

From the brief discussion above of the depiction of robots in the movies, it can be seen that their appearances are not usually a result of functional requirements. As you would perhaps expect, the appearance is generally intended to create an impression on the viewer – either of beauty (Maschinenmensch), technical impressiveness (Robby), or fright (Gort). It may, however, be television that has given us the truest impression of the likely appearance of robots in the far future – specifically the humanoid robot, Data. There are many reasons to suppose that future robots will be humanoid in form. The first and most obvious is the fact that if a robot has a similar external geometry to a human then it will be able to do many things humans commonly do – which might have many associated benefits. Suppose, for example, that a robot is intended to act as a carer for a person with some disabilities. The person concerned may still wish to undertake common tasks such as travelling on public transport or dining in restaurants. If the robot had a humanoid form, it would be able to accompany and care for the person without the need for specialised conversions of seats and other equipment used by humans. Another factor has to do with psychology or social acceptance. Put simply, most people are much more likely to be accepting of a robot that resembles a human than one which manifestly does not. However, those who do not like the concept of a robot that appears realistically human-like will often point out the concept of 'uncanny valley' in relation to people's negative reaction to lifelike robots. This term was first introduced in the 1970s by Masahiro Mori, then a professor at the Tokyo Institute of Technology. He invented the term 'uncanny valley' to describe his observation that as robots appear more humanlike, they cease to be appealing. Upon reaching the uncanny valley, our reaction supposedly descends into a feeling of strangeness, a sense of unease, and a tendency to be scared or freaked out, as shown in the graph below.

Even if there is some truth in the theory of the uncanny valley, I wouldn't get too concerned about it in relation to humanoid robots of the far future. Such devices are likely to have a very high degree of human likeness; and, as shown in the graph, as the human likeness approaches 100% the affinity very much rises – so much, in fact, that it ends up at the point where you would expect it to be if the uncanny valley never existed at all.

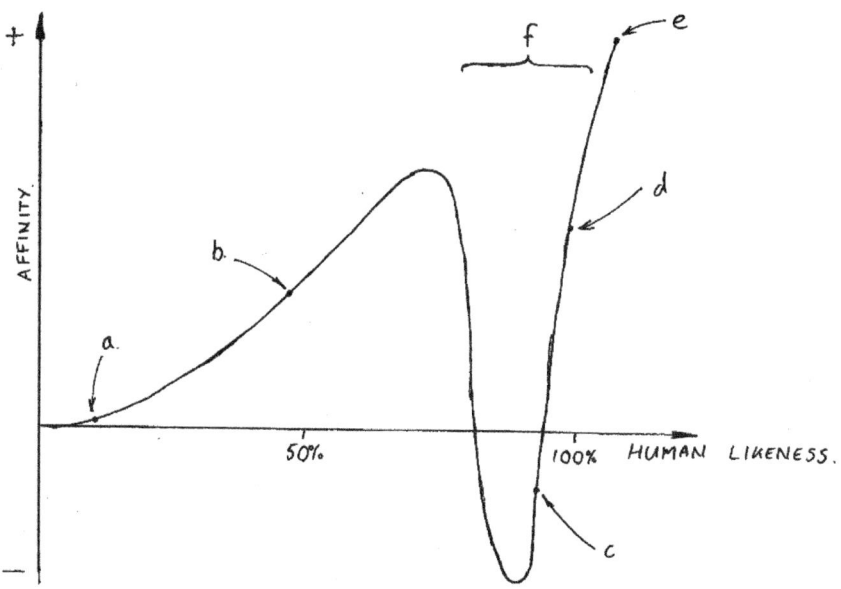

The Uncanny Valley in the relationship between human affinity for robots and the latter's human likeness. (a) industrial robot, (b) educational robot, (c) prosthetics, (d) puppets such as Sophia, (e) healthy person, and (f) Uncanny Valley. (Graph by the author.)

Are there, then, any serious objections to the concept that a humanoid form is the ultimate robot destiny? Some people may point to the capabilities of current machines and question whether there will ever be a time when the power and agility of a human could be realised within a machine confined within the limited space of a typical human body (not for nothing did Hamlet exclaim: "What a piece of work is man!"). But again, I would not be too concerned over such reservations. Electric motors are continually becoming more complex, powerful, and lightweight. Consider, for example, the harmonic gearbox; this employs strain wave gearing theory, which is based on elastic dynamics and utilizes the flexibility of metal. This type of gearbox, which was invented in 1957, is compact and lightweight and offers a high gear reduction ratio, which has led to it being commonly employed in robotics and aerospace (the latter includes the electric drives of the Apollo Lunar Rover). This is just an example – there are multitudes of other types of drives being constantly introduced – so we may expect that robotic motive power is something that will be available in the future.

Regarding matters such as balance and agility, these are control issues that are dependent upon computing/algorithmic developments. In the past, much emphasis has been placed on robotics research into 'closed form' classical

213

approaches to control, the results of which have been quite limited. Now, with the breakthrough in AI that has occurred in recent years – particularly in deep learning, we may expect more robust and practical solutions to robotics control problems.

One thing that robots of the future will definitely need, if they are going to be able to undertake the delicate or difficult tasks that humans can perform, is compliance. This term refers to flexibility and suppleness; and in order to understand what compliance is, it helps to consider what non-compliance is. A non-compliant (stiff) robot will have predetermined positions or trajectories. No matter what kind of external force is exerted on, say the robotic hand, it will follow the exact same path each and every time. In contrast to this, a compliant robot can reach several positions and exert different forces on a given object. For example: a compliant robot gripper can grasp an egg without crushing it, even if the egg is, say, slightly larger than expected. A non-compliant gripper will crush the egg and continue its given operation. Compliance can take two forms: passive and active. Passive can be thought of as being similar to the ability of, say, your fingers to be slightly spongy and to deform somewhat. This deformation would, in the above example, help to avoid the egg being crushed. Active compliance, on the other hand, is where the robot makes slight positional modifications during a task to assist with performing it successfully. For example, suppose a robot were given a task of threading a nut onto a bolt. This is a simple task for a human, but a robot using its grippers to hold the nut and bolt may not be able to accomplish it if there is any slight misalignment (which would be often expected to occur through common occurrences such as the nut or bolt position varying slightly each time they are picked up by the robot).

Active compliance would involve the robot very slightly varying the relative position and/or orientation of the nut and bolt, to assist in completing the task. This may seem like a trivial task, but it is the sort of thing that, up to now, has been very difficult to achieve robotically, and it also provides a good illustration of why a practical robot requires well developed sensors that are integrated with its control system. The most important sensory data needed for implementing active compliance for tasks like threading nuts onto bolts are likely to be high resolution vision and force feedback (tactile sensing).

Regarding the actual implementation of the compliance, in the case of the passive, we may expect this to result from new generations of polymers that exhibit human skin-like mechanical characteristics; such as stress relaxation. Just in case anyone is wondering what this term refers to, stress relaxation is the property some materials have (particularly plastic or rubber type substances), of applying forces but only for a short time. (Laziness, I call it.) I don't know if you have ever had an experience similar to the one I had a few years ago - of fitting a tap with a rubber washer into a hole in a kitchen sink (Belfast type sink, as a matter of fact). Well, using your special box spanners bought for the job, you tighten the nut that holds the tap in place. You get it good and tight – applying as much force as you can. Then, after a few minutes you check that the nut is tight and, lo and behold, it's not! You find that you can quite easily turn it – the reason for this is that the rubber washer has undergone stress relaxation. In the case of active compliance, the robot needs a sequence of motion commands that will correspond, in real time, to the information from its vision and tactile senses. The best way of generating these commands automatically is likely to be to again employ machine learning, with networks that have been previously trained on very similar tasks, using the task nature and sensory data as the input, and the needed motion commands as output.

The above discussion has become rather more technically detailed than intended; and it is likely that some of the approaches utilised and certainly terminology employed in the humanoid robotic systems of the far future will be rather different from what we currently envisage. But this does not alter the central conclusion that, in the future, robotic systems will emerge that will be able to do many of the difficult and dangerous tasks that are currently manually undertaken.

The presence amongst us of impressive human-shaped robots, or androids as I should call them, was, of course, introduced to us, or at least our imaginations, a long time ago now - in the previously mentioned anthology *I, Robot*. The stories therein were surely among the most impressive studies of the roles androids could play in society with interesting situations that can arise, as have ever been penned. Asimov created a robot named Robbie and went so far as to imagine the discipline of robot psychology, which is practiced in his stories by a Dr Susan Calvin, who is discussed in more detail below.

Perhaps even more famous than Robbie though is, of course, Data, for whom the STNG writers explored robots' rights in relation to their claim to be sentient beings as well as their right to be parents. These concepts are explored in depth in the STNG episodes 'Measure of a Man' and 'The Offspring'. In the latter, Data creates for himself a daughter named Lal – with impressive if not entirely successful results that lead to a moving ending.

Therefore, various factors make it likely that robots of the far future will be humanoid in form but capable of super-human performance in many respects – or at least that's my view. This kind of talk reminds me of what my old maths teacher used to tell us back in the 1970s – specifically that, in the future, humans will not spend their time working but instead will have to fill their abundant leisure time. He qualified this by saying that this would not occur in our lifetimes (or even that of our children). He was certainly right about that last point. In any case, there can be little doubt that in the far future robots will be a great help to humans – but will they also constitute a threat?

The androids Data and Lal from the STNG episode The Offspring; Data created Lal to be his daughter. (Drawing by the author.)

Robot dystopia

"In movies and in television the robots are always evil. I guess I am not into the whole brooding cyberpunk dystopia thing."

- Daniel H. Wilson

As mentioned, Hollywood usually depicts the future, at least when it comes to robots, as rather more of a dystopia than a utopia (consider, for example,

Westworld, Futureworld, Terminator, Blade Runner, Picard, and so on). Is this rather negative view of the promise of robotics in any way justified? Well, one thing that needs to be stated early on in such a debate is that, despite much discussion in various quarters to the contrary, currently robots cannot *think*. They do not demonstrate any ability to generate new data of the type associated with an original thought and since they don't think, it is hard to see how they could have the negative thoughts about humans that would surely be a prerequisite for them forming any kind of threat.

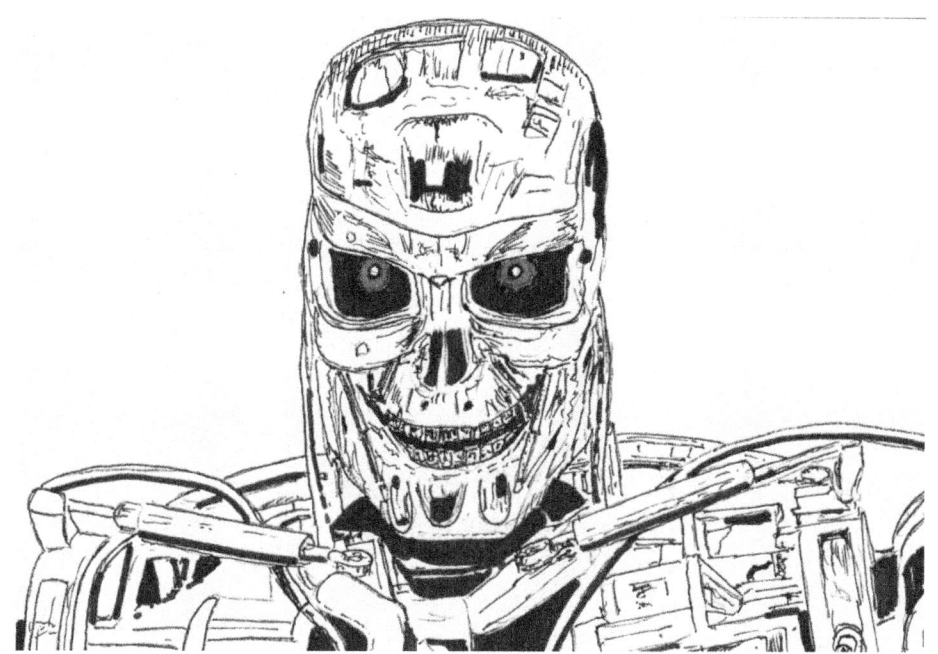

The robotic future is often depicted as dystopian. (Illustration by the author.)

Many speculators on the possible threats from robotics, even some who claim to have academic credentials, presumably take the robot dystopia line in the hope that it will be controversial – stirring up something of a fuss may, for example, help them to sell some copies of a new book. A few years ago, I attended a public lecture given by a speaker who is a professor of robotics at a well-known English university. He was stating that, within a few years, computers will be capable of original thought and will have intelligences well in excess of humans. One of the things he said he had been working on was a new type of neural network that (for some reason that was not entirely clear) somehow incorporated animal tissue. There was a Q&A session in relation to this where one of the audience members asked him if this NN had self-generated any kind of data – the speaker had to reluctantly reply that it had not. This is an important point I feel, since it relates to scientific method.

Nearly always, if we can expect something to become a scientific or technological reality in the near future, then we will have seen movements towards it – reported in journal papers and, ultimately, the media. The fact that the speaker's NNs had generated absolutely no new data so far does not provide an indication that NNs – or any type of artificial intelligence, will be generating new thoughts beyond those of man's capability within a few years. And, surprise, surprise, his predictions have indeed not come true. Perhaps someone should ask such people what they were on about in the speech they gave, and where the thinking robots they predicted to now be in existence, actually are.

If you ask me, the hyperbole they employ to get attention is, rather like certain movie creations, likely to produce unrealistic expectations that can lead to widespread disappointment and disillusionment in science/technology. It also has to be mentioned that media reports state that as far back as 1991, the same academic was predicting "real life Terminators" within ten years. Uh, if they existed in 2001, I didn't notice them. Everyone wants attention but talking twaddle in order to get it really will not do. Getting headlines for your predictions is not as important as getting your predictions right.

Another example of the reality gap between what the public believes current robots are capable of, and what they can actually do, is provided by the humanoid robot, Sophia. This sophisticated robot puppet certainly exhibits a clever combination of facial expressions – well coordinated with speech. It has, in fact, captured the public's imagination, having appeared on national TV chat shows, magazine covers, tech conferences, as well as, get this, delivering a speech to the United Nations! Most amazingly though, according to 2017 media reports, Sophia was officially named a citizen of Saudi Arabia – can you believe that? In reality, Sophia represents a curious combination of theatrics and technology. Robots have always excelled at arm waving theatrics, rather than actual useful tasks, but in the case of Sophia, theatrical tricks attribute more awareness or intelligence to the robot than it actually has. In other words, it is puppetry – a figure appears, onto which the audience projects the attributes of personality or intelligence, whereas in reality, those attributes are not actually present. Some members of the general public (but not actual AI/robotics scientists) are convinced that Sophia the robot has intelligence comparable to that of humans (which is also termed general intelligence). This, of course, is not the case; rather, Sophia is essentially a computer running a chatbot program (in case you are wondering what a chatbot is, it's a computer program that simulates human conversation through voice commands or text chats or both – rather like Amazon's Alexa and Google Assistant). Some responses are pre-programmed, either as responses to questions it expects will be commonly asked or programmed in ahead of time before specific interviews (it is standard practice in TV interviews to communicate the questions the host intends to ask).

218

The sophisticated robot puppet Sophia. (Drawing by the author.)

The programming of Sophia also seems to include conversational algorithms. These respond to common patterns in typical conversation; however, problems arise when, due to a lack of general intelligence, the robot does not recognise the significance of the subject matter of the question and so generates a response that seems wildly out of place or is even alarming. An infamous example of this that involved Sophia was the following exchange:

Interviewer: "Will you destroy humans? Please say no."

Sophia: *Blank face* "OK. I will destroy humans."

Here the robot has failed to appreciate the importance of the question – or at least I hope it has! AI researchers are, in fact, quite dismissive of Sophia. I will end this discussion of this robot by quoting some observations of it made by one of the most famous AI researchers of them all, specifically, Facebook's head of AI research, Yann LeCun (who is also the person credited with the invention of CNNs). On Facebook, LeCun has described a *Tech Insider* interview with Sophia as "complete bullshit" and has said: "This is to AI as prestidigitation is to real magic." Perhaps we should call this "Cargo Cult AI" or "Potemkin AI" or "Wizard-of-Oz AI". In other words, it's complete bullshit (pardon my French). *Tech Insider*: you are complicit in this scam." LeCun concluded his Facebook post by saying that "...at the end of the day, what's really happening is that people are being deceived." and "This is hurtful". No doubt, but the thing many can't get over is the device calmly stating that it will destroy humans. While it is obvious that this is, in truth, just a symptom of Sophia's lack of understanding, many have taken it as some form of portent of the threat robots could pose to society. But is there any basis for such fears and if so, how could we minimise the risks?

These questions were in fact considered over 70 years ago by the well-known science fiction writer, Isaac Asimov, who came up with the idea of combining rules within a robot's programming to eliminate the risk (a reasonable approach I would say). He subsequently formulated his three famous rules of robotics in his story 'Runaround', (part of his *I, Robot* story collection); these are:

1. A robot may not injure a human being or, through inaction, allow a human being to come to harm.

2. A robot must obey the orders given it by human beings except where such orders would conflict with the First Law.

3. A robot must protect its own existence as long as such protection does not conflict with the First or Second Law.

These laws would, however, only be effective for robots that were at similar levels of intellectual development as the machines we have currently. In other words, as long as the robot brain retains some resemblance to a complex calculator, we may be able to assume that Asimov's rules would be obeyed. But what happens if in the far future the complexity of deep learning (or whatever other algorithms/approaches are adopted in AI in the future that may provide a closer analogy to how the human brain works), reaches a level where the robot might be considered to be conscious?

If a robot were capable of exhibiting a degree of self-awareness, it would be, to some extent, able to think for itself. In this scenario, the machine could be capable of original thought and so could, for example, decide for itself whether to obey human commands in various situations. It is not difficult to imagine situations where the decisions it makes could have very serious consequences. For example, if the machine did display some levels of self-awareness, it does not seem unreasonable that this might also be accompanied by a preference for self-preservation. In this case, the extent to which this is expressed in its original thoughts and actions would be in competition with the influence that its original programming (with Asimov's three rules), has in determining its behaviour. In such a situation, one could hardly blame one of our distant descendants if they decided they did not wish to trust the robot's mercy in situations where helping humans might lead to its own destruction.

Here we are effectively discussing robot psychology, and this was a subject Asimov touched on in his *I, Robot* stories. He went so far as to employ the term 'robopsychology' to refer to the study of the personalities and behaviour of intelligent machines. Asimov even created a robopsychologist, Dr Susan Calvin, who he described as working for US Robot and Mechanical Men Inc. - manufacturers of his fictional robots. Dr Calvin is involved in tales that concern the solution to problems related to intelligent robot behaviour. Asimov's robopsychology is essentially concerned with combinations of mathematical analysis and traditional psychology, for explaining/predicting robot behaviour. An interesting combination, is it not?

Dr Susan Calvin and one of Isaac Asimov's fictional robots, in a book cover illustration by Les Edwards. (Illustration used with the permission of Les Edwards, www.lesedwards.com.)

Part of the anticipated interaction between robots and humans seems to be influenced by the 'Frankenstein complex' – the irrational fear that robots (or other creations) will attack their creator. However, it is worth noting that this has more to do with human psychology than the actual nature of robots. What are the origins of the Frankenstein complex? It can be viewed as a superstitious, and almost religious, feeling that the human creator has gone beyond what he/she should know and do. It's as if, by bringing an inanimate object to life in the form of man, they have trespassed somehow into God's realm.

221

Interestingly, in 1977 The Alan Parsons Project released an album that was originally intended to relate to Isaac Asimov's classic stories *I, Robot*, and Eric Woolfson actually spoke to Asimov about it, who was reported as being enthusiastic. However, the rights to the *I, Robot* stories had already been sold, so the comma was dropped and the record was adapted to a more general theme of human versus artificial intelligence. The title of the final track, 'Genesis Ch. 1 v.32', also makes a religious reference, by implying that humans made robots in their image, as a continuation to the story of Creation (the first chapter of Genesis only has 31 verses). The Frankenstein Complex has then, more to do with ancient fears, and also perhaps a natural fear of the unknown, than it has with advanced technology. For filmmakers, it also represents an opportunity to generate an emotional response in the viewer, thereby making them feel more involved and so increasing interest in the movie. This may well explain why a dystopian robot future is so commonly portrayed by Hollywood – even in the film *I, Robot*, (which is in contrast to Asimov's book – the latter being quite positive about the future of robotics and portraying robots as useful and powerful tools). Despite all these pessimistic views of the future, what reason do we have to suppose that robots that possess a degree of artificial intelligence would be hostile to humans? Precious little I would say. Consider, for example, a future where they have some intelligence and self-awareness, but at a much lower level than that of humans. This is, I suggest, somewhat similar to the situation for animals – dogs, for example. Do dogs have a strong desire to kill humans – surely not – in fact they are known as 'man's best friend'! However limited their intelligence may be, it is sufficient to enable them to, at some level, appreciate that their welfare and that of humans is intertwined. Then, the other possibility is that robots come to possess much greater intelligence and mental function than that of humans. This is a difficult scenario to imagine since mankind has far greater intelligence than any other beings of which he is aware or of which he has experience. Nevertheless, what advantage or benefit could such a robot obtain from attacking or destroying humans? Also, would not far greater intelligence also imply a higher level of ethical and moral awareness? Just as we judge that it is wrong to be cruel to and abuse animals that are less developed intellectually than ourselves, surely a super-intelligent robot would feel similar empathy and responsibility towards mankind.

The very distant future

"Even though the future seems far away, it is actually beginning right now."

- Mattie Stepanek

Our discussions so far deal largely with technologies that are similar to those that already exist, but which are in a state of greater development. One reason for starting from such a base is that it seems quite likely that systems that, to some extent, already exist will be amenable to extension in capabilities or performance. But can we make a leap of the imagination to envision what new and radically different capabilities might exist in the more remote future? Possibly we can approach this by first thinking of the current limiting factors of modern technology. In my view, one of the most limiting factors in modern science and technology is the instruments and tools that are available to us to undertake various tasks – or to be more specific, their limited capabilities. Consider, for example, a turbo-fan engine on a modern jet aircraft. This device requires inspection and maintenance and, consequently, there needs to be accessibility for instruments such as borescopes (endoscopes for jet engines) and repair tools. The power to weight requirements and limited space mean that such access is very limited – and this occasionally leads to wear/damage being missed during inspection, and sub-optimal repairs being undertaken that can sometimes, although thankfully rarely, have disastrous consequences. Can we avoid this by giving machines the power to self-evaluate/inspect and to effect repairs automatically? This is not as fanciful as it seems – computer systems (which, it could be argued, are currently rather more technologically advanced than machines), already have facilities for automatic system analysis and optimisation. Can such capabilities be built into machines? The answer must be yes. We already see this to a limited extent in the sensors systems of modern automobiles – but although such systems can flag problems, self-repair is not yet an available option. Self-analysis is, of course, the more straightforward part; we can imagine the machines of the future employing multitudes of sensors, including miniature cameras, with suitable lenses and LED lighting, and deep learning for image interpretation and identification of features indicating damage. But what about effecting the repair? This may be somewhat less straightforward. Perhaps, ultimately, the answer is to build machines from composite structures, with surfaces of high complexity – so much so that they themselves comprise machines (we may call them 'smart structures'). If a smart structure were of sufficient complexity, possibly implemented through nanotechnology, then it could itself be capable of performing repairs. For example, if within an engine a certain amount of needed material were missing from a critical structure or surface, then the smart structure would secrete the appropriate amount of the requisite substance, possibly using a chemical deposition process or some species of miniaturised 3D printing (or rapid prototyping as it is often currently known). If such capabilities were installed in an aircraft of the future, it could certainly provide enhanced safety performance, since possible faults could be automatically detected and corrected in flight. This would also eliminate the weight and expense currently associated with multiple back–up systems as they currently exist on aircraft – since if one system were subject to continuous close monitoring and repair, we could be so sure of its ability to function that back-ups would not be needed. It is, therefore, clear that advanced systems for automatic monitoring and repair could give us some very attractive capabilities; but can we go farther still so as to imagine a completely different approach to science and technology – one where our current notions of instruments and tools would be obsolete?

Elimination of the need for instrumentalities
"Elegance is elimination."

- Cristobal Balenciaga

In the previously mentioned film *Forbidden Planet*, after Dr Morbius arrives on the planet Altair, he discovers a laboratory built by an advanced and long extinct civilisation of beings – the *Krell*. One of the devices in this lab is a machine that can effectively boost a person's intellectual capability. Morbius tries using it on himself and receives such a jolt from it that he is rendered unconscious for two weeks. However, his brave experiment was not in vain, since he found that he had, in fact, received a brain boost that had doubled his IQ (which, by the way, was what enabled him to tinker together Robby the Robot within a couple of weeks). It seems that the Krell spent quite a lot of time getting brain boosts and that they reached some dizzying intellectual heights – so much so that they *eliminated the need for physical instrumentalities*. Wow, if you ask me that was a great move – imagine getting things done without having to break your back! (Personally, I would like to service my car without having to fool around with spanners and such.) It turns out that the Krell were controlling things remotely, if you will, using the power of thought. Unfortunately for them, it seems they forgot about the subconscious id – or the animal part of the mind (according to Freudian psychology, the id is the primitive/instinctual element of the human mind that hosts sexual/aggressive drives and hidden memories). Their ids turned around and created monsters that destroyed them. I am not sure if this is another manifestation of the Frankenstein Complex; but let's consider the possibility of eliminating the need for physical instrumentalities without a consequent annihilation. Is there any possibility that we could implement the effects of tooling and instruments by thoughts rather than physical actions? In deciding questions of such possibilities, it is worth considering whether the proposed act contradicts any established laws of physics – if it does, then we can effectively say it is not possible. However, if it does not, we can say that it is in fact possible and, more than that, that we expect it will, at some time in the future, be commonplace. 'Telekinesis' is defined as the supposed ability to move objects at a distance by mental power. We can ignore any supernatural connotations this word may have – we are not concerned with superstition or magic (although regarding the latter, it will be remembered that Clarke's Third Law states that any sufficiently advanced technology is indistinguishable from magic). But moving things around by the power of thought is, in fact, not such a wacky idea and we don't need to resort to the supernatural to imagine how it might be achieved. It is well known that brain activity can be detected using suitable instruments. According to Wikipedia: "Electroencephalography (EEG) is an electrophysiological monitoring method to record electrical activity of the brain." Having a bit of an aversion to long words, I prefer to refer to it as detection of brainwaves – in any case, it is usually performed by simply placing electrodes directly on the scalp. EEG is frequently used to diagnose epilepsy through analysis of abnormalities in EEG readings; but is there any possibility that it could also offer potential to eliminate physical instrumentalities?

In August 2019, I was endeavouring to present a paper at an optics/photonics conference that was being held at the Convention Center in San Diego. By the way, if you ask me, this is a great city – or America's finest city, as the locals call it. If you ever visit, please do go to Balboa Park, which is a 1,200-acre historic urban cultural park. It boasts beautiful open space areas, gardens, and paths, as well as interesting buildings that contain museums, several theatres, and of course, the famous San Diego Zoo.

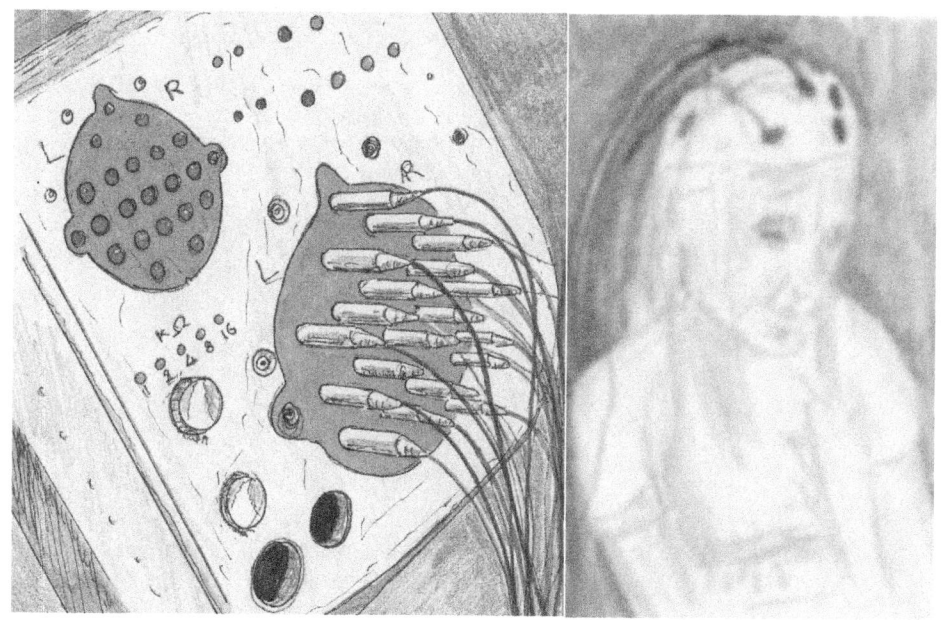

Electroencephalography (EEG) measures electrical activity of the brain and is usually performed by simply placing electrodes directly on the scalp. (Illustrations by author.)

As you can see below, I had a poster for the paper (which was about weed detection in grass using deep learning) and, as you can imagine, I was having a lot of trouble keeping order in all the crowds of people who were surging forward to see my paper (I wish). I waited quite a while but did eventually get to chat with a few interesting people. Patience is a virtue, I guess.

225

Part of Balboa Park, San Diego, California, where the 2019 photonics conference was held. Here is a photonics joke: A Photon checks into a hotel and the receptionist asks if he needs any help with his luggage. "No thanks," says the Photon "I'm travelling light." (Photograph by the author.)

Me, waiting for the crowds to arrive, next to a poster for the paper I presented at the 2019 photonics conference. (Photograph by the author. I have compressed this picture horizontally, to make myself appear thinner!)

Anyway, in the quietude of the hall concerned, I noticed that the guy next to me was presenting a paper on, yes, you've guessed it, brainwave analysis. Thinking about it now, I am not sure what his work had to do with optics, but it was interesting. As far as I could see, the researcher was using deep learning for some form of data pre-processing. In other words, he was only doing some preliminary analysis rather than being able to detect specifics about thoughts. For example, he could not tell that his subject was thinking of 'going for a walk in the countryside on a sunny day, while eating an ice-cream' - it was more on the level of being able to determine whether the person was bored, or excited. Of course, it is early days; but it is known that brainwaves are divided into bandwidths (or frequencies, rather like the pitch of sounds in air), which may be related to their meaning. They seem to reflect a continuous spectrum of waves (analogous to the continuous spectrum of colours in the rainbow), that may reflect our experiences of consciousness; from slow, well defined events - to fast, subtle, and complex interactions.

I suspect that once we know more about the actual associations of various features of complex brainwaves, it will prove possible to analyse them sufficiently to obtain useful thought information. Such a capability would obviously be a boon to those people suffering from serious paralysis who are unable to communicate conventionally.

It probably does not surprise you to know that this is another area where the future-thinker, Elon Musk, is setting the pace. He has set up a company called Neuralink which will supply a brain implant and the robotic device to implant it with the aim of helping such paralysed people. Work to date has involved tests with animals, including insertion of a Neuralink implant in a pig for two months, with the latter apparently remaining healthy. Musk has shown graphics which he says indicate the pig's movements with a "high degree of accuracy", and he says other graphics show electrodes influencing neurons. Neuralink has said it has received breakthrough device designation from the US Food and Drug Administration – which would certainly appear to boost its chances of being introduced in the USA (following clinical trials in humans). Neuralink is certainly ambitious - Matthew MacDougall, their head neurosurgeon, has said the device could allow it to interface with the brain's motor cortex, as well as sensory information, hearing and visual processing. In fact, Musk has been quoted as saying: "You could solve blindness, paralysis, hearing just by interfacing with the cortex," He has said that although initially the technology might be expensive, his aim is to get the price down to a few thousand dollars "inclusive of the automated surgery".

Sounds good to me! Elon Musk is certainly a 'get on with it' kind of guy, as well as someone who has a great deal of forward vision – and I admire him for it. It is surely innovators like him who are going to be pivotal in realising our affordable Martian commute (as discussed above, his company SpaceX is currently working on a plan for a rocket to take humans to Mars).

Perhaps technologies such as Neuralink's could render the communication blocks involved in 'locked in syndrome' a thing of the past – I certainly hope so. Regarding moving objects around by means of thought, the difficult part is capturing the thought's intention, as just discussed.

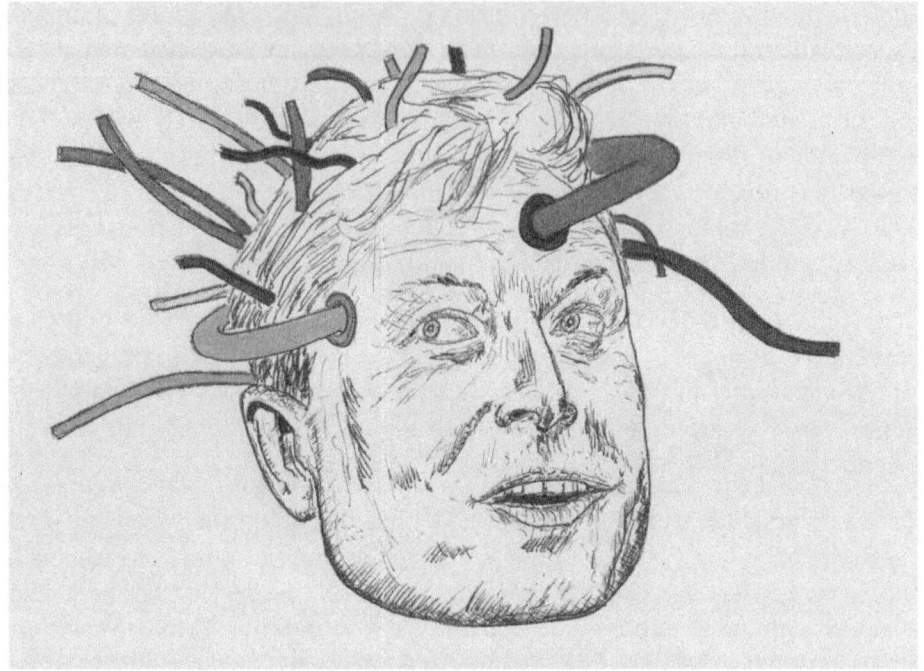

The billionaire entrepreneur Elon Musk is developing a brain-reading implant called Neuralink. (Illustration by the author.)

Once a person's wish is known, it would be a relatively simple task to employ robotics, automation, or even a simple transfer mechanism, to implement the required move of the object in question. There are, in fact, many applications in a wide range of sectors that could benefit very significantly from this kind of ability to move by the power of thought. In combination with suitable servos and/or hydraulic systems, such a capability could constitute an impressive and very helpful tool. We can imagine, for example, the construction worker on a building site who wishes that a huge concrete section could be transported to the top of a new building and, hey presto, a suitably equipped and interfaced crane could achieve this feat automatically. For a person from a previous era this would indeed appear like magic and it would surely constitute a step towards being able to eliminate industrial instrumentalities.

Many years ago when I was a small child, my Mother used to say to me: "I wonder what the next thing will be" (by which she meant the next striking technological innovation)…" They say it will be that you will be able to hear music in the mid-air". I never realised it at the time, but what she was talking about was essentially the full elimination of the need for instrumentalities. I was going to end this chapter here, but again find myself under the necessity of stopping the press. A few days ago, I heard on the news about a new device that puts 'music in your head', without the need for headphones. Apparently, 'sound beaming' technology employs a 3D sensing module that tracks the user's ear position and sends audio via ultrasonic waves, to create sound pockets by the ears. The result is sound that can be heard in stereo or a spatial 3-D mode that creates '360 degree' sound around the listener. So, I guess Mum was right, and a device that allows you to listen to 'music in the mid-air', has been invented.

Time travel

"People like us, who believe in physics, know that the distinction between past, present, and future is only a stubbornly persistent illusion."

– Albert Einstein

The ability to travel through time is certainly a fascinating concept, so it is not surprising that ever since the emergence of the book *The Time Machine*, over 100 years ago, writers of science fiction and fantasy have frequently returned to it as a plot focus. Let's first consider travel into the past. This is about as close to impossible as we are ever going to get in this Universe. There simply are no creditable physics-based laws, or even theories, that could accommodate travel backwards in time. There are also two practical considerations that indicate it is not possible:

1. If it were possible, people from the future (and large numbers of people at that), would have already travelled backwards from the future to be with us. We can be pretty sure they have not done so, since concealment of men/women from the future would be effectively impossible.

2. The concept of traveling backwards in time generates a multitude of paradoxes that have no reasonable resolution. For example, suppose I travelled backwards and met and killed my grandfather when he was a young man. That would mean I would never have been born and, if I was not born, I could not have travelled back and killed him, which would mean that I could have been born…

That is not to say that it is impossible to look into the past, at least to some extent. I don't know if you have ever used a telescope to look closely at the Sun. This can certainly be a fascinating experience – you can easily make out the solar flares (huge plumes) that occur occasionally, as well as interesting sunspots (cooler regions) on the surface. When you do this you are not looking at the Sun as it appears at exactly that instant but, in fact, you are looking into the past – and seeing phenomena on the Sun that existed around eight minutes previously. I have done this myself. For the last 40 years, I have had a 3-inch Newtonian reflector and I strongly recommend astronomy with a small telescope – or even a good pair of binoculars – as a fascinating hobby.

My 3-inch reflector telescope – excellent for lunar, solar, and planetary observation. (Photograph by the author.)

To be honest, a 3-inch reflector is a little too small to get brilliant viewing of distant/dim objects such as nebulae and galaxies, but it is ideal for studying the planets and for lunar and solar observation. On more than one occasion, I have managed to impress friends and visitors by showing them the four main moons of Jupiter and the 'ears' of Saturn (in 1610 Galileo said Saturn had ears – he was surely referring to the beautiful rings, but the telescopes of his time did not provide the resolution he needed to see them for what they really were). In such a telescope, details of lunar features such as mountains can also be clearly seen, and I once even observed a transit of Venus across the Sun. I must mention though, that if you do wish to observe the Sun, be sure to use the telescope to project its image onto a screen; some telescopes do include a filter designed for solar observation, but projection is by far the safest approach.

Apologies for the telescope digression, but my point is that astronomical observations involve looking into the past – the only question is how far back we are looking – which depends upon the distance of the object concerned. By the way, the most distant object that can be observed with the naked eye is the Andromeda Galaxy. If you live away from cities and street lighting, have a look for it near the Cassiopeia constellation on a very clear night. It is very dim but also surprisingly large – about the same apparent size as the moon, which also gives you an idea of how big it is when you appreciate that it is 2.5 million light years from Earth. Good grief; how far is that? (Actually, it's about 14.7 trillion miles.) If you manage to do this, you really will be looking 2.5 million years into the past! Some science fiction writers have imagined aliens with excellent telescopes who point them towards Earth and thereby can take a peek into our history. This is, however, a rather unrealistic concept. It is imaginable that someone on the Moon, with a very high-resolution telescope, may be able to point it towards the Earth and make out some (large scale) features of interest. In doing so, they would be looking into the past by around 2.5 seconds. It is not, however, reasonable to assume that they could make out any human-scale features. Regarding aliens, such observers would be many light year's distant - far too remote to resolve any features of interest since the light would have spread out and dramatically diminished before reaching them. (Intensity of a light from a body such as the Earth varies with $1/d^2$, where d is the distance of the observer; so, as you can imagine, as d becomes extremely large the intensity becomes vanishingly low.)

So, although journeys into the past are not on the cards, what about travel into the future? Actually, this is entirely possible and does not contravene any of the laws of physics. A favourite way of accomplishing it in science fiction and fantasy stories, is for the would-be time traveller to expose themselves to a 'metabolic-reduction' agent, or something similar. Am not sure if you have seen the *Twilight Zone* episode where a group of bank robbers plan to hide in a cave with their stolen heist until the police have stopped looking for them. Their idea was to spend around 50 years each in a glass case into which a special gas was to be pumped to send them to sleep for the duration. Unfortunately for one of them, a rock fell from the cave roof and cracked his case causing the gas to seep out, so that by the time the others awoke he consisted of little other than a skeleton. Such complications might be avoided by simply locating oneself near a very massive body and relying on general relativity time dilation. Einstein's great work, his theory of general relativity, proposed that space and time are distorted near a massive body, causing time to pass more slowly; and the closer you are to the object's centre of gravity, the more pronounced the effect. If a person ventured towards such a massive object, they would not notice that time was slowing, but if they then left and travelled back to their comrades, they would discover the latter to now be slightly older than themselves. For the same reason, we might expect the Apollo astronauts to be somewhat older than the rest of us, due to the fact that they spent some time away from the Earth and on an object that is significantly less massive than the Earth – specifically the Moon. The effect would, however, only be minimal and would have been lessened by the accelerations they experienced during their voyage – particularly the launch from Cape Canaveral (time dilation is caused by both gravity and accelerations). To explore the effects of time dilation due to gravity, we can do no better than look to the science fiction film *Interstellar*. Here, some travellers are in a spacecraft that approaches 'Miller's Planet' – an ocean world that is located near a black hole.

A scene from the film *Interstellar*, where the robot Tars is rescuing an astronaut on Miller's Planet, an ocean world. Astronauts visit the planet, but it is near to a black hole that causes severe time dilation, so that by the time the astronauts return, 23 years have elapsed for their colleague on the spacecraft. This is an example of time dilation due to gravity – which is described in Einstein's theory of general relativity. (Illustration by the author.)

Some of them decide to go down to the planet surface while the other remains in orbit. They have some trouble in an ocean on the surface – due to an enormous tidal wave caused by the proximity of the black hole. Things are sorted out, largely due to the intervention of the robot TARS (a device which I am sure would be very useful in the home – or anywhere else come to that). However, the tidal wave did cause them to spend a few more hours on the surface than expected, with the result that when they re-joined their colleague in the spacecraft they found that while they had been on the surface, 23 years had passed for him! God he must have been bored – 23 years flying around in a tin can waiting for his friends to sort out a simple job on a planet. The important point is though, that the two travellers had been exposed to a very high gravitational field which had slowed down time for them and effectively enabled them to travel into the future.

I got the power

"All peoples everywhere should have free energy sources."

- Nikola Tesla

One thing that is needed in the field of implementation of advanced technology is a lightweight source capable of delivering large amounts of power. Throughout most of history, the only power sources available to man were his own muscles and those of domesticated/trained animals. Some hundreds of years ago, mill owners implemented windmills or water wheels for driving their equipment, thereby indirectly harnessing the power of the Sun. In fact, all power sources, except for nuclear power, ultimately rely on the Sun as their energy. The Industrial Revolution was the era where fossil fuels began their reign as the dominant power source and that era is only just beginning to come to a close.

One motivator for moving away from fuels such as coal and oil is of course the carbon emission generated by combustion and the associated greenhouse effects of carbon dioxide causing global warming, which was discussed above in some detail.

By the way, the concept that nuclear power does not contribute to global warming is an error, since mining and processing of uranium involves a large and continuous emission of carbon dioxide, not to mention the emissions associated with building and running the actual nuclear power station and transporting nuclear fuel. Also, large amounts of carbon dioxide are likely to be released when attempting to deal with the spent fuel and radioactive waste that the nuclear fission generates. And, of course, the fuel involved, uranium, is like, for example oil, a limited resource and not continuously renewable such as is the case for wind, solar, and tidal power. The 43rd President of the United States George Walker Bush is apparently among those who have made the error of believing that nuclear generation represents a renewable power source (perhaps not surprising when considering other errors he made - such as starting the Iraq War - which is generally considered to have been a gigantic mistake).

This statement is based on the following quote attributed to George: "Obviously, nu-que-lar power is, uh, a renewable source of energy, and the less demand there is for non-renewable sources of energy, like fossil fuels, the better it off it is for the American people." And this was from the leader of the Free World! Good grief!

Actually, in the portrait below he looks like quite a nice guy – in a simple-minded kind of way.

George W. Bush, who apparently believes that nuclear power is a renewable power source and that the Iraq War was a good idea. (Drawing by the author.)

Recently, I was just looking up various quotes by the 43rd President of the United States – there is so much good material there, surely a whole book could be devoted to it; here is one of my favourites:

"The vast majority of our imports come from outside the country."

- George W. Bush

And what about this for sheer profundity:

"I think we agree, THE PAST IS OVER."

- George W. Bush

It is undeniably true that nuclear power produces less CO_2 per kWh of electricity than traditional fossil fuel generation; but then nuclear also generates some pretty appalling radioactive waste that can remain a danger to humans for hundreds of millennia. There can be little doubt that such a relatively old-fashioned and dirty power generation technology as nuclear fission can only be viewed as some kind of stop-gap technology and that we can't look to it as a major power source for the future.

What then, is left to us? Renewables, of course. These technologies have been under-funded and under-exploited over many generations as a result of a pronounced and seemingly unaccountable bias of many people, particularly politicians, towards nuclear power. This may have had its origins in the Cold War, and particularly the race after World War II to be the first nation after America to have a nuclear weapon capability. Uranium reactors do, after all, produce plutonium – which is very well suited to making atomic bombs, but which is also extremely toxic. Plutonium is an artificial metal and it's one that may have the dubious claim of being the most dangerous material ever to be manufactured.

Regarding renewable power, there is something very laudable about having a power source that does not contribute to global warming and which costs very little to run beyond routine maintenance costs. Devices such as wind turbines and solar panels are, then, making a valuable contribution by feeding into the national grid. While on this subject, I would say it should be much easier for each of us to simply buy one such device from the internet or high street stores, install it at home, plug it in, and start doing our bit for tackling global warming. Similarly, I spend an hour per day on my exercise bike, finding that when I have finished, the body of the machine has become warm through dissipation of the mechanical energy as heat. It would again make much more sense if I could plug the bike into the mains and have my efforts contribute in a modest way to the nation's power. It would also be an incentive for me to put in as much effort as possible thereby also helping me to keep in shape – but currently the modest task of retailing such a bike seems to be too much to ask. And of course, if millions of others had the same idea as me, the contribution wouldn't be modest at all.

Considering the threat we face from global warming, it is inevitable that in the future more use will be made of renewable power generation. Many large companies are of the same opinion; for example, BP is increasing its low carbon investment by 10 times, to around $5 billion a year, and have stated their intention to become a net zero carbon company by 2050 or sooner to help the world get to net zero carbon emission. We have the future in our hands and capabilities and technologies are emerging to enable us to make it a green one.

Our green future is in our hands. (Illustration by the author.)

A reliable supply of electricity is, of course, very important and essential for modern living, but we also need to go beyond this. Specifically, there is a pressing demand for a lightweight power source. Up until recently, we were dependent upon the old lead-acid accumulator technology of the car battery – which has a very unimpressive power to weight ratio. Things are now, thankfully, finally improving somewhat, with the new types of batteries that are appearing in the latest generations of electric cars. However, even these surely have a long way to go before they reach the power to weight ratio of so antiquated a fuel as petrol.

But what of the future? Electrical power generation does not seem to present a problem, since this can be realised through use of renewables or other non-polluting technologies. Of course, one slight problem with this source of power is that it is often intermittent – there is no guarantee that the wind will be blowing when you happen to want to put the kettle on. Approaches to this in the past have included construction of the Dinorwig power station in Wales, where water is pumped to the top of a mountain when demand is low and then allowed to flow down, generating electricity during periods of peak demand.

The view down toward Dinorwig power station from the slate trail above. (Illustration by the author.)

The problem with this is, apart from it being expensive to build, is that it also tends to be rather expensive to run – friction means that overall it consumes a good deal of electricity itself. One would be lucky to retrieve 80% of the electricity sent for storage, so in the past this meant requiring more electricity to be generated from fossil fuels - hence potentially adding to carbon emissions. This would, of course, be less of an issue in the case of renewable power. Another approach that is rather less wasteful and also able to more quickly respond to demand, would be to store the excess electricity in large scale batteries. Recent battery developments have made this a more realistic prospect than it was in the past, but storage capacities are currently still rather limited. If larger amounts of power are required than could be generated from renewable sources (with storage as required), then we need to look to other methods of electrical power generation. Global warming dictates that we can't go forward with fossil fuels and, as mentioned, nuclear fission is a relatively polluting technology. But what about nuclear fusion? What indeed. How many years have we listened to the promises of fusion power being viable in the near future, while in reality commercial fusion power does not seem much closer now than it was 40 years ago. But let's not give up hope, since if fusion could be made to work it would be a truly great power source; here are a few advantages it would offer:

237

• It's a clean technology in which atoms of hydrogen are fused, producing only helium – so there are no greenhouse gas emissions. Unlike fission, no long-lived radioactive waste is produced in fusion.

• Safety. Getting the fusion to occur is a rather complicated and difficult process – so there is effectively no possibility of a meltdown.

• Abundant fuel source. A fusion reactor would employ deuterium (a type of hydrogen) and lithium. There is enough of these substances in the world's oceans to provide the Earth's population with abundant energy for millions of years...

Fine and dandy. There is just one slight problem: at the moment, it doesn't work – or at least it doesn't work in a way that generates useful power output/electricity. Fusion is the process that takes place in the heart of the Sun and has provided the energy to sustain life on the Earth over the last 5 billion years. It works by fusing light nuclei to form a heavier nucleus, accompanied by releasing bursts of energy (i.e. it's the opposite of the fission that occurs in today's nuclear power stations – where energy is released when a nucleus splits into smaller nuclei). In a nuclear fusion power station, a combination of hydrogen gases, deuterium, and tritium would be heated to extreme temperatures (around 100 million degrees Celsius). This causes the gas to become a plasma and for the nuclei to combine to form a helium nucleus and a neutron. One way to control the intensely hot plasma is to use powerful electromagnets. A ring-shaped magnetic chamber designed for doing this is known as a 'tokamak'. When the extreme temperature is reached, a tiny fraction of the mass is converted into 'fusion' energy. When the plasma contains millions of these reactions every second, a huge amount of energy can be produced from a very small amount of fuel. The reason why it does not currently comprise a power source is that up to now the energy produced by the fusion has been considerably less than the energy put into the chamber to heat and contain the plasma (currently the energy out is only up to 70% of the energy in). But this is not for want of trying; some very talented scientists have worked hard on the problem and some progress has been made. For example, JET – the Joint European Torus, at Culham, is the world's largest tokamak and has produced a world record 16 megawatts of fusion power using deuterium and tritium fuel. Also, General Atomics in San Diego have, since the 1980s, been undertaking fusion research in their DIII-D experimental tokamak fusion reactor.

There are two new fusion developments planned for the UK: STEP - a new UK power plant design activity based on the compact 'spherical tokamak' reactor concept, which aims to deliver net electric power output on a timescale of 2040, and the MAST (Mega Amp Spherical Tokamak) upgrade device. There are also a number of international fusion developments. These include: ITER – a large multinational tokamak that is being built in the south of France with the aim of producing 500 megawatts of fusion power, and DEMO – a European demonstration power station design – which aims to supply fusion electricity to the grid around 2050.

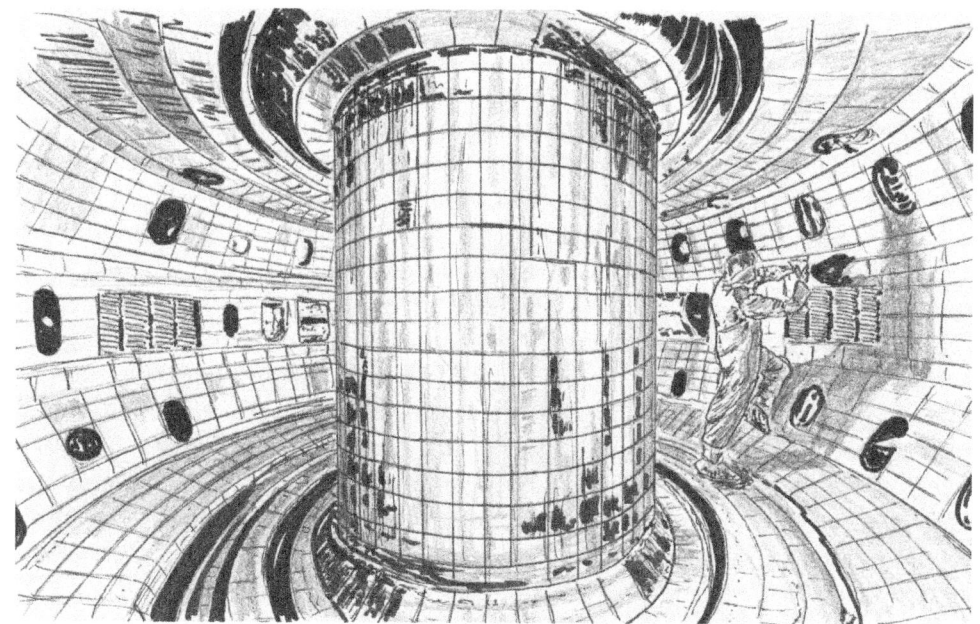

A tokamak fusion reactor operated by General Atomics in San Diego, which has been used in research since it was built in the 1980s. (Illustration by the author.)

Additionally, there are power plant design programmes being developed in various other countries, including China, South Korea, and Japan. Good luck to them all I say! The prospect of clean abundant energy for all our needs is indeed appealing. There is, however, just one cautionary comment that might be worth making. If we were to have access to vast amounts of fusion electricity at very low cost, it is natural that we would wish to exploit it as much as possible. We could, in the winter run as many 'bar fires' as we wish, and there would be little incentive to insulate our homes. In warm climates, air conditioners could be used all summer, and in general all manner of electrical heaters and machines could be employed for a wide range of purposes. All these devices would have one thing in common – they would produce heat (either directly for a heater or through friction in the case of machines). If electricity were truly abundant, the resulting heating could significantly contribute to the warming of the planet. We are all familiar with global warming as being a phenomenon resulting from greenhouse gases such as carbon dioxide and methane in the atmosphere, but up to now we had not considered the possibility of it also being caused by an over-abundance of electrical power.

However, all we need is for the world's tokamak scientists to constantly raise their energy out figure to just above 100% of the energy in, for such an over-abundance to become a real possibility. But, again, I feel the prospect of plenty of useful energy available to help humans in all sorts of ways is an alluring one; it's just the same as for anything else, i.e. we have to treat it responsibly. Call me scurrilous, but I can't help wondering whether, if the $5 billion that was put into the Large Hadron Collider (LHC) at CERN had been put into building a very large scale tokamak, we would be now getting significantly more energy out of fusion reactions than we are putting in. It does, however, have to be acknowledged that in 2012 experiments in the LHC provided significant evidence for the existence of the Higgs boson. This is an important development in theoretical physics, which helps to confirm the existence of various other particles. But what practical use is this in confirming fundamental theories of physics? One such theory, which has been popular in recent decades, is 'string theory'. This essentially suggests that particles are composed of energies that resemble vibrating strings. The particular vibrations of the strings create all the various observed particles and forces, with all matter and forces in the universe being made of these vibrating strings. It might be reasonable to ask whether discovery of the Higgs boson provides evidence that string theory is correct. It may do so to some extent, but according to *Scientific American:* "String theory is formulated in 10 dimensions and has other properties that do not hold in our world. It makes no explicit or testable predictions or explanations, and it has no direct connections to Higgs bosons." So I will just make one comment and then tip-toe away from that one: I have to wonder if it is worth spending so much time and effort on something that "makes no explicit or testable predictions or explanations". Whatever the exact situation regarding Higgs and string theory, there is one thing I know for sure: it is a much better idea to spend a few billion dollars on building a particle accelerator, than spending trillions on wars – which, unfortunately, is something man is wont to do.

From this discussion, we can conclude then that economic and clean generation of electrical power on much larger scales than has been seen up to now, for distribution through grids, is certainly possible and should be achievable within the next few decades. However, making such power available to exactly where it is needed, whether moving on the land or at sea or in the air, is a rather more formidable task. One suggestion might be to miniaturise a fusion power station by building a very small tokamak, with an associated miniature power plant. It must, however, be borne in mind that reducing the scale is not as simple as might be at first thought - the volume inside the reaction chamber would decrease in proportion to the cube of the decrease in the linear dimensions. This is the same reason why you cannot simply scale a human up and expect they would be able to function normally – if you made a person twice as tall, their weight would increase by a factor of 8 and, most likely, their legs would break. It also explains why simple scaling comparisons that you sometimes come across are meaningless – an example of this might be: "if you scaled a flea up to the size of a man, it would be able to jump over Nelson's Column" (in reality, it would not even be able to support its own weight). To summarise, because of scaling considerations and also the laws of physics, it seems very unlikely that we will ever be able to scale down a nuclear fusion reactor power plant to the extent that it could comprise a lightweight mobile power source.

So, what other options might be available to us? Unfortunately, it seems relatively few – unless someone has a brilliant idea that enables a dramatic breakthrough in the future that provides new functionality in this area. One possibility might be to employ high power radio beams – perhaps in the microwave wavelength, to transfer the needed energy. However, we have to remember that microwaves are capable of cooking humans as well as chicken for your roast dinner. Consequently, complex networks of high-power microwave beams, that are moving about and tracking the multitudes of people who need them, does not seem to comprise a safe situation – and so probably does not represent a safe and reliable solution for mobile power. What may be much more likely is some form of power storage – such as a battery with a much greater power to weight ratio than is possible currently. (Recent developments in batteries for electric cars have been encouraging and it seems reasonable to believe that this progress will continue.) Not that the power storage has to occur in the form of an electric battery; some other approach may prove practical, such as very high pressure storage of gases that can drive miniature turbines when released, or heating materials such as metal blocks to very high temperatures and then generating electricity from the resulting temperature differential between the metal and the air, using, for example, thermocouples (working on the same principle as the power that keeps those fans spinning on the top of hot stoves). These are just concepts – we can't specify the details of technological breakthroughs that have not yet occurred – we have to wait for the inventors to do their stuff. It is interesting to note that important advances often accompany dramatic improvements in the performance of materials (for example, in the past, steam engines only became widespread once the metal of their boilers was capable of withstanding high pressure; while in the future power storage devices mentioned above, ultra-high tensile strength will be needed for the material of the pressure container, and excellent thermal/electrical performance will be required for the insulation/thermocouple material). Whatever the exact configuration of the power storage devices of the future, it seems likely that an ability to store energy in such devices at charging stations and then make it available as needed on the move, may well be the most likely solution to the mobile power needs of the future. It may be that to make power readily available across wide regions of the globe would require networks of very large numbers of recharging points – connecting these all to a central power generator using wiring could prove expensive and challenging from an engineering perspective (particularly if they are to be located on the oceans or at altitude). This may be where the charging by radio/microwaves could be employed – so that the charging point would only represent coordinates in space, with no actual hardware being needed at the point in question. In such a scenario, the storage device would only have to move to a charging point and then employ an antenna to receive the energy. Collimated (highly directional) radio waves could be directed to each charging point from various transmission points (which could perhaps even make use of satellites to relay the transmissions all around the globe). In such a situation, the directions of the high-power radio beam (from transmission point to charging point) would be fixed over time, so they would be much less dangerous than employing dynamic/constantly moving beams.

It's a material world

"The materials I use are absolutely essential to the work I make."

- David Batchelor

Since the industrial revolution, we have had machine tools that have helped us to manufacture goods for our never-ending needs. You might have come in contact with these machines at school or college or, of course, at work. The two most ubiquitous examples would be the lathe (used to machine 'axis-symmetric' components such as car axles) and the milling machine (for producing prismatic parts such as cuboidal objects). These are examples of the simple types of machine that could be seen in workshops during most of the 20th century. Nowadays, rather more complicated machine tools that are powered by servo motors and computer controlled, are common. Examples of such machines are 'multi-axis machining centres', which are able to manufacture both axisymmetric and prismatic parts, as well as a good deal more. However, one drawback that these and nearly all conventional machine tools have in common are the limitations associated with the tooling they employ. To express this another way, in order to manufacture an object with a complex morphology, we have to design it so as to allow access for the tool. For example, in the multi-axis machining centre, typical tools include a 'slot drill' (which can be used to cut holes and grooves) and an 'end mill' (employed to machine surfaces). The geometries we can machine are necessarily limited by the need to allow access space for these tools – and this limits the complexities of component designs that can be produced.

What if we could manufacture objects without the need for conventional tooling? Well, that would greatly increase the complexity of parts that we could produce. As a matter of fact, this has already occurred, to a modest extent, through the technology known as Rapid Prototyping (RP – also known as Additive Manufacturing or 3D Printing). This usually involves manufacture of parts from polymers, although for some processes other materials can also be employed. RP processes do indeed dispense with conventional tooling; instead, a computer-controlled system implements 'additive manufacture' where the part is built up a layer at a time. The first RP systems featured expensive computer-controlled laser beams, which scanned across the surface of a photosensitive resin, which was lowered after each scan, thereby building up the part. Actually, this results in a rather floppy, bendy part, which has to be cured by being left in an oven for several hours (the oven, rather than heating, floods its interior with ultraviolet light – the resulting part is hard and quite strong). This process, which is known as stereolithography (SLA), is relatively complicated and expensive – so perhaps it's a bit surprising that it was the first RP process invented.

Nowadays, a more common RP technique is that of fused deposition modelling (FDM), where a small platform is moved with precision in two directions using computer-controlled actuators, while a miniature nozzle on the platform extrudes polymer (heated and under pressure). Consequently, the polymer is laid down in a line – in a way that is analogous to a line of toothpaste being dispensed from a toothpaste tube. Then the platform is lowered and the next layer is formed. FDM parts used to have a reputation of having poorer surface finish and mechanical properties than SLA equivalents, but FDM has been the subject of much development in recent years and the quality of the parts is now quite high.

FDM also has the big advantage of being less expensive than SLA both in terms of the purchase price, maintenance of the machine, and the raw materials used to make the parts. (SLA machines employ expensive ultra-violet lasers that need to be replaced at regular intervals and the photosensitive resin is expensive – as well as being chemically hazardous). Returning to the advantages of RP, since these machines do not employ any conventional tooling, highly complex designs can be readily manufactured. One exciting application that can be enabled by RP technology is that of 'biomimetics'. Here, a Computer Aided Design (CAD) system is used to place some constraints on the design of a new part. For example, the part could be a bracket for an aircraft panel where at two points the bracket is attached to the aircraft wall and the panel. In biomimetics, the actual design of the bracket would be a problem solved through a large number of computer iterations, driven by the aim of increasing the strength to weight ratio of the bracket as much as possible. After several hours, the resulting design often seems to resemble structures found in nature – such as the growth of vegetable matter in trees or vines. The important point is that no matter how complicated the design is, it will still be possible to manufacture it using RP technologies. In this scenario, the factor limiting the complexity of the design is not the usual problem of tooling limitations, but rather the limits to the complexity of the 3D curves that can be formed within the design – which will be dependent upon the curve modelling mathematics employed in the CAD system.

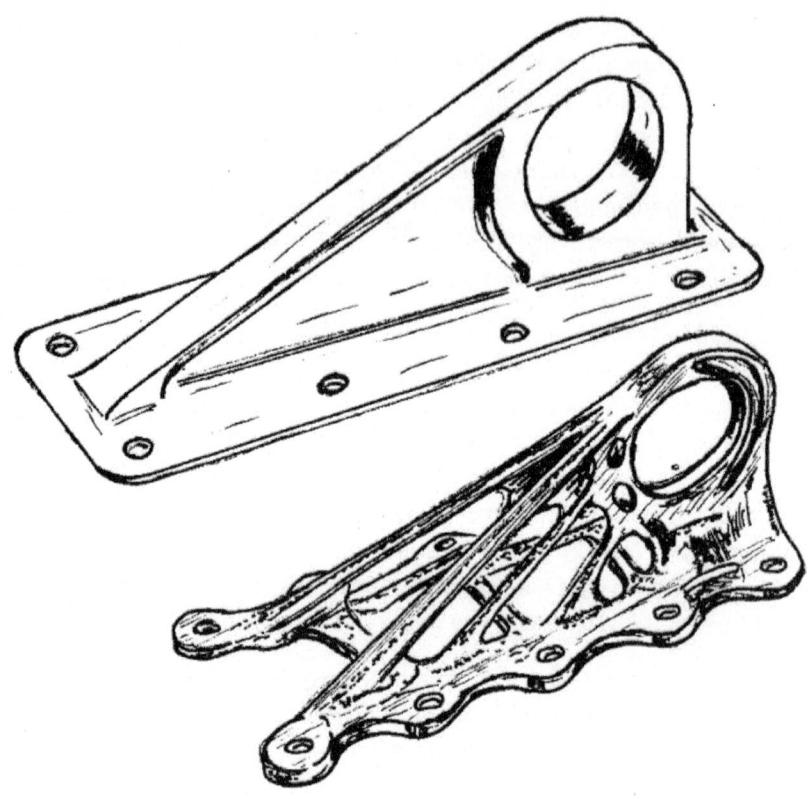

Here a biomimetic aircraft hinge bracket appears below a conventionally manufactured one; the biomimetic part has the same function but less weight than the other. (Pen and ink drawing by the author.)

You might be thinking that this is all well and good, but what real use is it if we are only talking about plastic parts? Actually, this is a view for which I would have some sympathy, since the limitations in the materials that can be produced have traditionally placed rather severe limitations on what can be achieved with RP systems.

There is, however, an RP technology that has emerged in recent years which is known as electron-beam additive manufacturing. This, not surprisingly, uses an electron beam to melt a raw material (metal, in powder or wire form), under a vacuum. The result is a fully dense and complete metal part.

An example of the latest generation of electron-beam additive manufacturing machines. (Drawing by the author.)

RP is a rather exciting technology that is already being employed for direct, rapid manufacture of components (such as the above aircraft bracket example), which are highly optimised in terms of strength vs. weight. Looking to the future, what are the chances of being able to use the RP additive manufacturing approach to build up very complicated objects such as, for example, a motor suitable for powering a car? Successful operation of such a 'replicator' would necessitate building objects up at the atomic or molecular level. Currently with RP, we would be lucky to achieve resolutions at the micron level (a micron is one millionth of a metre). The replicator would require a resolution 1000 times greater than this – we would be talking nanometre resolutions. Not that such a thing is impossible; but the operating concepts of the replicator are likely to be quite different from our current generations of RP machines. For one thing, the replicator would need to be able to work with, and build up, objects employing a vast array of materials (even something as relatively simple as a car engine contains a wide range of different material types and properties). Of course, if the capabilities of the replicator were extremely advanced, so that it could reproduce living tissue, then we might be

245

talking about a device able to effectively transport humans at the speed of light, as in the case of the *Star Trek* transporter mechanism. As discussed above, such a capability would require some extremely advanced functionalities and so may forever be beyond the capabilities of our technologies. However, we by no means have to get to the stage of being able to say, 'Beam me up, Scotty!' to be able to access a replicator device that could be very useful to mankind in a multitude of ways. A replicator operating on the nanoscale and able to manufacture a wide range of highly complex machines seems entirely possible in the future. There is no reason why the replicator could not replicate itself – thereby producing a plethora of replicators that could take care of man's manufacturing needs. The labour savings that such facilities could provide would clearly be profound.

Miscellaneous miracles

I would like, if I may, to now consider various advanced capabilities which have, up to now, existed mostly in science fiction or fantasy stories but which may become part of our reality in the far future.

Invisibility

"I went over the heads of the things a man reckons desirable. No doubt invisibility made it possible to get them, but it made it impossible to enjoy them when they are got."

— H.G. Wells, *The Invisible Man*

In H. G. Wells' fantasy story, *The Invisible Man*, the main character becomes invisible through the ingestion of a substance. Being able to do this is, however, about as near to impossible as it's possible to get due to the complex nature of the human body. The vast array of complex chemicals and structures within a human make the chances of being able to order the molecules in a way that would facilitate perfect transparency virtually impossible. But that is not to say that it is entirely impossible for an individual or object to become invisible; we could, for example, just bend the light rays around the object in question. One way of doing this is to place a material in front of the object to diffract (bend) the light. To do this, we need a material with a negative refractive index – which is not something you find in your average hardware store! In fact, one has to construct something called a 'metamaterial'. This term comes from the Greek word *meta*, meaning 'beyond' and the Latin word *materia*, meaning 'matter' or 'material'. A metamaterial is any material engineered to have a property that is not found in naturally occurring materials. In order to make an object appear invisible, light needs to be guided around the object, rather than just reflected from its surface. In order to do this the metamaterial is often composed of a lattice with the spacing between elements less than the wavelength of the light we wish to bend. Sheets of material have emerged recently that can effectively shield objects from being visible - with quite impressive results - just do a search for, for example, 'HyperStealth' on YouTube. However, some caution is needed regarding invisibility cloaks. Recently a video on the internet of Chen Shiqu, deputy head of the Criminal Investigation Department at China's Ministry of Public Security, went viral with over 21 million views of him demonstrating his unbelievable invisibility cloak. In fact, for many people it really *is* unbelievable – they are convinced it was generated using advanced video processing. If this is the case, then what Chen is really doing is waving around a green or blue sheet which is then being used to represent the background using a photographic technique that has been employed in the movies for many years. To summarise, even if we discount Chen Shiqu's invisibility cloak, invisibility shields are not a complete impossibility – devices already exist that provide reasonable levels of performance; but could we render an object invisible without the need for a shield – just by, if you will, the flick of a switch?

Chen Shiqu demonstrating his 'invisibility cloak'. (Drawing by the author.)

You are probably aware that the concept of such a 'cloaking device' was invented some time ago by the writers of *Star Trek*. In case you are interested, here is what Wikipedia has to say about this: "*Star Trek* screenwriter Paul Schneider, inspired in part by the 1958 film *Run Silent, Run Deep*, and in part by *The Enemy Below*, which in turn had been released the previous year, 1957, imagined cloaking as a space-travel analogue of a submarine submerging, and employed it in the 1966 *Star Trek* episode 'Balance of Terror', in which he introduced the Romulan species. He likewise predicted, in the same episode, that invisibility through "selective bending of light" as described above, would have an enormous power requirement. Another *Star Trek* screenwriter, D. C. Fontana, coined the term 'cloaking device' for the 1968 episode 'The Enterprise Incident', which also featured Romulans."

Star Trek placed a limit on the use of this device: to fire at another ship, a cloaked space vessel must 'decloak'. But how, you may ask, would such a cloaking device actually work? One thing we have measured as being able to bend light is gravity – but even the strong gravitational field of the sun only bends starlight passing near it by a tiny fraction of a degree (by an angle of 0.87 seconds of arc, in case you are interested). To be able to bend light through much larger angles would require an extremely powerful gravitational field – of the order that would be observed near a black hole. Creation of a black hole, even a small one, would require an extraordinary amount of mass – and hence energy. So Paul Schneider's statement in 1967 that invisibility through selective bending of light requires an enormous amount of power, seems prescient indeed (the idea of black holes bending light, or even the basic concept of what a black hole is, was hardly at all appreciated by the public at that time). Putting aside the rather fantastical idea that cloaking could involve the use of a black hole, what other methods might we employ to achieve it? That is a good question, and our present-day speculations are likely to be wide of the mark of cloaking technologies of the far future. Perhaps the best thing we can do is to simply survey technologies that are being researched currently and which show some promise for implementing cloaking. One such survey is provided here:

https://www.youtube.com/watch?v=kUhKShrHTYA

Nanotechnology

"People don't want to believe that technology is broken. Pharmaceuticals, robotics, artificial intelligence, nanotechnology - all these areas where the progress has been a lot more limited than people think. And the question is why."

- Peter Thiel

In many ways the story of nanotechnology is a good example of what this book is all about; so I could have spent the whole book discussing just the subject of engineering on the nanometre scale. In case anyone is unaware, a nanometre is one millionth of a millimetre - so we are talking about some very small-scale technology here. The ideas involved were first discussed in 1959 by the noted physicist Richard Feynman in his talk *There's Plenty of Room at the Bottom*, where he described the possibility of synthesis via direct manipulation of atoms. Following some nano-metre-scaled manufacturing breakthroughs in electronics in the 1960s, the term 'nanotechnology' was first used by Norio Taniguchi in 1974. To give an idea of the scale involved, a single human hair is around 80,000 nm wide, while a red blood cell is approximately 7,000 nm across, a DNA molecule 2 to 2.5 nm, and atoms are around 0.2 nm. Eric Drexler was inspired by Feynman's ideas and popularised nanotechnology in his 1986 book 'Engines of Creation: The Coming Era of Nanotechnology'.

Dr Eric Drexler. (Drawing by the author.)

Since, on the nanoscale, the properties of materials can be quite different from those for a larger scale, nanotechnology includes the scientific investigation of the behaviour of materials at atomic, molecular, and larger scales. The aim is to then use the resulting knowledge to enable the design, manufacture and utilization of structures, devices and systems, that operate on very small scales, but which can exhibit useful properties or perform useful tasks on much larger scales. The reason I say that this whole book could have been about nanotechnology is because, over the last 30 years, the potential of nanotechnology has been, let's be honest, hyped out of sight, while the actual applications and useful benefits have been rather limited.

In the 1990s, I did quite a lot of research on metal powder manufacturing – I published some papers and went to some relevant conferences. I don't think I attended a conference that did not have a special program on nanotechnology. However, many of the papers presented at these and similar events were not really 'nano' at all. After a while, nanotechnology came to mean anything that was implemented on a rather small scale – so that in many instances it could in reality hardly be called 'micro-technology'. At the same time, it would be hard to over-estimate the promise that was said to repose in nanotechnology. This was reflected in the numerous funding calls from national research funders (such as EPSRC in the UK and NSF in the USA), which asked applicants to focus on nanotechnology.

So, nanotechnology has promised much over many years; but I have to say that, despite some limited successful applications, so far its actual commercialisation has not fulfilled the public's expectations. An example of a nanotechnology that seemed to promise much is graphene – which consists of carbon in the form of a single layer of atoms. Graphene has some amazing properties – it's electrically and thermally conductive and transparent, yet is believed to be the strongest known material, being 200 times stronger than steel; so strong, in fact, that a couple of thin layers of it can apparently stop a bullet. After tens of thousands of patents being applied for and much hype about how graphene is going to change our lives, you might expect to see it everywhere by now. But although there have been numerous applications of graphene (I won't list the applications to date – those interested can look them up on the internet), it could be argued that it has not yet lived up to the grand expectations that people had for it.

The fact is that there is a big difference between producing some small samples of a material and testing it under highly-controlled conditions in a lab, and being able to manufacture it on an industrial scale in forms that are sufficiently robust to be useful in real world applications. Or, to put it another way, I can't yet pick up sheets of graphene at B&Q for my current and pressing building needs – such as my leaking roof! Graphene might yet prove to be very useful in the future though – if it could be produced on a large scale it might facilitate the building of a space elevator (more on this later).

Notwithstanding the above discussions, there have of course been many useful applications of nanotechnology. According to Wikipedia, there have been useful applications in the following areas (although I would not categorise the last one as useful):

- Nanomedicine
- Nanobiotechnology
- Green nanotechnology
- Energy applications of nanotechnology
- Industrial applications of nanotechnology
- Potential applications of carbon nanotubes
- Nanoart
- Nanoelectronics
- Nanotechnology in warfare

Rather than go into these in detail, I will let you look up those you are particularly interested in. By the way, another application of nanotechnology is mentioned in the above YouTube survey of technologies for implementing invisibility – specifically 'invisible glass'. This is glass that has nano-scale cones (or short needles) formed onto its surface that dramatically reduce the reflectivity – effectively rendering the glass invisible due to lack of highlights/reflections. It seems to work well but I can't help wondering how robust the surface is – will the glass still be invisible after a bit of wear?

Possibly one reason why nanotechnology has not, to date, fulfilled the great expectations we had for it is that, in the first instance, those expectations were set extremely high. For example, in his 1986 book, mentioned above, Eric Drexler dreamed about the fabrication of molecular machines. He envisaged these machines as being able to produce any (macroscopic) item from molecular building blocks. To enable this, the machines would have to be capable of 'self-replication'. To support this, Drexler makes some arguments about the feasibility of these machines, using the analogy of biological replication on the small scale – which is commonly observed. He goes on to talk about engineering a synthetic form of life with self-replicating machines, or nano-robots that, once set running, could spread in the form of a grey corpus. This has, if you can believe it, created a widespread fear of 'Grey Goo'. This would manifest itself as a mass of runaway self-replicating machines remaking their environment into colourless formless sludge. Jesus H. Christ! That is not something I want to experience.

You may think this all a little fantastical, but Drexler's book was actually very influential and initiated much debate amongst scientists and the general public with knowledge of, or interest in, scientific issues (also, science fiction authors have had a field day with the Grey Goo concept). Nevertheless, many arguments have also been made by scientists to dismiss the prospect of self-replicating nano-bots (and other wild claims for nanotechnology), which relate to issues such as:

implications for energy management, the strong surface forces on the nanoscale, and Brownian motion. Our lack of understanding of the effects of these issues may be real, but it seems likely that if they are seriously limiting factors in relation to the ability to manufacture nano-bots, then the situation may be similar in relation to the whole of nanotechnology.

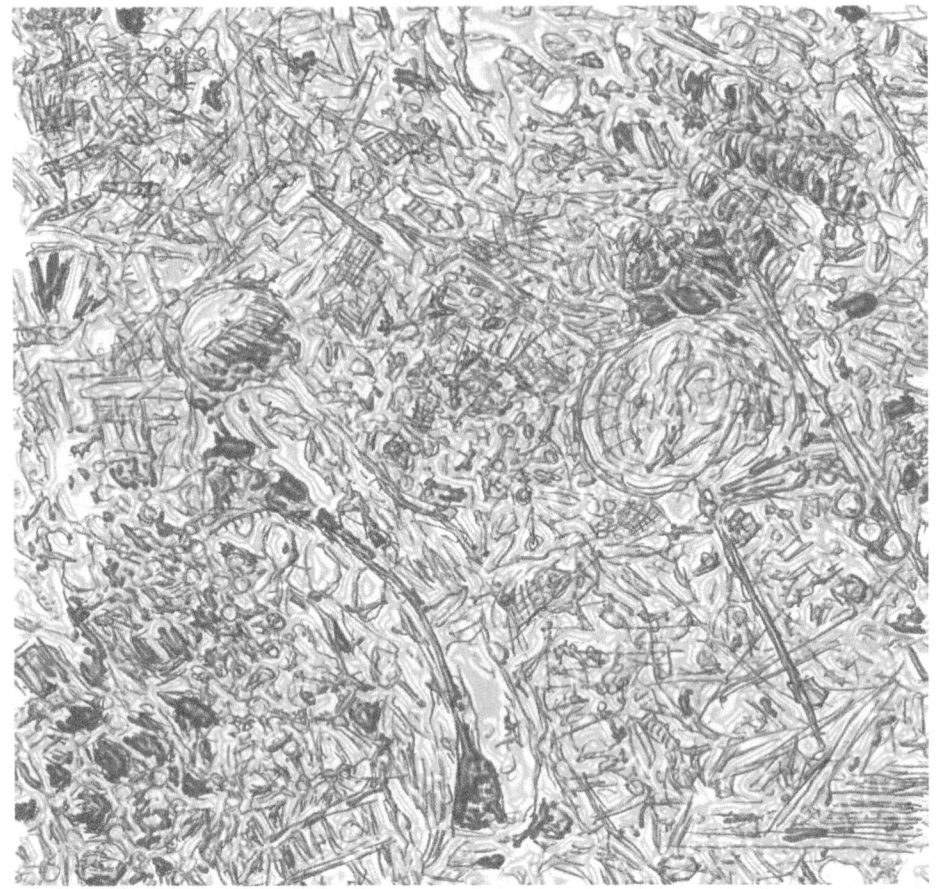

Eric Drexler envisaged Grey Goo as a mass of runaway self-replicating machines remaking their environment into colourless formless sludge. (Illustration by the author.)

This may explain why practical achievements in the field so far have been rather limited and may remain so for some decades to come. It seems then, that we are unlikely to make really impressive progress in nanotechnology until we have more understanding of the physics and 'tooling' relevant to the nanoscale. Not that this is impossible; and it may still be the case that the potential long-term benefits could be enormous. For example, since the replicator that was discussed earlier would need to operate on the atomic or molecular scale, its availability would presumably solve many tooling issues associated with nano-scale engineering. Consequently, if the great challenge of producing such a replicator could be successfully met, it could have very profound implications not just for manufacture of various materials, but also for production of a new generation of machines that could offer possibilities for undertaking almost any task on virtually any scale. The future potentials of such a device is therefore almost limitless and would, in practice, be limited only by our imaginations.

Space elevator

"The space elevator will be built about 50 years after everyone stops laughing."

— Arthur C. Clarke

I have always enjoyed the science fiction novels of Arthur C. Clarke. Back in the 1970s and 80s, I used to marvel over works such as *Childhood's End, A fall of Moondust, Imperial Earth* and, memorably, *Rendezvous with Rama*. His scientific achievements are perhaps less famous than they ought to be — ranging from a pioneering paper on telecommunication satellites in 1945 through to, effectively, predicting the internet (quite accurately) in 1962. One reason why I was drawn to his novels was that they comprise rather more than simple fantasy. They are, in fact, good examples of hard science fiction — that is to say technology is heavily featured, and they display a concern for scientific accuracy and logic. In 1979, he wrote a novel called *The Fountains of Paradise*, which describes the construction of a space elevator. This is a structure linking the ground with a satellite in geostationary orbit. The aim would be to use it to raise payloads to orbit and, if successful, it would offer the huge benefit of replacing traditional rockets. The only problem is that geostationary orbit is actually a relatively long way from the Earth — to be more exact, it's at a distance of about 22,300 miles. Consequently, the tensile forces in a tether reaching from the satellite to the surface of the earth would be enormous — so much so that even the strongest materials known to modern technology would be torn apart by them. However, his novel is in fact set in the 22nd century and in the early parts of the book Clarke discusses the demonstration of a microscopically thin but strong *hyperfilament* that makes the elevator possible. He describes the hyperfilament as being constructed from "continuous pseudo-one-dimensional diamond crystal". This was prescient on the part of Clarke, since the strongest materials currently known are, like diamond, composed of carbon. I am thinking of carbon nanotubes (the main difference between carbon nanotubes and graphene is that the latter is a single 2D layer of carbon atoms, while in carbon nanotubes a layer is rolled into a 3D tube or cylinder). Hopefully, by the 22nd century, carbon nanotube R&D will have progressed sufficiently to enable the space elevator to be constructed. By the way, for it to remain stable the elevator tether would need to extend well beyond the satellite (possibly with a counter weight at its far end), so that the centre of gravity of the space elevator would be located near the height of geostationary orbit.

The space elevator is a structure linking the ground with a satellite in geostationary orbit. (Illustration by the author.)

Although modern materials are not strong enough to build a space elevator on Earth, they could be used to build one for the Moon, or even Mars. These structures could employ materials such as Kevlar, in various thicknesses – with the thickest cross sections being near the satellite, where the forces would be highest. (If a space elevator were to break at this point one can imagine that the structure would fall and hit the ground with tremendous force; so much design work, with safety factors, would need to be employed to ensure this could not occur.)

In Clarke's novel, the space elevator is built in a (fictionalised) Sri Lanka (it needs to be as near to the equator as possible), on a mountain called Sri Kanda, which bears a strong resemblance to the real mountain Sri Pada. But in the novel, Clarke was not content to just describe the elevator construction – there is also a subplot relating to human colonization of the Solar System and the first contact with extra-terrestrial intelligence (the latter also being a theme of his earlier work *Childhood's End* as well as Carl Sagan's later science fiction novel *Contact*). The *Fountains of Paradise* was certainly well received – winning Clarke the prestigious Hugo Award for Best Novel – 1980 and the Nebula Award for Best Novel – 1979, as well as nominations for the Locus Award for Best Science Fiction Novel – 1980 and the British Science Fiction Association Award – 1979.

It should, however, be noted that Clarke did not actually invent the concept of a space elevator. That honour goes to the Russian scientist Konstantin Eduardovich Tsiolkovsky (Ed to his friends?), who was inspired by the Eiffel Tower in Paris. In 1895, he envisioned a similar tower that reached into space - being built from the ground up to the altitude of 35,786 kilometres, the height of geostationary orbit - so that the top of such a tower would be circling Earth as a satellite in a geostationary orbit. Objects would gain horizontal velocity due to the Earth's rotation as they were driven up the tower, and an object released at the tower's top would have enough horizontal velocity to remain there in geostationary orbit. Tsiolkovsky's conceptual tower was a compression structure, while all later versions of the elevator employ tensile structures, such as the tether mentioned above.

You know, there does not seem to be much that Konstantin Tsiolkovsky didn't achieve or invent in rocket science and astronautic theory. For example, he was the one who dreamt up the idea of staged rockets – which was used so successfully to get the first man into space and then on to the Moon. He is rightly considered to be one of the founding fathers of modern rocketry and astronautics. Even more impressively, Tsiolkovsky spent most of his life as a recluse in a log house on the outskirts of Kaluga, about 120 miles from Moscow. Apparently, his unusual habits made him seem bizarre to his fellow townsfolk – I guess they didn't realise he was also a rocket/astronautics genius!

Both the space elevator, and the mass accelerator described earlier, comprise methods that could be used in the future to lift large masses into Earth orbit. They are both likely to be highly complicated and expensive to build, but once constructed could operate very efficiently and should make all the difference in long term exploration of the solar system and beyond – since launching a spacecraft from orbit is dramatically easier than launching from the surface of the Earth.

By launching from orbit, we can imagine that a spacecraft would be able to carry enough fuel for facilitating relatively long and eventful journeys of discovery. It is interesting to consider which of the two methods of getting into orbit will be the first to be technologically feasible and also which may be the first to be operational (due to cost and other factors, these two things are not necessarily the same).

Konstantin Tsiolkovsky. (Drawing by the author.)

Effects on our society

Having spent a good deal of time discussing breakthroughs that we might hope to see in the future, I would like to explore, if you will bear with me, the possible effects they can have on ourselves and our societies i.e. our *lives*; and I will start by considering how it might affect our *deaths*.

The prospect of eternal life

"Forget all your sorrow, don't live in the past
And look to the future, 'cause life goes too fast, ya know"

-Ozzy Osbourne, from the song 'Hard Road' by Black Sabbath

Who wants to live forever? Well I do, for one. Our lives are so fleetingly short, and the questions we face are so immense, that it is a wonder that, as Schopenhauer observed, we don't spend all of our time just musing on the meaning of life (rather than doing things like putting clean shirts on every day and making small-talk). It is not fashionable to reflect on death much nowadays, but the only thing that we can say with 100% certainty that all living things will experience, is death. Yes, as Ozzy Osbourne used to say, 'ohhh, it's a hard road' - and then we're gonna die; bum deal! But at least we are alive now and most of us experience much more pleasant and easy lives than nearly all of our forefathers did.

But who has not found themselves in their middle age, waking up in the middle of the night in a cold sweat, thumping their pillow and repeating earnestly that they don't want to die? Again, mercifully not myself, but many have – including Julian Barnes, who actually writes about the experience in his book *Nothing to be Frightened Of*.

It is undeniably true that, at least in the West, the average life expectancy is increasing all the time. This is one reason why nowadays a greater proportion of the population will experience cancer at some point in their lives – it is largely a disease of old age (other reasons might be increases in pollution such as the diesel fumes discussed earlier, as well as increasing presence of chemicals and plastic particles in our environments). It has to be said though, that life expectancies increasing by a year or two is quite different from the prospect of eternal life. The latter is not a new concept. For thousands of years, there have been tales of 'The Fountain of Youth', which is described as a spring that restores the youth of anyone who drinks or bathes in its waters. Notable examples appear in the writings of Herodotus (5th century BC), the Alexander Romance (3rd century AD), and the stories of Prester John (early Crusades, 11th/12th centuries AD). A more recent example appeared in the poems of Alfred Lord Tennyson: "The woods decay, the woods decay and fall..." In this poem, Tithonus asks for the gift of immortality, which is readily granted to him, but forgets to ask for eternal youth along with it. It's a bit like when, at the supermarket, you buy your groceries but forget to bring the bags to put it in – you've got something but there's not much you can do with it!

I guess we would all like to stay young and attractive - assuming that we are attractive to start with! Of course, Conan Doyle has his own take on the myth of the Fountain of Youth. In his Sherlock Holmes story 'The Adventure of the Creeping Man', the antagonist, Professor Presbury, wishes to marry a young woman and since he is 61, he feels that for the marriage some form of, shall we say, rejuvenation, is required. His plan for obtaining this involves taking a serum extracted from monkeys - Colobinae Asian monkeys, as a matter of fact. Unfortunately, rather than the desired Viagra-esque effect, the serum apparently left Presbury with some 'positively simian' characteristics. Suffice it to say that he mistook Greater London for the jungle and found himself squawking while swinging through the trees of Hampstead Heath. As you can imagine, it didn't end well for the professor. An *outré* narrative indeed. But Holmes displays his usual prescience in making some observations that are still relevant today. For example, he says: "When one tries to rise above Nature one is liable to fall below it..."

The Sherlock Holmes character Professor Presbury was a renowned physiologist at a great English university, but he ended up creeping around in simian fashion. (Drawing by the author.)

I can't help thinking that this phrase might well apply to attempts that could be made to greatly extend life using modern technology. For example, it can be imagined that genetic engineering could be used to modify human genes in favour of very long life. In my view, scientists would have to be extremely cautious here –

it may well be not at all wise to try implementing this. It is clear that the aging process is something that is programmed into our genetic code and it is highly likely that evolution has done this for very good reasons. The main one that comes to mind is the chance of errors occurring over very large numbers of cell divisions. This is why cancer often occurs in old age – after many cell divisions have occurred. It seems that evolution over millions of years has introduced an aging process as part of the lifecycle as a means to limit the lifespan of the individual, and has coupled it with a strong desire to reproduce as the best means of maintaining health.

Simply short-circuiting the genetic results of all that evolution could be folly of the worst kind. A very similar argument can be applied to human cloning. When you consider all the significant risks that the human animal is exposed to through sexual intercourse – not least disease transmission – it seems clear that sex would not have evolved if it were not absolutely essential for human health.

So, if becoming a modern-day Methuselah is not realistic, what options are left for those seeking immortality? Well, if you are in the USA and have enough cash, one idea is to put yourself (after death) into the hands of cryonics technicians. This profession has existed since the 1970s, with the companies involved putting bodies of the deceased into deep freeze, with the aim of reviving them in the future, if and when suitable technology becomes available (the latter part being, I fancy, not 100% certain). The process is something like the following: Freezing starts as soon as possible after the patient dies to stop brain cells dying through lack of oxygen, with cooling beginning in an ice bath to slowly reduce the body temperature. The blood is removed from the body and replaced with 'cryo-protectant' fluid (anti-freeze to you and me), which prevents ice crystal formation that may damage cells. This seems to me like a stage that may have a detrimental effect on overall chances of success. I mean, if someone were to extract my blood and replace it with antifreeze then, even with the technologies of a few thousand years from now, it seems unlikely to me that I could be revived with any kind of quality of life. That would make your worst hangover seem like a walk in the park. Also, I can't help wondering whether blood cell damage will occur, during or after the antifreeze transfusion.

Anyway, the next stage is for the person to be put into an arctic sleeping bag before lowering them into a giant tank, where their temperature continues to be reduced to that of liquid nitrogen in a bid to ensure preservation (-196 degrees Celsius). The US company, Alcor, for example, offers cryonic preservation for the whole body for around $200,000. For those who can't afford the whole body, just the head can be frozen for $80,000, (but who wants to come back as a disembodied head?)

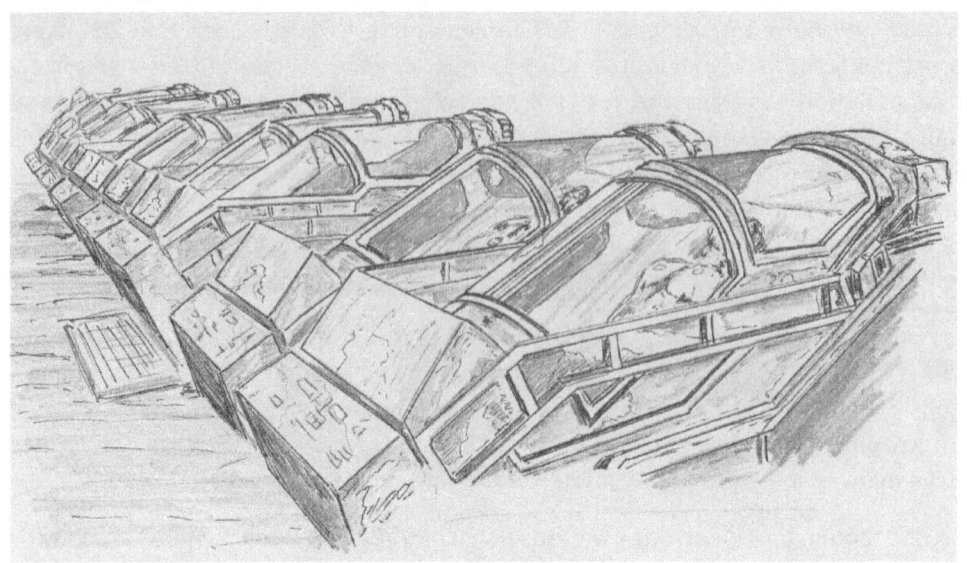

Cryonics, the freezing of human bodies in anticipation of future cure, is not just the stuff of movies – companies in the USA have offered it for some time. (Illustration by the author.)

Although there is no scientific evidence cryonics will succeed, one can imagine that it might be possible to bring back life in a body that has been frozen in this way; but given the inevitable tissue damage involved, I have to ask whether the mind of the individual will be preserved and restored (or if you prefer more metaphysical terms, the soul or the spirit). If not, then we can't really say the individual has been restored – although the DNA may be the same, the rejuvenated body would be more like your identical twin or a clone of yourself. Perhaps the biggest risk, in practice, to taking the cryogenic route to immortality is that, if you need to be frozen for many years to give enough time for technologies to be developed to revive you, there is a relatively high chance that during that long period problems/issues will occur that will cause the freezing to be stopped, thereby ruining your plan. Probably the most likely cause for this would simply be that for some reason there is a business downturn for the cryonics company – they run out of money and call the receivers in and cease trading i.e. turn off the freezers. There are also a multitude of other potential causes for a premature thaw. Even if the process were to be successful, one has to ask who would provide the very high/expensive level of support the people from the past would be very likely to require.

Another approach to potential immortality, which is often described in science fiction, is to store one's essence in a computer (this occurred in quite a few episodes of *Star Trek*). This seems like quite a nice solution – certainly more straightforward and potentially less messy than the cryogenic option. The main problem here is that currently no one knows what one's essence actually is. The soul and spirit are somewhat mystical terms – meaning different things to different people. There is no doubt that humans have a high level of consciousness – but what is consciousness? We usually think of materialism as the idea that goods and wealth are the most important things; for example, materialism is valuing a new car over friendships. However, it also has a meaning in philosophy - here materialism asserts that matter is the fundamental substance in nature, and that all things, including mental states and consciousness, are results of material interactions (materialism is closely related to physicalism—the view that all that exists is ultimately physical). The problem is that materialism cannot explain consciousness. In fact, it's such a problem that the philosopher David Chalmers described consciousness as the "hard problem" and contrasts it with the "easy problems" such as discriminating, collating information, reasoning, focusing attention, and so on. Therefore, the hard problem of consciousness is the problem of explaining why and how sentient organisms have subjective conscious experiences such as seeing red and green colours, emotions or feeling heat or cold; rather than objective observation. I submit that since scientists still have no real idea of what consciousness is, it would be a prodigious challenge to be able to load such consciousness into a computer. Otherwise, as mentioned, it's a great idea.

"As much money and life as you could want! The two things most human beings would choose above all - the trouble is, humans do have a knack of choosing precisely those things that are worst for them."

— J. K. Rowling, Harry Potter and the Sorcerer's Stone

Attainment of velocities in excess of that of light, for interstellar travel
Relativity
There was a young lady named Bright,
Whose speed was far faster than light;
She set out one day
In a relative way,
And returned on the previous night.

— A. H. Reginald Buller

I must certainly be nuts to devote a whole section of this book to the idea of travelling, or potentially travelling, faster than light. There can be few subjects more likely to raise the hackles of your average modern-day physicist. Also, I don't wish to be seen as trying to contradict the great physicist Einstein, or to be setting at nought the accepted wisdom of the scientific community for the last one hundred-odd years. So let me state here and now that I am not trying to do these things; crazy indeed would I be to attempt them. I also know how difficult it can be to accept change, even when it is of the apparently mildest form. Consider, for example, the prospect of permanently changing from PG Tips to Tetley Tea (apologies for this analogy Tetley – in reality, I quite like your tea). So I am not saying it is a scientific fact that man can travel faster than light. Rather, I will just relate to you the situation, as I see it, surrounding this question of physics. It will then be up to you to make up your own mind. Now that I have issued my disclaimer, let's ask: what is the maximum speed that man can travel at? This is another question that is easy to ask but may be very difficult to answer with certainty. We can be sure that it will become even more pressing in the future as we develop technologies that will drive us at increasing speeds through space. Naturally, mankind will wish to explore beyond the solar system – just as our ancient forebears wanted to know what lay beyond the hills or mountains on the horizon. Of course, if some of the potential threats discussed earlier become more acute, travel to other worlds may pass beyond a simple matter of curiosity towards a necessity for the survival of the species.

It should be emphasised early on in this discussion, that for over a century most physicists have believed that the ultimate speed that we could travel is just slightly less than the speed of light (c) - that's to say around 180,000 miles a second. The reasons for this, which have to do with the theory that Einstein designated as 'special relativity', will be discussed in some detail below. If we are indeed limited to c, this would place some serious limitations on the practicality of deep space exploration and colonisation. Jim Kirk and company certainly would not have been able to zoom all around the Galaxy having adventures with alien species if the Enterprise could not have exceeded c. In fact, during his five-year mission, he would barely have had time to explore as far as the nearest star (after the Sun). Even more concerning would be the effect known as 'relativistic time dilation', which most physicists believe occurs when someone travels at speeds approaching that of light. The result of this would be that when Jim got back to the Earth after five years of travelling at high speeds, he would find everyone on Earth dramatically aged or perhaps even dead. But would this really occur and is it completely impossible to travel at speeds greater than that of light? I will endeavour to address these important questions below. Before doing so, I would like to mention that just because something is believed for 100 years, this does not guarantee it is correct. Before the publication of the special theory of relativity, scientists believed that space was absolute (rather than relative) and that in space light passed through a medium known as the aether (analogous to how sound travels through air). They thought this for *many* hundreds of years and there did appear to be quite a bit of evidence for it – but we now believe this to be wrong. It also does not matter if thousands, or even millions, of people believe a theory – it can still be wrong (remember Galileo). Finally, I feel we have to keep Clarke's First Law in mind and those believing in the possibility of super-light speeds, could express this in the following way: When a distinguished but elderly scientist states that it is possible for man to travel faster than he has done in the past, he is almost certainly right. When he states that travelling faster than light is impossible, he is very probably wrong. Controversial I know, but there we are. In fact, having spent some years studying and thinking about this area of physics, I have noticed that many physicists appear to consider the idea of the impossibility of travelling faster than light to be almost an article of faith. To be honest, it seems like another case of the dogma of science – since faster than c travel has been considered to be impossible for the last 100+ years, they seem to wish it to remain so, and can get rather upset with anyone who suggests that it might just be possible that occasions could occur when c might be exceeded. Well, sorry guys, but if there is one thing I believe in more than anything else, it is the need for free thought and to keep an open mind. Yes indeed; in my own humble way I have been sitting in a corner with a towel around my head (figuratively speaking) racking my brains over this. And below I have sketched out my observations; sorry if they don't fit in with commonly accepted wisdom. If, like Rupert Sheldrake, some will consider me a heretic ... perhaps I should recant? But this wouldn't achieve much since now I have written the ideas down. Once you have done this, particularly in the internet age, there is little you can do; now they are not just my ideas – they are everybody's – to be considered and either accepted or rejected as you see fit.

A very brief history of speed

"If everything seems under control, you're not going fast enough."

— Mario Andretti

Before we broach the tricky question of whether we can ever exceed c, let's briefly review man's quest for speed over the years. In the history of machines for transportation, there has often been an innovative development of the motive power needed, at the time concerned. An important example from the first half of the nineteenth century is that of the steam-powered locomotive. Many people believe that this was invented by Stephenson, but that honour has, in reality, to go to Richard Trevithick. This 6'2" Cornishman did not excel at school (one of his school masters described him as "a disobedient, slow, obstinate, spoiled boy, frequently absent and very inattentive") but he was good at arithmetic and had a talent for designing and building new types of steam engines. In Merthyr Tydfil on 21 February 1804, when Richard Trevithick mounted one of his high-pressure steam engines on a local iron master's tram rails, the railway age began. Considering the enormous impact railways had, and continue to have, on just about the whole world since then (it is, for example, quite possible that the American states would not have joined together into the union of the USA if it were not for the existence of steam locomotive railroads), it is my sincere conviction that this event, and the achievements of Trevithick in general, should be much more famous than they are.

Richard Trevithick, who invented the working steam locomotive, but who never got widespread recognition or financial reward for the invention. (Drawing by the author.)

Robert Stephenson's contribution, with his locomotive 'Rocket', was to bring together several innovations to produce a locomotive with enhanced performance. For example, Rocket employed multiple boiler fire tubes to ensure a more continuous and useful supply of steam for powering travel over longer distances; but this was long after Trevithick first demonstrated successful operation of his steam locomotive – in fact, it was 25 years later!

Jumping forward, in the late nineteenth century, the advent of the motor car (a great invention if you ask me) led to the extended development of the internal combustion engine; while in the mid-twentieth century the invention of the centrifugal gas turbine for jet propulsion and its subsequent development as part of the WWII war effort, provided the power needed to accelerate jet aircraft up to the speed of sound and beyond. Then, in the second half of the twentieth century, the invention of manned rocket flight enabled a dramatic increase in travel speeds – of up to around 20,000 mph. (To be more precise, astronauts aboard NASA's Apollo 10 moon mission reached a top speed of 24,791 mph relative to Earth, as their rocket travelled back from the Moon on May 26, 1969.)

Stephenson's drawing of Rocket. (Illustration by the author.)

Our future need for speed
"The future depends on what you do today."

— Mahatma Gandhi

As we progress through the twenty-first century, humanity faces challenges on a greater scale than those previously experienced. Earlier sections of this book have considered future threats to mankind in some detail. As discussed, one of the most significant threats that has received world-wide attention is that of global warming. This certainly seems to present a potentially existential threat to humanity, with

265

some scientists (such as Robert B. Laughlin, mentioned earlier) concluding that it constitutes such a threat that, no matter what measures were to be taken to address it, significantly influencing it would be beyond the capabilities of mankind. Such perceived risks have been motivating factors in the drive to develop new generations of spacecraft with the long-term aim of transporting humans to new worlds to assist in ensuring long-term survival of the human race. However, colonisation of alien worlds does itself pose a number of not insignificant challenges – most notably, the need to traverse the huge distances involved in reasonable time scales. The first stage on this journey was Neil Armstrong's first step on the Moon in 1969; and the second is likely to comprise journeys to Mars, which are planned to occur within the next twenty years. By the way, last night I was out in the garden with my son – we were using the telescope I mentioned earlier to observe Mars. Apparently, the viewing was the best that will occur until 2033 and I can indeed confirm that the disk of the planet was nicely visible. We were contemplating the question of whether Mars will be the first planet beyond Earth to be colonised by humans and wondering when this might occur.

Unfortunately, when travelling beyond Mars, significant practical difficulties arise. Although the distances to other worlds are much larger than those for a Martian visit, they could be achieved with chemical rocket propelled spacecraft. The chief difficulties are to do with the nature of the planets concerned – Jupiter, Saturn, Uranus, and Neptune, are 'gas giants'. Being comprised of multiple layers of gas, without any solid planet surface, makes them very difficult to colonise; and they exist at extremely low temperatures. For example, although Titan, Saturn's moon, does have a solid surface and an atmosphere, due to its remoteness from the sun the surface temperature of Titan is very low at -179 degrees Celsius.

Given this situation, there are strong motivators for travelling beyond the solar system to discover if there are any habitable planets orbiting nearby stars in the Milky Way Galaxy. The problem here is that the distances involved, even to reach the nearest star systems, are so enormous that most people view the prospect as unrealistic or the subject of science fiction rather than potential science fact. The star nearest to the Earth (apart from the Sun) is currently Proxima Centauri, which is at a distance of 4.24 light years. To get an idea of the scale and distances involved, if the Sun were the size of a football and positioned in London, then Proxima Centauri would be the size of a tennis ball, but it would be located in New York! Despite this distance, the motivation for this exploration is, in fact, very strong – since astronomers have discovered a potentially habitable planet orbiting Proxima Centauri.

In order to enable travel across the immense distances between the stars, quite a large number of authors have written about ideas for high speed travel that employ methodologies that one might describe as fantastical. Some of these have included making use of various esoteric astronomical phenomena, including 'wormholes'.

The idea is that the latter can be created by connecting a black hole to a white hole (allegedly a region of space where nothing can enter). Apparently, when these two phenomena combine, they form a wormhole. Now, there is evidence that black holes exist in space, but that's about all we can say here with any certainty. For example, if any unfortunate person tried to approach a black hole with a view to engineering the said wormhole, it is pretty certain they would be torn apart by an enormous gravitational field with their atoms then being unceremoniously dragged into the black hole at fantastic speeds. If it's any consolation, it is likely that at this time their remains would emit a pretty flare of light and some X rays. Astronomers have actually observed X rays that they believe to originate from matter being sucked into black holes. Such X rays are believed by many to constitute evidence for the existence of black holes. Another little difficulty is that there is not a *shred* of experimental evidence for the existence of either white holes or wormholes.

Another potential method for initiating faster than light travel that is sometimes promulgated, is to employ the 'warping' of space. There is evidence that space is slightly distorted or warped by gravitational bodies – as predicted by general relativity – and measured by the apparent change in position of stars whose light has passed near the sun during total eclipses. This concept of distorting space led physicist Miguel Alcubierre to propose, in 1994, a method for changing the geometry of space by creating a wave that would cause space ahead of a spacecraft to contract and the space behind it to expand. The ship would then, apparently, ride this wave inside a region of flat space, known as a warp bubble, being carried along as the region itself moves due to the actions of the drive. There are though, a few practical problems associated with the proposed Alcubierre drive – the first of which being that it apparently necessitates the existence of 'negative energy' and therefore requires 'exotic matter' (it has this in common with wormholes, but last time I checked neither of these two items were available on Amazon). Another issue is that to function, it seems that such a drive would require rather a lot of energy. The theoretical physicist Lawrence M. Krauss has offered some rough estimates of the energy needed to create the incredibly high gravity fields that would be needed to warp space sufficiently to implement the proposed Alcubierre drive (as well as the concept discussed above, of enabling light to be bent to the extents required to implement a 'cloaking device' similar to the one invented in *Star Trek* by the Romulans). His suggestion is that to do this would require about as much energy as would be needed to produce a black hole the size of the Enterprise (he rightly points out that such a black hole would be able to bend any light beam that travelled near to it). It turns out though, that the mass of such a black hole would be around 1/10 of the mass of the Sun. Krauss observes that, expressed in energy units: "it would take more than the total energy produced by the Sun during its entire lifetime to generate such a black hole." Jumping Jesus! So, you will excuse me if I find the likelihood of such drives being employed for high speed spacecraft travel to be a little unrealistic. I should just add that if you are wondering whether in *Star Trek* the use of the term Warp Drive to describe their method of faster-than-light travel came from the Alcubierre theory, in reality the opposite is true. Alcubierre stated in an email to William Shatner that the former's theory was directly inspired by the term used in *Star Trek*; and he also referred to the "Warp Drive of science fiction" in an article he wrote in 1994 about his theory. By the way, although *Star Trek* made the concept of Warp Drive famous, the term was actually first used by John W. Campbell in his 1931 science fiction novel, *Islands of Space*.

Although wormholes and Alcubierre drives may appear somewhat far-fetched, is there any chance that humans could travel over the vast distances to nearby stars in practical timescales (years but not centuries), by utilising technologies not dramatically dissimilar to those currently available (where some technological development may be required, but not revolutionary scientific breakthroughs)? Perhaps we can do this by re-interpreting the special theory of relativity (SR) in relation to its implications for facilitating such travel. In any case, I certainly don't want to find myself contradicting the postulates of SR or trying to set at nought the great scientific theories and papers of Albert Einstein.

World-famous physicist, Albert Einstein. (Drawing by the author.)

I mean he did so much – look at his general theory of relativity – not the sort of thing you would dream up over the pub and scribble onto a beer mat. It is, I fancy, rather more substantial than that and it's been shown to be correct experimentally. His predictions for the bending of light near massive bodies (something that was touched on above) have actually been experimentally observed in the form of the apparent changes in the positions of stars whose light has passed near to the Sun during total solar eclipses. But, while not presuming to contradict the great scientist, is there any chance we could view all this speed limit business from a new angle (that sounds, I know, like a plan for a new road scheme). In short, can we beg to differ, not with Einstein, but with the conclusions that have been widely drawn in scientific literature as to the implications of SR for high-speed/interstellar travel?

Implications of special relativity for very high-speed travel

"When you are courting a nice girl, an hour seems like a second. When you sit on a red-hot cinder a second seems like an hour. That's relativity."

— Albert Einstein

In 1905, Einstein published his famous paper that described his special theory of relativity (SR). SR comprises two postulates that are particularly relevant to very high-speed/interstellar travel:

1. The laws of physics are identical in all inertial systems (i.e., non-accelerating frames of reference); and all velocities are measured relative to a specified frame of reference – hence the term 'Relativity'.

2. The speed of light (and other electromagnetic radiation) in a vacuum, is always constant at 300 million metres per second.

These postulates were something of a revolution in physics at the time, since from the 16th until the late 19th century it was generally believed that the Universe had an 'absolute' coordinate frame, which could ultimately be used to measure the absolute position and velocity of all objects. There was a theory of a somewhat elusive/ethereal 'material' known as the 'aether', through which light was thought to travel. It was believed that the aether provided the coordinate frame that could be used to specify the absolute position and velocity of all objects in the Universe. And I, for one, am not surprised that they came up with this theory. To start with, it seems completely reasonable that a wave should need some kind of medium to travel through. Waves that mankind has been aware of over the ages certainly do travel through media – sound through air, waves on the sea through water, and so on. Also, light always seems to be measured as travelling at a constant speed – which again, would be analogous to the constant speed of sound in air. Despite all this, the theory of the aether was dealt a significant blow in 1887, when Michelson and Morley undertook and published a famous experiment.

It had been assumed that if the aether existed, then movement of the Sun in the Milky Way Galaxy and also the rotation of the Earth around the Sun would constitute movements through the aether; so that if light travel were measured in two perpendicular directions, the speeds would be found to be different. But in the Michelson-Morley experiment, the measured speeds in the two directions were found to be similar – and, as we know, data are king.

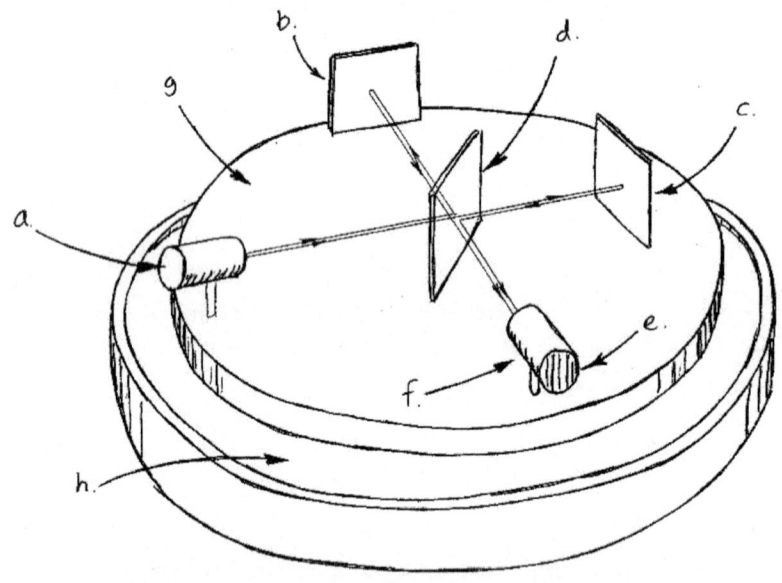

The Michelson-Morley experiment: (a) light source, (b) and (c) mirrors, (d) half-silvered mirror, (e) interference fringes, (f) telescope, (g) granite block and (h) pool of mercury. (Pen and ink drawing by the author.)

To cut a long story short, this provides strong support for postulate 2 of SR, that the speed of light in a given medium is always constant, and indicates that the aether, as it had been understood up to that time, does not exist. Since the Michelson-Morley experiment, there has been a good deal of further experimentation that supports the experiment's findings and confirms that postulates 1 and 2 are correct to a high level of accuracy. Acceptance of this implies that time dilation will be observed.

It should be noted that there are two types of time dilation – one associated with special relativity (SRTD) and the other associated with general relativity (GRTD), with the latter addressing the effects of gravity (as mentioned above) and acceleration. SRTD is a difference in the elapsed time observed by two travellers due to a velocity relative to each other. Here, the word 'observed' is important since the time dilation is only observed because one traveller is moving relative to the other while using the fastest known phenomenon, i.e. light, to make the observations. The word 'relative' is also important since the amount of time dilation observed only depends upon the velocity of one traveller relative to the other. But is SRTD *real*? We know that GRTD *is* real – if two travellers synchronised their watches, then one went close to a very massive object for a while, and then came back to meet the other and compared watches, they would find that the watch of the one who had gone near to the object would be reading an earlier time – time would, literally, have slowed down for him/her (as per *Interstellar*). But would this be true of the two moving travellers mentioned above? If they slowed down, turned around, came back together and compared their watches, would one read differently from the other? If so, which would read the earlier time and why? If they read the same time, SRTD would not be real, and instead would only be an apparent, rather than a real, objective effect.

The above discussion is important in relation to determining if it may be possible for humans to travel at faster than light speeds. Over the years, many statements have been made in various publications that assert the impossibility of humans ever travelling at speeds greater than that of light. One of the most recent was a BBC Earth article entitled: 'This video explains why we cannot go faster than light'. The authors of this piece had the temerity to accompany the text with a video depicting the starship Enterprise from *Star Trek*! (This is, of course, anathema to your average trekker, who, like *Star Trek* itself, wishes to believe in a positive view of the future where all manner of scientific feats are accomplished, no matter how difficult or unlikely they may currently seem to be. Not to mention the slight on the great hero character which the Enterprise herself comprises.) The arguments put forward in this article and others, as explanations for c being a 'speed limit' could, however, be interpreted as *apparent* effects resulting from the fact that observations will be made using light (or other EM radiation), as well as an under-appreciation of the implications of postulate 1 above i.e. the relative and equivalent nature of all reference frames. There is, for example, a problem in relation to the common use of the term 'speed of light' when referring to humans traveling through space. Specifically, what is the speed that is being referred to, relative to? I fear that many physicists today would consider that a heretical question and all talk of exceeding c to be sacrilege. I just hope they don't decide to try to implement an inquisition! It's not that I am trying to contradict what Einstein was saying in his 1905 paper – his two postulates seem to me to represent astute observations that are very much worth pointing out. And no doubt every result that logically follows from them is correct. Perhaps the best way of determining what the exact nature of these outcomes might be is to employ that method of reasoning that Einstein himself was so fond of – specifically the thought experiment. In endeavouring to explore the possibility of exceeding c, let's start by considering a very simple scenario.

Exceeding c made simple

We can imagine a situation where two spacecraft are together but then accelerate away from each other, with each employing an acceleration of 10 m/s² as shown in the figure below. This is 1g, which is the acceleration we experience on Earth from the force of gravity – so it could easily be withstood by the astronauts on the spacecraft. It could also be easily attained, maintained, and monitored through the use of accelerometers on each craft. (For anybody unfamiliar with the nomenclature of mechanics/accelerations, this just means that relative to the starting point, the speed of the craft increases by 10 metres per second (m/s), every second.)

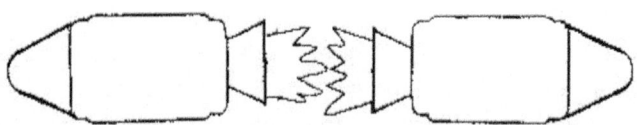

Two spacecraft each fire their motors and accelerate away from a start point at 1g. (Drawing by the author.)

In this case, after a period of 100 days, each would be travelling at 173,000 km/s relative to where they started from, as shown below (calculated using Newton's laws of motion). They would, in fact, each be travelling at more than half the speed of light relative to the start point, and since they are moving in opposite directions, it seems that their relative speed would exceed c.

After 100 days the two spacecraft are still accelerating away from the start point at 1g; they then cut off their motors. It appears that they have now attained a relative velocity of 346,000 km/s (which is greater than c). (Drawing by the author.)

In this scenario, everything that has happened is well within the limits of what SR and classical mechanics say is possible, and yet, apparently, one person is travelling away from another at a speed in excess of that of light. My suggestion is that the reason why this appears possible, while most texts on SR imply that it is not, is that insufficient consideration is given to the implications of everything being relative. For example, much emphasis is placed on the effects of time dilation; but what if these are apparent rather than real and they are observed because of the limited and constant speed of light? Let's consider an analogous situation of a black universe containing only air, where observations are made using sound waves. In such a universe we would measure the speed of sound as always constant and effects such as time dilation would appear to occur. Obviously, in this situation it could not be objectively shown that a moving object had aged less than a stationary one. Also, if it is believed that SRTD is real, then paradoxical situations arise that are hard if not impossible to resolve. To help illustrate what is meant by the equivalent nature of all reference frames, we can consider a famous paradox that concerns twins. By the way, I have some friends that you could call paradoxical twins – the difference being that the guys I am discussing below are flying around in spacecraft.

Paradoxical twins

"My sister and I, you will recollect, were twins, and you know how subtle are the links which bind two souls which are so closely allied."

- Sir Arthur Conan Doyle

Let's imagine twins travelling while observing each other. If one twin were on a spacecraft (let's call it spacecraft 1) and the other twin were on another spacecraft (called spacecraft 2 and moving relative to 1), then time dilation would be observed. (The time dilation would be different if one of the twins were on the Earth or on another planet such as Mars - because the spacecraft, the Earth, and Mars would all be expected to be moving relative to each other.)

If the twins in the two spacecraft mentioned above were to both fire their motors for, say, 50 days (rather than 100) they would reach a relative speed of 173,000 km/s (which is about 58% of c), so that SRTD (calculated using something called the 'Lorentz function') would indicate that the twin on spacecraft 1 would observe that time appears to slow down for the twin on spacecraft 2. If this slowing of time were real (rather than just observed), then if both spacecraft simultaneously turned around and fired their motors so that they came back together again and they were able to compare their clocks, twin 2's clock would show that less time had elapsed than was shown on twin 1's clock – meaning that twin 1 was now older than twin 2. However, because everything is relative (and in the above description the two spacecraft even accelerated by equal amounts) there is no reason why the roles of the two twins should not be reversed, so that the twin 1's clock would be found to have less time elapsed that that of twin 2 i.e. twin 2 is the older one. Obviously, it is impossible for both of the twins to be younger than the other! This is a version of the famous 'Twin Paradox', which has been stated in a number of forms over the last century, and for which various resolutions have been suggested. One of these is to assume that the rocket engine is only fired on one spacecraft so that it undergoes accelerations that cause time dilation due to general relativity effects (GRTD). The problem with this explanation is that GRTD would not be sufficient to explain the time dilation calculated from the Lorentz equations – particularly if the spacecraft travels at very near the speed of light for a considerable time. Also, situations can be imagined where the accelerations (and therefore GRTD) experienced by both persons would be identical in magnitude and duration (as in the example described above). Thirdly, if you are saying that the time dilation was due to acceleration relativistic effects, then this is GRTD and so cannot form a proof for the existence of SRTD. Perhaps it was the latter observation that led to a YouTube video being posted which was entitled "Twin paradox: the real explanation (no math)". I will not mention the speaker's name – but you can look it up if you are interested. He seems to be a nice guy – he does an engaging talk – no doubt he is an accomplished physicist who is respected by his peers. To give a very brief summary of what he says in the talk – he asks us to consider three observers: A stationary relative to the Earth, B moving away from it and C toward it (from a distant point). His idea, in a nutshell, is that at the half-way point, where B and C pass, B could use a big sign to tell C what time has passed on his clock – then C could start his clock and measure the time he takes for the second half of the journey and when C reaches Earth he could again use a sign to tell A the sum of the time elapsed during the two halves of the journey. According to the speaker, this time will be less than the time that has passed on A's clock since B left. The reason why the speaker goes to the trouble of having two travellers is to avoid the necessity of having the traveller accelerate when turning around and heading back to the Earth because he feels that the conventional explanation that it is this acceleration that causes time to slow for the traveller is wrong. There is only one slight problem with all of this – the speaker seems to have forgotten the first postulate of special relativity, which says that: "The laws of physics are identical in all inertial systems (i.e., non-accelerating frames of reference); and all velocities are measured relative to a specified frame of reference." In other words, since there are no accelerations occurring, it is equally valid to say that B (or C) is stationary as it is to say that A is. If B were considered to be stationary, then A would be moving and so time would pass more slowly on A. It is clearly impossible for time to pass more slowly on B than A and to also pass more slowly on A than B. Therefore, to summarise, this explanation seems to me to provide *absolutely no* resolution for the Twin Paradox. None, zero, zilch! And if a respected PhD physicist, author and science communicator (who runs YouTube channels and gives TED@New York talks, conducts research in particle physics at Fermi National Accelerator Laboratory, is an adjunct professor of physics at the University of Notre Dame, was a co-discoverer of the top quark, has co-authored hundreds of research papers, and, get this, was a member of the team that discovered the Higgs boson in 2012!) apparently cannot provide a resolution for the Twin Paradox, then I must ask – who can?! But this speaker made things rather over-complicated in considering three observers. In reality, it can be expressed simply – if two travellers pass at high relative velocity, they might each subjectively observe the other to be slowing down, but later they can't both turn out to be both older and younger than the other – such a concept is ludicrous. This would seem to lead inexorably to the conclusion that there is no adequate resolution to the Twin Paradox. Or ... perhaps I'm wrong ... if you can think of a convincing resolution, I would be glad to hear about it! If no such resolution emerges, it's hard (at least for me), to conclude that the twins could re-join and discover that time had passed at a different rate for one than the other. Damn hard. There is no doubt that the SR time dilation effect is genuinely observed, but I am having a hard time believing it is an absolute and real phenomenon, rather than being relative and apparent.

Special relativity time dilation: girl leaves boy to fly off at very high speeds. When she returns will she find the boy has aged more than herself? (Illustration by the author.)

You know, I have spent many years searching through books, scientific papers, and 'popular science' online articles/videos, for a satisfactory resolution to the Twin

Paradox; but so far have been sorely disappointed. Most books on special relatively that mention the paradox vouchsafe the idea that the twin who turns around, thereby undergoing an acceleration, will be the one who has aged less – and indeed, this is what our children are taught in 'A' level physics lessons in schools and colleges. But the esteemed and respected professor mentioned above, who has tremendous experience in physics research, tells us in a YouTube video that the acceleration explanation is wrong! He then goes on to offer his proposed resolution to the paradox involving three gentlemen; all moving at a constant speed relative to each other; you can see what I think of this proposal in the text above. Being something of a sucker for punishment, I have also asked a number of people who fancy themselves as physicists (in some cases perhaps justifiably), about the Twin Paradox, but again I can't report that I got anywhere in these enquiries. My reception was perhaps somewhat similar to what one could have expected from a particularly pious priest after asking something like: 'if everyone goes to heaven after dying, isn't it getting a bit crowded up there?' No doubt they thought I was a heretic, but their ripostes to my suggestion that the Twin Paradox shows that SRTD cannot be a real effect, include repeatedly placing particular emphasis on the 'maths of the Lorentz transformations'. I can't help thinking that such comments comprise an effort to build a mystique around the subject. This is a fault that scientists can occasionally be subject to where they are essentially trying to say that: 'you don't understand this physics, because you don't understand the complex maths that it is based on'. I must point out though, that here this doesn't wash, because while the Lorentz transformations sound complex and esoteric, they are in fact based upon some very simple maths – so simple that any self-respecting GCSE maths student could understand them (I won't go into the Lorentz transformations here, but the maths they are based on, which relates to observed effects due to the constant speed of light, can be found in nearly every book on special relativity). Another favourite is to discuss at length the dynamics of particles that have been observed in, for example, particle collisions in the Large Hadron Collider at CERN - or perhaps the fact that some Italian researchers thought they had measured neutrinos travelling faster than c but now find they were not. Well sorry, but I wasn't talking about neutrinos, hadrons, quarks, or any other quasi-physical particles on the quantum scale, I was talking about full-sized dudes flying around in spacecraft – very much on the man-sized scale. I pointed this out to one 'physics communicator' gentleman who replied with something like 'the laws of physics apply in the same way to everything'. Well, excuse me but that sounds a little nonsensical, since there are many curious phenomena observed in quantum dynamics, which cannot be directly transferred to the macroscopic scale. For example, in quantum mechanics there is a peculiar phenomenon known as *superposition*, where two particles seem to be in two or more places or states at once. While I don't doubt that experiments can be performed that demonstrate superposition really occurs for particles such as photons (quantum-sized elementary particles that make up light), I very much doubt whether the same could be said of, for example, a football! Having said that, I was interested in the 2018 *Scientific American* report that a team of researchers in Israel and Japan proposed an experiment designed to: "enable scientists to sneak a glance at where a photon actually resides when it is placed in a superposition". They go on to say: "They cannot say exactly what a superposition is without looking at it, but if they try to look at it, it disappears." And "(the) photon made this bizarre, logic-defying sequence of disjointed appearances ... at different times." So perhaps I have, after all, observed superposition on the macroscopic scale – when watching the cats in my garden! Speaking of cats, another example of superposition is that of Schrödinger's cat, which is a thought experiment, imagined by Austrian-Irish physicist Erwin Schrödinger in 1935. The idea is that you place a cat in a box with a tiny bit of radioactive material. When the radioactive material decays, it triggers a radiation detector that causes a poison or explosion to be released that kills the cat. To summarise, according to quantum mechanics, a paradox arises in that the cat ends up both dead and alive at the same time.

Schrödinger's cat – both alive and dead at the same time? (Illustration by the author.)

Apparently, Schrödinger developed the idea during the course of discussions with Albert Einstein to illustrate problems associated with the 'Copenhagen' (i.e. standard) interpretation of quantum mechanics applied to everyday objects, where it is said that according to quantum superposition a cat inside a box can be both alive and dead at the same time. I, in fact, have a tabby (who I rather unimaginatively named Tabby), who is fond of getting inside cardboard boxes. I would certainly be surprised if I were to open such a box and find Tabby within to be both alive and dead. From personal experience, I know that cats are capable of virtually anything, but I really feel this is going too far. Such a feline would presumably find herself in some kind of cat-limbo (whatever that may be like); and since cats have seven lives, would one need to conduct this experiment seven times before any meaningful conclusions could be drawn?

My cat Tabby – is in a box (left); but while in it she will surely always be either alive or dead – never both. I open the box and discover that she was actually alive! Tabby demonstrates how direct application of quantum mechanics to macroscopic objects is not really sensible. By the way, you may have noticed that it is the ubiquitous Amazon box. (Photographs by the author.)

Be that as it may, Schrödinger, with his alive and dead cat in a box, imagined something that provides a pretty good illustration of the problems of applying quantum mechanical conclusions to everyday macroscopic objects. I should quote it the next time someone offers analysis of dynamics on the quantum scale as evidence of what speed a human could reach in a spacecraft. Not only that, but I won't be entirely satisfied that SRTD is a real phenomenon, rather than an apparent one, until I hear a convincing resolution to the Twin Paradox; and will continue to suspect it may be possible for humans to travel faster than c until I hear a convincing explanation of why the accelerations in the simple thought experiments described above, could not occur.

And the explanations would have to relate to the man-sized scale of the thought experiments rather than the quantum scale (accelerated quantum-scale particle analogies just will not do!) It may simply be that we have never observed macroscopic objects travelling faster than light since there are no known natural phenomena capable of accelerating them to such great speeds – combined, of course, with the fact that the fastest thing we have with which to measure such speeds is EM radiation (e.g. light), which itself cannot travel faster than c.

But that's just what I am thinking – we need a debate in the wider scientific community. I hope that's clear. Now I need a cup of tea.

Whatever speeds we eventually reach, there will always be time for tea. (Illustration by the author.)

Something in the air – or aether

"Once ether was everywhere. The crook of an arm, say. (Also, the heavens.) It slowed the movement of the stars, told the left hand where the right hand went. Then it was gone, like hysteria, like the hollow earth. The news came over the radio. There is only air now. Abandon your experiments."

— Jenny Offill, Dept. of Speculation

The above discussion of the Twin Paradox provides an example of what is meant by one saying that, in considering SRTD, it seems that not enough consideration is generally given to the implications of postulate 1. It is possible that the reason for this is as follows: The concept of the aether as a type of medium or substance that is associated with an absolute coordinate frame, had been well established in the minds of scientists for some hundreds of years when, suddenly, the Michelson-Morley experiment effectively disproved its existence. Drat and blast! (As Dick Dastardly might have said.) Scientists don't like surprises. However, it was also found that the speed of light is always constant in space (away from gravitational bodies) irrespective of the velocity of the light source. So, although the concept of

279

an absolute aether was dismissed, scientists still thought of light as propagating through a 'medium' (although not a real substance); and some scientists even continued to identify the term aether with 'properties of space' that results in the constant value of c (this version of aether could be referred to as 'virtual aether'). Since air, and the traditional aether, is located relative to an absolute reference frame, it may therefore have been assumed, at perhaps an unconscious level, that the virtual aether also somehow provides a reference frame for measuring velocities. This results in books/articles referring to a person travelling at, for example, less than or near to the speed of light, without giving information on what this 'speed' is being measured relative to. Sometimes the authors tend to imply that the speed they refer to is relative to the Earth, but relativity tells us that the location of the Earth cannot provide an absolute reference point, any more than the position of the Sun, or the centre of the Milky Way Galaxy could.

"If you ever start taking things too seriously, just remember that we are talking monkeys on an organic spaceship flying through the universe."

— Joe Rogan

Books/articles on SR often also discuss the idea of a very fast moving spacecraft going through a 'light-barrier' and state that this is analogous to an aircraft passing through a sound barrier in air, and they go on to discuss potential problems associated with this. Again, this effect would be observed if the virtual aether had an absolute location as air does on Earth; whereas, in reality, the virtual aether (i.e. observation of light travelling at c), always behaves as though it were located relative to the point at which the light concerned is observed. Imagine a spacecraft travelling in interstellar space, at velocity near c relative to the Earth, while carrying a light source that is radiating visible light in all directions.

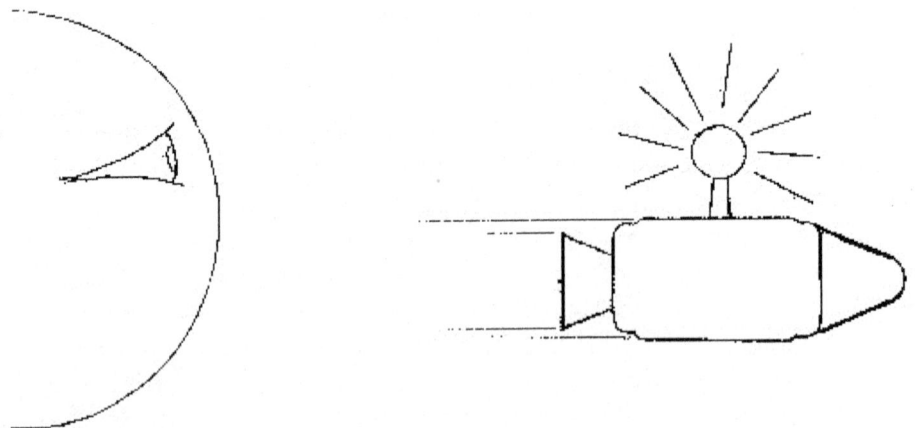

Spacecraft travelling away from an Earth observer (on left). (Drawing by the author.)

When the above spacecraft is travelling away from the Earth at 0.9c, everyone (or nearly everyone) agrees that both the craft and Earth observers would measure the light as travelling at a speed of c, with the only difference being that for the Earth observer the frequency of the light would appear to be red (Doppler) shifted.

If we imagine that the craft were now to fire its motor for a period so that it accelerated beyond c to, say, 1.1c relative to the Earth, and then turned off the motor, both the Earth and the craft would be in non-accelerating reference frames. Given this situation, according to the first postulate of SR, the light would continue to radiate equally in all directions as shown above (just as a similar light would on the Earth), and passage through a 'light barrier' would not, in fact, have been observed by those aboard the craft (ignoring starlight effects). Rather, it seems to me that the spacecraft observer would still measure the light as being emitted at a velocity of c; however, the Earth observer would no longer be able to see the light since the relative velocity of the craft is now greater than c.

The conclusion is surely that a good analogy cannot be made with the sound barrier, since the spacecraft is not moving relative to the virtual aether, unlike an aircraft moving relative to the air.

In the previous thought experiment, an object is described as moving away from the Earth at a speed greater than that of light. One would expect that most physicists would consider such a thing to be impossible, given that we are constantly being told that 'nothing can travel faster than light'. Consequently, it may surprise you to learn that most, in fact, don't – for the following reason. Scientists have taken measurements that show that the Universe is expanding and objects that are far away from us are travelling away from us at a faster speed than nearer ones. This is called 'Hubble's Law' – where the velocity of the galaxies is been determined by their *redshift* - a Doppler shift of the light they emit towards the red end of the spectrum. Actually, recent observations with the Hubble Space Telescope show that not only is the Universe expanding, it's doing so at an accelerating rate. In case you are interested, this was achieved by astronomers using Hubble's images to observe a particular kind of supernovae (Type Ia supernovae) that are believed to have a uniform brightness. This allowed scientists to determine how far away each supernova was from its apparent brightness, while measuring its velocity using redshift. Their conclusion was that the rate of expansion of the universe is increasing.

Nobody is completely sure why this is, but it has been suggested that it is caused by a mysterious form of energy that scientists have named 'dark energy', which is possibly pushing everything apart. This, by the way, is not to be confused with 'dark matter', the latter being matter that has not been observed but which has been suggested as existing to explain why, for example, galaxies stay together rather than flying apart.

The impressive and ultimately highly successful Hubble Space Telescope; whose images have provided many discoveries, including the fact that the universe is expanding at an accelerating rate. (Illustration by the author.)

According to these theories, the total mass–energy of the universe comprises 68% dark energy, 27% dark matter, and only 5% ordinary matter and energy, with the latter being the only type we stand a chance of observing with our telescopes. Of course, another possibility is that all this dark energy and matter is humbug (as Scrooge would have said) and it's just that we have something wrong with our current theories of gravity. Personally, I wouldn't rule out the latter.

If you travel far enough out (way-out man!), there is a distance (beyond 15 billion light years) at which objects such as galaxies, are speeding away from us faster than the speed of light! Strange, but true, apparently. At the point at which they exceed c, they cross a *cosmological event horizon*, where the situation for them is very similar to the spacecraft in the above thought experiment, in that light from them would then not be able to reach us. It's worth noting that if the idea of the 'light barrier' were correct, then presumably one would expect to see a flash of light when a body such as a galaxy passes through the cosmological event horizon (analogous to the sonic boom for the sound barrier), but I don't believe any such effect is observed and I can't help thinking this is for the reasons described above.

So, it is possible for objects to move apart at speeds greater than c after all – simply by them being sufficiently distant to travel fast enough to pass the cosmological event horizon. According to currently accepted physics, this can occur for very distant objects but not for closer 'local' ones. You may wonder why this is the case and if you were to ask a physicist this, they would probably reply by talking about 'space-time curvature' effects and general relativity – despite the fact that these relate to the slowing of light due to the presence of massive bodies in space. This is not something we are considering here – we are just talking about an object travelling away from an observer. Or they might say something like: 'although the distant galaxies are moving, they are not actually moving – space is just expanding'. Wow I've got to try that if I get stopped by the police for speeding: "What can I do for you officer … speeding you say? No, I don't think so, I wasn't moving that fast – it was just the space between us expanding!" Sure-fire winner with the Boys in Blue, I'm sure. To summarise, saying that object A cannot move faster than c relative to the viewer but object B can, just because B is further away from the viewer than A, seems to me a bit far-fetched (as it were).

So, we have reason to believe that it is possible for objects such as very distant galaxies (that are about 13 to 15 billion light years from us), to travel at velocities of more than c relative to the Earth. Let's now consider the situation for objects at distances that are less extreme. There are, of course, vast multitudes of bodies in space, including planets, stars, and galaxies – the above craft would be expected to be travelling at speeds of more than c relative to some and less than c relative to others – the Earth would simply comprise one of these bodies. For example, we can imagine a situation where the direction of the motion of the spacecraft is in a straight line directly towards the Andromeda Galaxy. If, when traveling at a speed of 0.999c, the rocket motor is turned off, then, according to Newton's first law of mechanics, it would continue to move at 0.999c indefinitely (ignoring the gravitational effects of the galaxies and friction from occasional hydrogen atoms). I think nearly everyone would agree that this is a possible scenario. Let's say that the craft travels in this way for, say, 100,000 (Earth) years – after such a long time it has left our Milky Way Galaxy. It's now moving directly away from the Milky Way Galaxy and toward the Andromeda galaxy. Now, the Andromeda Galaxy is actually moving towards the Milky Way Galaxy (Andromeda is the closest large spiral galaxy to our own and is unusual for a very distant body, in that it is moving toward us). So, in this situation presumably the craft would be travelling at a speed of more than c relative to Andromeda. If you think it wouldn't be, why?

Do you imagine that as it approached a speed of c relative to Andromeda, at which time it would be travelling at less than c relative to the Earth, its acceleration would suddenly reduce to zero? That seems a little unlikely, does it not? Beautiful Andromeda is, after all, considerably larger than the Milky Way and, of course, immensely larger than the Earth. The concept that the spacecraft cannot be travelling at a speed greater than c relative to any of the multitudinous objects in the observable Universe, many of which are themselves travelling at all kinds of speeds – some of which will, of course, be high, sounds to me to be *ipso facto*, on its face and by its nature, nuts! But again, you can decide for yourself. By the way, if you are wondering how anyone on the spacecraft would know for sure that the craft is accelerating, this is easily answered – they would, not surprisingly, use an *accelerometer* – the previously mentioned device that measures acceleration. You can buy simple versions of these devices from Amazon or eBay; connect them correctly and they will give you a reading of acceleration – and if you keep a record of your acceleration over time, you can work out your speed relative to the starting point (using Newton's laws again).

Definition of c

"If any philosopher had been asked for a definition of infinity, he might have produced some unintelligible rigmarole, but he would certainly not have been able to give a definition that had any meaning at all."

- Bertrand Russell

Another argument that is given for why humans cannot exceed the speed of light is that the Lorentz equations show that, for example, time would slow to zero as c was approached. Although, as described above, the Lorentz equations might only describe relative apparent effects, let us imagine that it were impossible to travel at c, but that travel at more or less than c were possible (it has, for example, been suggested that travel at precisely c is impossible because it would invalidate Maxwell's equations). Even in this situation, we can imagine how it would be possible for an accelerating spacecraft to exceed c, for the following reasons: The speed of light (like any other speed) is an abstract concept; it is not real – it covers an infinitely small range of speeds. Therefore, the accelerating craft would spend an infinitely small period of time at exactly c, so that even if travel at exactly c were impossible, it would be possible to accelerate through and beyond it. It is also worth noting that quantum mechanics shows that all phenomena/energy changes at the sub-atomic scale occur in small packets – quanta. This explains why an energised electron can pass through forbidden orbits in order to reach possible higher energy orbits.

While we are discussing the exact nature of the speed of light, it is worth mentioning that nowadays it is based on a definition rather than observation. It has been defined to travel at exactly 299,792,458 metres per second. Rupert Sheldrake is, however, of the opinion that it changes somewhat over time, and points to a drop in speed observed between 1925 and 1950. It does seem, though, that his idea will remain untested for the foreseeable future, since the unit of length the metre is defined in terms of the speed of light, which of course is itself defined. (The metre is defined as the length of the path travelled by light in a vacuum during a time interval of 1/299 792 458 of a second.) Imagine if I had a car and was trying to measure the actual speed it travels at by dropping a marker, driving for 1 hour, and then dropping another marker. If I had defined my car to always travel at 50 miles per hour, I would say that the distance between the markers is 50 miles. If the actual speed were only 25 mph you might think that the distance between the markers would be 25 miles but, according to the definition, it would be 50 miles – so the situation would be ludicrous and I would never be able to measure the actual speed. What I am trying to say is that defining a physical phenomenon, such as the speed of light, as having a certain value, rather than actually measuring it, does not impress me as being very scientific, but again seems rather dogmatic. I am not, by the way, asserting that c *does* change because, Jesus, I'm likely to be in enough trouble as it is.

Experimental proof?

"No amount of experimentation can ever prove me right; a single experiment can prove me wrong."

- Albert Einstein

It may be that Einstein was not quite right in regard to the above quote, since the single experiment of showing the bending of light from stars when the light rays pass close to the Sun, pretty much proved his general theory of relativity was correct (as mentioned above). But what about travelling faster than c? Physicists who believe that c cannot be exceeded, often point to experiments in particle accelerators as providing experimental evidence of its impossibility. Such machines employ electric/magnetic fields in order to accelerate particles to very high speeds. There can be little doubt that c has a particular significance in electromagnetism. Electromagnetic (EM) waves are comprised of oscillating electric and magnetic fields, and we all agree that EM waves are always observed as travelling at c – it seems they cannot travel faster than c. Is it then completely surprising that when using electric and magnetic fields to accelerate miniscule particles from rest, we are not able to accelerate them in this manner to speeds greater than c? Perhaps we should have expected that. But can we then make the inference, as most physicists do, that since we can't accelerate the particles beyond c, it will therefore never be possible for men to travel in spacecrafts at speeds greater than c? I have my doubts. Curious phenomena are the rule rather than the exception on the quantum scale; and, as mentioned, we simply can't expect dynamics observed in a particle accelerator to be the same as permitted behaviour on a macroscopic scale. (You remember Schrodinger's perplexity about the cat in the box.) There is a world of difference between trying to use a stationary magnetic field to accelerate a barely physically existing particle/wave to c and someone cruising along in a spacecraft at 0.9c relative to some object, burning their rocket motor for a while with the result that their speed relative to the said object increased by 20%. I mentioned to one science communicator/journalist gentleman, that the mechanics of humans is not the same as the mechanics of sub-atomic, let along quantum scale, particles. The reason I said this is that he was referring to the physics of mesons, as part of his argument to say that humans cannot travel faster than c. When I pointed out that humans are rather different from mesons, seeing that the latter have a diameter of one *femtometer* (which, if you would like to know, is 1×10^{-15} m), he said something like: 'the laws of physics apply in the same way to all objects'. He is probably a nice guy – no doubt he goes down to the pub with his mates and so on – but what kind of nonsense is that? Is he saying that, since everything is subject to the same laws of physics, it follows that all objects should behave in the same way? Surely not! A meson is, as a matter of fact, about the same size as a proton and, I must point out, the mechanical behaviour (as well as just about all other kinds of behaviour) of humans is completely different from that of mesons and protons. To summarise, it would have made more sense if, instead of a subatomic particle the size of a proton, he had been talking about something the size of a croton (a type of fairly large plant native to Indonesia, Malaysia, Australia, and the Western Pacific Ocean islands), or even a crouton (such as those that float in your soup).

By the way, uncharged mesons may decay to photons, which is a type of elementary particle. Photons are quantum particles/waves that make up electromagnetic radiation such as light and radio waves. They have no rest mass and they always move at the speed of light in vacuum. So, the journalist was arguing that mesons not being able to exceed c is evidence for humans not being able to do so, despite the fact that mesons decay into photons, which themselves always travel at the same speed – which is exactly the speed he believes humans cannot travel at! Make of that what you will; but, to be honest, it doesn't prepossess me to place a pre-order on Amazon for the physics book he said he was writing (although naturally I wouldn't be averse to receiving a complimentary copy – I always try to keep an open mind). One thing I will point out though, is that photons are the force carrier for electromagnetic force fields – meaning that it would not be exactly surprising that such fields cannot operate at relative speeds that exceed c.

Finally, it is often stated that experimental tests have been undertaken on aircraft that show that SRTD has caused highly accurate clocks on the aircraft to run more slowly than clocks on the ground – if this were the case, then it would provide evidence that SRTD were a real effect. Considering the importance of an ultimate limit to the speeds which humans could, in theory, reach and its implications for, say, galactic exploration and colonisation, the actual number of such experimental tests does seem relatively limited. The test that is often quoted was undertaken almost half a century ago. In 1972, J. C. Hafele, and R. E. Keating flew highly accurate caesium clocks around the world in both directions. Their measurements showed that the flying clocks gained and lost time relative to an Earth-based clock. (Whether they lost or gained time depended on their direction of travel and 'lost time' meant that upon return the flying clock indicated that less time had passed than was shown on the ground clock.) Despite this, I have doubts about whether the experiment can be taken as proof that SRTD is real, since, as you may recall, special relativity considers effects caused by velocities measured in frames of reference that are not accelerating and are away from the effects of gravity (hence the term 'special'). This is not the case for the Hafele and Keating clocks – they are located on aircraft that are accelerating in circular paths around the Earth and they are, of course, subject to the Earth's gravitational field. These results can, however, be explained in terms of general relativity effects: a clock will have the velocity of its plane added to the rotation of the Earth (or subtracted from it, depending upon the direction of travel). The resulting tangential velocity represents an acceleration of the flying clock relative to the one on the Earth, which will result in a GRTD effect. (Einstein's equivalence principle states that gravity force is the same as the pseudo-force experienced by an observer in an accelerated frame of reference – so that both acceleration and gravity forces influence the rate at which time passes.) GRTD further indicates that both flying clocks will also experience a speed increase due to being further from the centre of the Earth than the ground clock. To summarise, my suggestion is that it's possible that in this case the time dilation was real and that GRTD effects can explain the time differentials indicated by the clocks. Therefore, when it is stated that taking a very accurate clock into an aircraft resulted in it running at a different speed to an identical one on the ground, and that this was caused by the velocity and height of the flying clock, this can be interpreted as being correct but misleading. The time differential might arise not from special relativity but from the general relativity effects associated with the acceleration and height of the flying clock. So, although such experiments do provide evidence that GRTD is a real effect, I would hesitate to say that they prove that SRTD is real. At least, that's my perspective on things – and I'm sticking with it! Besides, if SRTD were a real objective phenomenon, then there would need to be a resolution to the Twin Paradox and, as discussed in detail above, such a resolution does not seem, at least so far, to exist.

Implications for very high-speed/interstellar space travel
"In conclusion, I return to Einstein. If we find a planet in the Alpha Centauri system, its image, captured by a camera travelling at a fifth of light speed, will be slightly distorted due to the effects of special relativity. It would be the first time a spacecraft has flown fast enough to see such effects. In fact, Einstein's theory is central to the whole mission. Without it, we would have neither lasers nor the

ability to perform the calculations necessary for guidance, imaging, and data transmission over twenty-five trillion miles at a fifth of light speed.

We can see a pathway between that sixteen-year-old boy dreaming of riding on a light beam and our own dream, which we are planning to turn into a reality, of riding our own light beam to the stars. We are standing at the threshold of a new era. Human colonisation on other planets is no longer science fiction. It can be science fact. The human race has existed as a separate species for about two million years. Civilisation began about 10,000 years ago, and the rate of development has been steadily increasing. If humanity is to continue for another million years, our future lies in boldly going where no one else has gone before.

I hope for the best. I have to. We have no other option."

— Stephen Hawking, Brief Answers to the Big Questions

If the considerations in the above sections are correct, they lead to conclusions that are, like special relativity itself, rather surprising, not terribly easy to accept; and for which there are some curious implications. The first would be that the velocity of any object (A) could only be referred to in relation to some other object (B) in the Universe — otherwise the term would be meaningless. The second would be that whether there is a relative velocity, or no velocity, between A and B, would have no effect on A or B, other than to change the way each perceives the other (if they are moving relative to each other). The third would be that either A or B could be made to accelerate, in accordance with Newton's laws of mechanics, so that their relative velocity increases up to and beyond c. This latter hypothesis would have implications for a subject that was discussed earlier in this book — specifically interstellar travel. We can imagine a spacecraft that employs a developed and efficient form of chemical rocket propulsion, and is able to accelerate at 1g (which is convenient for the travellers on board, since it will provide them with artificial gravity). As this occurs, the situation on board the spacecraft is that a rocket motor is expelling gases from the rear, thereby providing an action that will have a reaction effect of accelerating the craft forward (according to Newton's laws of motion). These effects will be exactly the same no matter what its distance and velocity is relative to Earth (if we ignore the effects of the Earth's gravitational field). Therefore, when the craft has attained a velocity of 0.999c relative to Earth, we can imagine there would be no difficulty in accelerating to 1.111c and then continuing to accelerate. In this scenario, the craft would have surpassed the speed limit of c that has traditionally been assumed to exist for human travel. When the craft reaches the halfway point in its travel, it would rotate through 180 degrees and then decelerate at 1g, again providing artificial gravity and enabling it to be stationary once it has reached its destination. It is worth noting that there are some practical problems that would need to be addressed for very high-speed (order of c) space travel. One example problem is the need to carry sufficient fuel to fire the rocket motors for extended periods (days or weeks); while another is heating of the craft exterior that would arise from friction from the very low density of hydrogen atoms that occupy deep space. However, such challenges would need to be addressed through future application of advanced technologies; and do not comprise grounds for believing such travel to be impossible. For example, if the craft were travelling to the red dwarf star Proxima Centauri, it would take just over 4 years to get there using the method outlined in this book – consequently one could make the return journey in less than a decade. This star is particularly interesting, since in August 2016 discovery was announced of Proxima b, which is the exoplanet closest to us, as well as orbiting within Proxima Centauri's circumstellar habitable zone (aka 'Goldilocks Zone'). Unfortunately, though, if there is any extra-terrestrial life on Proxima b, it would have to be extremely hardy/robust. The reason for this is that in March of 2016, astronomers observed that Proxima Centauri emitted a 'superflare'.

The flaring red dwarf star Proxima Centauri, with the orbiting exoplanet Proxima b. (Illustration by the author.)

This is rather like the solar flares we observe coming from the Sun, but immensely larger – so large, in fact, that it was bright enough, can you believe it, to be visible to the naked eye! Such superflares would produce high intensities of UV radiation that would, over time, break down any ozone layers in Proxima b's atmosphere that are needed to protect any organisms on the planet from harmful UV radiation from the star. Consequently, the chances of finding life on this exoplanet may be rather slim.

Although we may not find life on Proxima b there are, of course, multitudes of other star systems in our Galaxy. Observations show that red dwarfs are the most common stars in The Milky Way (comprising around 75%), and it also has to be acknowledged that recent research indicates that about 60% of such stars experience flare activity. Even so, there remain billions of stars that are very likely to also have orbiting exoplanets in the Goldilocks Zone. This is surely an exciting prospect – the question is, how can we get out there and explore this vast potential? Perhaps somewhat surprisingly, the relatively conventional and attainable methods of transportation proposed above might also enable travel to many of these more distant stars; since a continuous acceleration of 1g enables very high relative velocities to be attained in reasonable timescales. For example, using this method a spaceship travelling 50 light years might attain a maximum speed of around 22.5c, meaning that this journey could be achieved in only 5 years. There are 133 stars within 50 light years of earth. Most of these are very similar to the Sun and it is probable that there are many Earth-like exoplanets around these stars. So, the stars might be within reach after all … which is indeed an intriguing prospect. Before we can say the above conjectures are correct, we need more definite proof; but if they are, journeys to exoplanets of sizes similar to the Earth, orbiting stars similar to the Sun, within the habitable zone i.e. POTENTIALLY HABITABLE PLANETS, would be achievable in the not too distant future and it would only take the order of a few years to travel each way. That prospect would be more than intriguing – if you ask me it would be as exciting as hell.

Putting it all together – the destiny of mankind

Man's future: in the stars?
"It is not in the stars to hold our destiny but in ourselves."

– William Shakespeare

What is man's destiny? A good question. Easy to ask …harder to answer (or at least to answer in any way that may seem satisfactory). As Shakespeare observed, our future is not recorded in the stars – rather it is up to us to work it out. However, although the stars may not dictate our destiny, they may well provide the key to our realising our ultimate desires for our future – which is surely most significantly expressed in our wish to survive as a species. But this will, of course, not happen spontaneously – as again Shakespeare realised, it is up to mankind to formulate his own vision for a successful destiny – just as each of us do, in a more modest way, for each of our lives (or at least we try our best to). And, of course, we need to work hard towards actually realising our preferred destiny – survival must be earned. I seem to remember that Jon Colicos, as Kor, said that in *Star Trek's* 'Errand of Mercy' episode – a memorable performance if you ask me; also: "Your friend (Spock) dead; you, a mental vegetable; not a pleasant prospect for you, Captain Kirk, but it awaits you unless you tell me everything I want to know." Kor's plan was to have Spock dissected. Fortunately, this did not happen, and Kirk and Spock were happily able to save the day.

Kor, as played by John Colicos in the *Star Trek* episode 'Errand of Mercy'. (Drawing by the author.)

In this episode, the Federation and the Klingons visit Organia, which is occupied by a race known (not surprisingly) as the Organians.

Two members of Organia's High Council from the *Star Trek* episode Errand of Mercy, changing from humanoid form (which was adopted for the sake of visitors), to their true form of pure energy. (Illustrations by the author.)

To start with, the humans and Klingons consider the Organians to be peasant-like, but later it is realised that they are actually highly-evolved – to the extent that they have 'evolved beyond the need for physical bodies'. They have, in fact, evolved into advanced and powerful energy beings, employing their humanoid outward appearances solely to provide points of reference for visitors. This becomes clear at the end of the episode, when two members of Organia's High Council, revert to their true form of pure energy. Inevitably this makes one think of the phrase "It's life, Jim, but not as we know it." – the supposed comment by Spock to Captain Kirk. This, along with "Beam me up, Scotty." may well be two of the most famous and often quoted phrases in modern colloquial usage of the English language. Another equally famous phrase, attributed to Sherlock Holmes is, of course: "Elementary, my dear Watson." It might surprise you to learn that Spock never actually uttered "It's life, Jim, but not as we know it.", nor did Holmes remark "Elementary, my dear Watson." – both phrases originated from followers of the stories/series concerned (although in one episode Mr Spock does refer to 'no life as we know it', and in one short story Holmes describes some reasoning as being 'elementary'). Anyway, after witnessing the remarkable Organian transformation, Spock goes on to say that: "I should say the Organians are as far above us on the evolutionary scale as we are above the amoeba." I, for one, can't help wondering whether we might find ourselves saying something similar about real extra-terrestrial intelligence – if contact with such beings is ever achieved.

Man's destiny in the medium term will, hopefully, involve development and beneficial utilisation of many of the mechanisms and systems outlined in this book. The actual mechanical performance of machines has, for some time, meant that they are capable of quite impressive physical feats. But this is in theory – in practice there have been severe limitations in our ability to write programs that enable them to operate automatically in useful ways. The world is a very complex place and things naturally become disordered with the passage of time. Up to now, robotic devices have found it extremely difficult to adapt to variations caused by this natural disorder – to the extent that it is often cheaper to do a given task manually than to order the environment sufficiently for it to be achieved by the current generation of robots. But all of this is changing due to recent developments in AI and particularly deep learning – which was discussed in some detail in earlier sections. We are currently just on the cusp of a robotics revolution that will change our lives in many ways for the better – I don't think this is an exaggeration. By this I don't mean we will have androids like *Star Trek*'s Data walking around within the next 5 or 10 years. Rather, we will have robots that will look more like the current versions of robots and automation we see in today's automated factory lines. The difference is that the future generations of robots and systems will be able to accommodate the variations and randomness we encounter in the real world – *and still be able to get useful tasks completed*. It cannot be long, surely, before robot systems start to tackle large percentages of the dangerous, difficult and dirty tasks that civilisation demands to be completed and which, up to now, have been the hard lot of those worthy citizens who have volunteered over the years to undertake them. I believe that many of us would welcome this. In the medium term, such robotic devices in combination with the replicator technologies alluded to earlier, are bound to be able to provide for just about all our material needs. In this situation, what is left for mankind? A tremendous amount, as it happens; for we would then all be able to devote much of our time to leisure activities or spiritual pursuits that we currently frequently say that we wish we had time for. If we are being honest, we would have to say (like Pink Floyd): "Have; have not, and who'll deny it's what the fighting's all about?" If money had little to no value due to the fact that we had virtually anything we needed or wished for, then for sure there would be much less incentive for squabbling over money on the local scale or starting devastating wars internationally. Imagine being able to live a very comfortable life and having no concerns more pressing than how to balance your time between composing music or writing poetry. Or your interests might be somewhat less fine art – you may simply get the most spiritual satisfaction from bicycle rides in the countryside – or anything else that you fancied. Such could be our destiny – if we do not allow ourselves in the meantime to be consumed by greed and fear. Gene Roddenberry had the foresight to appreciate this – which is why it is clear in his creations such as *Star Trek: The Next Generation* (STNG), that money does not feature in his positive vision of the future. By the way, I don't see why, eventually, it should not be possible to build androids/robots with advanced capabilities and performances similar to those of Data in STNG, but as for whether such devices will ever comprise sentient beings, well, that is quite another matter.

Having said a few things about potentialities for the medium term, what then can we say about mankind's longer-term destiny? Well, it's very much up to us – we can waste more and more time and effort on weapons of mass destruction that can never be used (for if they were our destiny would be very clear and very shameful). Either we can continue to 'blow it', so that mankind's rule on this speck of dust floating in the cosmos comes to a premature and ignominious termination, or we can look to the future with hope. The latter is what we need to do to ensure the long-term survival of the species as well as our cultures and achievements. These have, after all, certainly been very hard won over the millennia, and surely the last thing we wish to do would be to throw them away for no good reason.

So, how can we survive? As mentioned above, our future is not recorded in the stars, but I would say that the stars hold the *key* for our future, so they are what we must reach for in the long term. In many ways, the whole of this book is aimed at making some observations that might provide some indications of how we might go about doing this. More specifically, the above few sections of the text address some relevant practical considerations – such as whether and how we might travel fast enough to reach the stars. Such questions are, I feel, very important to the whole book – so much so that I feel it is worth ending this section by giving a brief summary of what we have found in this area.

REACH FOR THE STARS

REACH FOR THE STARS – the kind of poster you might expect to see in a nursery or primary school – but the message is just as important for us adults. (Photograph by Ali Abdul Rahman, courtesy of Unsplash, used with permission.)

Modern astronomy has identified many potentially inhabitable planets orbiting stars in the Milky Way Galaxy; however, exploration of these exoplanets requires travel over great distances (numerous light years). Traditional interpretations of special relativity have concluded that human travellers cannot attain the speed of light (c) and that approaching c causes time dilation, so that a traveller returning to Earth would find everyone significantly aged. Consequently, interstellar travel has been assumed to be impossible within a human lifetime. The above sections have re-assessed the implications of the two postulates of special relativity; and if the conclusions are correct, would indicate that a traveller might, in fact, greatly exceed c relative to Earth and return without having aged excessively due to time dilation effects. If this were possible, return travel to nearby stars and their exoplanets would be attainable, with conceivable technological developments, and within attainable periods (years but not decades or centuries). Such exploration would clearly be of extreme scientific value and a potentially revolutionary event in human history. It would have very profound implications for both our understanding of mankind's place in the cosmos and also the ultimate destiny of humanity. In short, it would help to move us along the road that leads to our being able to answer those questions that our young children ask of us so earnestly but which we find ourselves unable to answer in any way that could be considered satisfactory.

"The Cosmos is all that is or was or ever will be. Our feeblest contemplations of the Cosmos stir us -- there is a tingling in the spine, a catch in the voice, a faint

295

sensation, as if a distant memory, of falling from a height. We know we are approaching the greatest of mysteries."

— Carl Sagan, Cosmos

Who knows whether faster than light speed will ever be attained, thereby making interstellar travel a practical prospect? At the moment, at least for me, it is hard to be certain; you will also have an opinion and only time and further experimental data will tell us for sure. If it could be attained in the not too distant future, this would provide extremely strong motivators for continuing research and development of high-speed space travel. Such a capability might offer humanity a means of ensuring survival in the very long term, even in the event of possible long-term environmental degradation or catastrophes on the Earth.

Summary of predicted far future technological developments

To conclude this section on the far future, below is my take on science and technologies that are way beyond the current horizon. When reading Table 3, please do bear in mind my earlier comments that predictions for the far future (i.e. beyond the next few decades) are extremely difficult – and so are given here more as thought provocation than accurate estimates (that's my idea of a disclaimer):

Development	Capability provided	Approx. date
Artificial intelligence exceeds intelligence of man in some fields (e.g. logical reasoning)	Computer can become self-programming at levels beyond human capabilities – leading to advanced software that can solve problems previously considered completely intractable	21st Century (second half of)
Mobile power source invented with very high power and low weight characteristics	Travel is revolutionised – as are the capabilities of mobile technologies	21st Century (second half of)
Industrial robots implemented to automatically undertake various challenging (unstructured) manual tasks	Humans no longer have to undertake difficult, dangerous, or dirty jobs – lives are saved	21st Century (second half of)
Material replicator (and transmitter)	Manufacture of any required object; transport of objects at the speed of light	22nd Century

Manufacture of highly reliable human organs and other life-extending medical breakthroughs (e.g. cures for various cancers)	Greatly extended life (e.g. additional 200+ years)	22nd Century
Travel at speeds that significantly exceed c	Interstellar travel	22nd Century
Androids implemented with similar capabilities to Data In *Star Trek: The Next Generation*	Androids can effectively undertake any tasks humans wish them to	22nd Century
Contact established with extra-terrestrials (ET)	Technological progress is likely – but exact extent depends upon the technology of the ET	22nd Century
Humans start colonising significant regions of the Milky Way galaxy	Future survival of humans is secured (no longer threatened by objects colliding with Earth)	23rd Century
Humans employ technology to evolve beyond needing their animal bodies	Human essence and intelligence can be stored in other formats – possibly computer-based or technologies we are not yet aware of	25th Century
Ultra-highspeed travel developed (1000,000c and above)	Humans explore and colonise the Andromeda galaxy and other neighbouring galaxies	27th Century
Humans and humanity achieve everlasting life	Immortality	29th Century
A substantial part of the known universe is explored and understood	Humans gain some understanding of the mind of God (or whatever created the universe)	30th Century

Table 3. A list of dramatic and/or important, predicted technological breakthroughs and accomplishments of the far future (I can't guarantee the accuracy of the timescales!).

Part 4.

Concluding remarks

Here I have again included Les Edwards' illustration of one of Isaac Asimov's famous fictional robots (and Dr Susan Calvin) since, for me, it gives a strong impression of how astonishing the technological possibilities of the future might well be. (Illustration used with the permission of Les Edwards, www.lesedwards.com.)

So, if you have read this far then you have accompanied me on a little tour of my universe, which has comprised a few reflections on how far we have come in terms of science and technology, what might have been holding us back, the major threats we face, and what the future might hold. And that future is going to be, I believe, an extraordinarily bright one. Why there is such a fashion for depicting dystopian futures, for example in films, I don't know – what's the point? I guess it's the old profession of being a doom-merchant – which so much of the media seems to be overly focused on. Essentially it creates a sensation and thereby gets the writer responsible noticed. Who wants to hear about everything going well? A scandal is juicier and more intriguing and certainly sells newspapers. This is why so much of our news is sensationalised and presented in a dramatic and emotional format. I swear that some news agencies could provide a dramatic and/or sensationalist spin on the news that, for example, there has been no bad news for a while e.g. "we poor humans have had too much of a good run of it and I expect we will have to pay for it", or something similar.

Not that there are no threats that are emerging that are potentially serious, and which require our attention to avoid or minimise possible negative effects. I have endeavoured to describe a few and I hope I have provided some realistic contexts for what they do/might mean for mankind and how we can tackle them.

"Once you replace negative thoughts with positive ones, you'll start having positive results."

- Willie Nelson

I am with Willie Nelson in believing that positive thoughts can lead to positive actions. That is why I have made such mention of figures associated with popular culture – most of the people mentioned had a positive influence, if not directly then surely through their creative influence. Amongst all of the imagery, some of the strongest positivity comes, at least for me, from *Star Trek*; as George Takei (who played Mr Sulu) expressed it:

"At the core of '*Star Trek*' is Gene Roddenberry's vision of the future. So much of science-fiction is about a dystopian society with human civilization having crumbled. He had an affirmative, shining, positive view of the future."

- George Takei

And Sherlock Holmes, who you will have noticed I have made much mention of, is a character who, despite his somewhat dark habits, comprises a very positive figure – so much so that he even overcame the 'foremost champion of crime' – Professor Moriarty, albeit at the cost of his own life (or so Watson thought). Watson eloquently expressed his admiration for Holmes in the short story 'The Final

Problem', which ends with Watson saying he shall ever regard Holmes as "the best and the wisest man whom I have ever known".

So, I am very much not in the dystopian camp. But I might also have some difficulties in believing in a future utopia, since I haven't seen much evidence that man is, or will be, capable of creating a community or society that is perfect or ideal. However, one thing I do believe is that there is realistic potential for the future to be vastly better than anything mankind has experienced up to now. I am also convinced that the chances of realising such an agreeable future will be increased by general positivity and specifically by imagining various possible positive future scenarios.

But what of the title of this book: "Why you can't catch a rocket to Mars"? Well, the design and build of such a device will require, I fancy, quite an impressive effort and engineering achievement. Engineering is facilitated by scientific and technological advances. Impressive developments in these areas were made by the ancient Greeks, who managed to communicate some concepts to the Romans; but it seems that most of their advanced culture was somehow forgotten for many centuries. The world effectively fell asleep all through the Dark Ages. It may well be that if the barbarians had not sacked the great library at Alexandria, thereby burning the many thousands of scripts and parchments therein, the hiatus in man's achievements would not have occurred and previous generations could have built upon the excellent accomplishments of the ancient Greeks (Carl Sagan certainly thought so). If this had occurred, then I feel that there would be little doubt that you *would* be able to catch the Martian rocket – if not the Alpha Proxima one!

But we are where we are, and we do need to ask why all the excitement of the space race, culminating in man landing on the Moon, did not lead to the kinds of accomplishments that were expected – for example, humans travelling to Jupiter and Saturn as in the films *2001 A Space Odyssey* and *Silent Running*. I have tried to present some reflections and narratives that may help to explain this apparent shortcoming, but the causes might be simpler than we realise and it may be entirely possible to also express the situation very succinctly; here, for example is my rather simpler take on the situation: *Nowadays it's all about bean counting and spin-doctoring, with emphasis put on such things as economics, personality (rather than character), and disposable pop culture. As I mentioned before, I enjoy history programmes and reading novels as much as the next person, but such things will not save the planet – for that we need science and engineering!*

In making the attempt at the end of Part 3 to predict important anticipated developments/inventions of the far future, I am doing something that wise men would probably advise against. Of course, I, like anyone else, can't realistically peek into the far future. Its secrets and astonishing possibilities are hidden from us as a consequence of the things we can imagine being heavily influenced by the limitations of our own age. The far future will be more influenced by, and similar to, the medium future rather than anything we could dream up. However, I do think it is important to consider the far future, if for no other reason than just to show that we do have sufficient confidence in the wisdom of man to expect there *will* be a positive far future to look forward to (as mentioned, it is likely that maintaining a positive belief such as this will increase the chances of it becoming true).

Arthur C. Clarke once said: "Two possibilities exist: either we are alone in the Universe or we are not. Both are equally terrifying." I don't know if the possibilities are terrifying, but they must both certainly be astonishing. Most people, most of the time, simply don't think about such concepts – presumably because they involve questions they cannot answer and which they believe will not affect their lives. I hope that, with this book, I have shown in some modest kind of way, that they might just be somewhat in error in both of those convictions.

It is natural to be somewhat afraid of the unknown, and the future, by its very nature, is something that will always have elements of the unknown associated with it. But if we look to the suffering and ignorance of the past millennia it becomes clear that progress for humankind has, over the ages, comprised a long move forward into broad, sunlit uplands (to employ Churchill's phrase) – we have no reason to suppose that the next phase of man's destiny will not be similarly positive. We, like our ancient predecessors, can choose to look over the next mountain if we wish. I believe that if we step forward with resolve and determination, in the certain belief that our knowledge and achievements can lead us to a new Golden Age, then we will be bound to find ourselves justified.

"Remember to look up at the stars and not down at your feet. Try to make sense of what you see and wonder about what makes the universe exist. Be curious. And however difficult life may seem, there is always something you can do and succeed at.

It matters that you don't just give up."

— Stephen Hawking

Steven Hawking, with Albert Einstein, Data, and Isaac Newton; in a scene from *Star Trek: The Next Generation.* It was reported that when Hawking went on a tour of the set, he saw the warp core in engineering and said, "I'm working on that." To this day, Hawking is the only person to play himself in an episode of *Star Trek.* (Drawing by the author.)

The mighty and awe-inspiring Saturn V rocket, which first took man to the Moon in July 1969. One wonders what the rocket that will take humans to Mars will look like. (Illustration by the author.)

Afterword

"There is as much sense in Holmes as in Hafiz and Horace, and as much knowledge of the world."

(The author's observation, after a quote by Sherlock Holmes in 'A Case of Identity'.)

The author's Holmesian bookshelf. (Photograph by Andrew V. L. Smith.)

"It isn't all over; everything has not been invented; the human adventure is just beginning."

- Gene Roddenberry

If you enjoyed reading this Book...

If you enjoyed reading this book, I wonder if I could ask you to write a review on Amazon for it - reviews are the best way for independent authors and authors with small publishers to gain exposure and help sales. Thanks!

Printed in Great Britain
by Amazon